Preventing
Problem
Behaviors

Bob Algozzine · Pam Kay

EDITORS

A Handbook of Successful Prevention Strategies

Preventing Problem Behaviors

Foreword by Jane Knitzer

A joint publication of the
Council for Exceptional Children
and Corwin Press, Inc.

CORWIN PRESS, INC.
A Sage Publications Company
Thousand Oaks, California

Council for
Exceptional
Children

For information:

Corwin Press, Inc.
A Sage Publications Company
2455 Teller Road
Thousand Oaks, California 91320
E-mail: order@corwinpress.com

Sage Publications Ltd.
6 Bonhill Street
London EC2A 4PU
United Kingdom

Sage Publications India Pvt. Ltd.
M-32 Market
Greater Kailash I
New Delhi 110 048 India

Printed in the United States of America

Library of Congress Cataloging-in-Publication Data

Main entry under title:
    Preventing problem behaviors: A handbook of successful prevention strategies /
edited by Bob Algozzine & Pam Kay.
        p. cm.
    Includes bibliographical references and index.
    ISBN 0-7619-7775-9 (cloth) — ISBN 0-7619-7776-7 (pbk.)
        1. Classroom management—Handbooks, manuals, etc.
    2. Problem children—Behavior modification—Handbooks, manuals, etc.
    I. Algozzine, Robert.   II. Kay, Pam.
    LB3013.P69 2001
    371.102'4—dc21   2001001033

        05   06   07   7   6   5   4   3

Acquiring Editor:	Robb Clouse
Editorial Assistant:	Kylee Liegl
Production Editor:	Diana E. Axelsen/Olivia Weber
Editorial Assistant:	Kathryn Journey
Copy Editor:	Kristin Bergstad
Typesetter/Designer:	Lynn Miyata/Denyse Dunn
Cover Designer:	Michael Dubowe

Contents

1

Promising Practices for Preventing Problem Behaviors   1
Bob Algozzine and Pam Kay

School administrators face daily and continuous challenges in efforts to establish and maintain safe and orderly classroom environments where teachers can teach and students can learn. Prevention strategies have the potential to reduce the incidence and prevalence of school-related problems. Prevention of emotional and behavioral problems involves several key features: (a) universal prevention measures that ensure that the school and classroom environment promote positive behaviors; (b) early and annual screening of children to determine who has been "placed at risk"; (c) early secondary intervention at the youngest age possible; and (d) cross-setting participation and collaboration in prevention programs encompassing individuals, families, teachers, peers, and community agencies. This chapter provides a brief overview of school-based programs to prevent emotional and/or behavioral problems from interfering with education.

2

Preventing Problems by Improving Behavior   11
Debra M. Kamps

This chapter focuses on proactive approaches to improving behavior for individual students with antisocial tendencies. When these supports are provided early in a child's life, the risks can be reduced and the outcomes improved. The reader will find a blueprint for promoting well-managed educational environments for all children, including (a) information about antisocial behavior, (b) tips for teaching rules and compliance, (c) tips for choosing rewards, (d) procedures for reducing inappropriate behaviors, and (e) information about using functional assessment procedures for children with chronic, more intensive needs for behavioral support.

Effective teachers organize their classrooms to support learning, safety, and appropriate social behavior. They have a strong academic focus and support students in setting appropriate goals, achieving high standards, fostering positive relationships with school staff and peers, and promoting meaningful school, family, and community interactions. This chapter uses examples from classrooms to describe how Total Quality Education is an effective model for creating a positive learning environment. Individually and as a class, students use self-assessment data to control their process and monitor their continuous improvement.

Social skills instruction in general education classrooms is an important prevention strategy. This chapter defines social skills, gives examples of research-based curricula, outlines effective instructional procedures and enhancements, and describes strategies to reinforce and maintain positive behaviors both inside and outside of the classroom. The programs described focus on (a) use of an instructional model in natural settings, and (b) the incorporation of peer groups as appropriate role models. A number of effective social skills programs are presented, along with four essential elements that must be present before any program can be effective.

Unified Discipline encourages firm, caring responses to management problems in the classroom and other areas of the school. Consistent attitudes, expectations, correction procedures, and team roles drive this approach to preventing and improving behavior on a schoolwide basis. Unified Discipline has demonstrated its effectiveness with improvements in office referrals, discipline demographics, classroom ecology, individual student performances, and general attitudes.

Foreword

In 1990, my colleagues and I wrote a book titled *At the Schoolhouse Door: An Examination of Programs and Policies for Children With Behavioral and Emotional Problems* (Knitzer, Steinberg, & Fleish, 1990). That report highlighted how very little attention there was to helping students who had been placed at either academic or behavioral risk achieve success. Thus, 10 years later, it is with a great deal of pleasure that I write the foreword for *Preventing Problem Behaviors,* edited under the able leadership of Bob Algozzine and Pam Kay.

This book, in my view, is important for several reasons. First, it turns the spotlight on the fact that there are actually tools that teachers and schools can use to achieve the goals that are so urgently called for by policymakers and politicians. Moreover, the tools focus not just on academics or on setting higher standards. Instead, the focus is on the behaviors that get in the way of learning as these are reflected in real learning environments. Thus the book brings an important perspective to the current, often simplistic debates about what it takes to craft learning environments that will promote success for all children—immigrant children, homeless children, middle-class children, children exposed to or victims of violence, too-aggressive children—all children.

Second, the book has, at its core, a commitment to research-based knowledge. The approaches described here have grown out of the work of six research teams funded by the Office of Special Education Programs in the Department of Education, and most of the chapters include data from, or references to, research-based findings.

Third, and very important, the book provides a framework to guide school personnel who are seeking to develop coherent procedures to promote positive learning environments. The interventions described range from classroom-based strategies, to whole school initiatives such as Total Quality Education, to partnerships between parents and teachers that promote shared understandings and actions. At the same time, underlying all of the interventions is this evidence-based belief: To help children whose behaviors are barriers to their learning, it is necessary to teach them new behaviors, set high expectations, reward positive behavior, and promote positive peer interactions. This is not how it is always done. In fact, this book even cites research findings that teachers spend much more time criticizing children than praising them.

Fundamentally, this book is a guide to thinking proactively about what schools can do to intervene for children at risk of behavioral problems. It presents information in a straightforward, no-nonsense, easily accessible style that often includes advice about what kinds of strategies work best under what kinds of circumstances. On a deeper level, the authors call for a fundamental rethinking of the usual and customary way in which teachers and educators do business. Its most important message is that the burden of change lies not just with the students, which is the most common view. Instead, it challenges us to take seriously a very sensible but hard-to-act-upon hypothesis: Teachers and other school personnel can help children become better learners only if they themselves are willing to change—to change the way their classrooms are structured and to change the way they interact with their students, and sometimes with the families of the students. As such, my hope is that this book will be an important resource for those across this country who refuse to give up on children and schools that are challenging.

—Jane Knitzer, Ed.D.
National Center for Children in Poverty
Mailman School of Public Health
Columbia University

REFERENCE

Knitzer, J., Steinberg, Z., & Fleish, B. (1990). *At the schoolhouse door: An examination of programs and policies for children with behavioral and emotional problems.* New York: Bank Street College of Education.

Acknowledgments

T he U.S. Office of Special Education Programs (OSEP) in the U.S. Department of Education supported the six research projects whose work forms the core of this book. The grants involved were H237F40012, H237F50014, H237F50019, H237F50028, H237F50036, and H023A40019, funded under the Individuals for Disabilities Education Act, or IDEA. Opinions expressed in these chapters are those of the authors, and not necessarily those of the U.S. Department of Education or offices within it.

We deeply appreciate the encouragement and support provided by Helen Thornton, Project Officer at OSEP. Her vision kept us moving forward through the years of collaborative work that produced this book and numerous other joint publications. Each of us thanks the principals, parents, teachers, and students who allowed us into their lives. In addition, the authors of the following chapters thank the specific individuals named:

Chapter 6: Marge Coahran, Margo Rabon, Gail Rose, Amy Ryan, Cyndi Snyder, Penny Bishop, and those who served as Parent Liaisons in the ABC project;

Chapter 7: Mary D'Ovidio, Jen Oppenheim, and Michelle Miller for their contributions to the development of the Linkages to Learning Program at Broad Acres Elementary School, the principals and teachers at Broad Acres, John and Margo Richters, and, most important, the children and parents at Broad Acres and at the control school;

Chapter 8: David Miller, Gary Matloff, Rowand Robinson, and Kristine Landry for significant contributions to the Conflict Resolution/ Peer Mediation Project's implementation and evaluation;

Chapter 9: Camilla A. Lehr, Ph.D., Colleen M. Kaibel, and past and present monitors for their contributions to the ongoing development and refinement of the Check & Connect model.

About the Authors

BOB ALGOZZINE is currently teaching in the Department of Educational Administration, Research, and Technology of the College of Education at the University of North Carolina at Charlotte. He has been a special education classroom teacher and college professor for more than 30 years in public schools and universities in New York, Virginia, Pennsylvania, Florida, and North Carolina. Textbooks he has written are used in teacher preparation courses around the country. He has been a featured speaker at local, state, national, and international professional conferences and is widely recognized as an expert on effective teaching and special education.

BOB AUDETTE is Associate Professor of Elementary Education at the University of North Carolina at Charlotte. His teaching, service, and research focus on the application of Total Quality principles in classroom settings. The use of these principles with students of elementary age results in their development of personal responsibility for their own learning and behavior.

SANDRA L. CHRISTENSON is Professor of Educational Psychology at the University of Minnesota. Her research focuses on enhancing students' engagement with school and promoting positive academic and behavioral outcomes for students through home-school collaboration. She is an author of books, chapters, tests, and journal articles, several of which focus on prevention and family-school collaboration, and serves on the APA Task Force for Dropout Prevention.

ANN P. DAUNIC has been involved for the past several years in research at the University of Florida about preventing or reducing aggressive behavior through problem-solving strategies. Her interest in conflict resolution and anger management with students at risk for school failure reflects her background in psychology and a more recent focus on cultural and minority issues. Experience as a non-public school administrator, counselor, and tutor contributed to her desire to support students with learning or behavioral difficulties in collaboration with their parents and teachers.

EDWARD D. ELLIS, JR., has served as both an elementary and secondary principal for a total of 20 years. He is currently the Principal of Crestdale Middle School, Charlotte, North Carolina. He has taught Language Arts, Social Studies, and U.S. History in Grades 7-9. He is a doctoral candidate at the University of North Carolina at Charlotte; his current interests include extensive research on behavior management and unified discipline programs.

DAVID L. EVELO served the Minneapolis Public Schools in a variety of roles for 30 years, including district program coordinator, teacher, school engagement and transition specialist, and district special education coordinator. He was the codirector of several U.S. Department of Education funded dropout prevention studies from 1990-1998. He is presently a consultant.

ROBERT J. EVERT has 25 years experience in cross-cultural work, education, mental health, and community organization. With a master's degree in Theology, he was a missionary for 10 years in Bolivia, serving also as the director of an educational radio station and a rural integral health project. After returning to the United States, he became a licensed psychotherapist and has worked in school-based mental health programs. The Linkages to Learning program at Broad Acres has allowed him to use his diverse training and experience in developing a community-based direct service and prevention program with a multicultural population.

MARTHA FITZGERALD's research, spanning more than three decades, has focused on ways that children, parents, and teachers can come together as partners in learning. Her home-based research in the seventies served as the prototype for Vermont's Essential Early Education. Later her research focused on school-based approaches to special education mediated by Consulting Teachers. She serves as Principal Investigator for Achieving, Behaving, Caring Partnerships, an approach that helps parents, teacher, and child work as a team. She and her husband Ed Knight are the parents of five adult children, one of whom has an emotional disability.

KAREN A. FRIEDMAN is a doctoral candidate in the Department of Special Education at the University of Maryland. Her research focuses on strength-based assessment of children with emotional and behavioral disorders and on parent/professional collaboration. She was involved with the creation of the Maryland Coalition of Families for Children's Mental

Health; she serves on the executive board of that organization and the Montgomery County Federation of Families for Children's Mental Health. She represents these groups at the Maryland Disability Law Center Advisory Board.

CHRISTINE M. HURLEY is a school psychologist and special education coordinator for the Minneapolis Public Schools. Her research interests include school climate, dropout prevention and school engagement for adolescents, family involvement in education, and educational issues related to homeless youth and families. She is an author of technical reports, procedural manuals, journal articles, and book chapters, including authorship of the "Keeping Kids in School" Check & Connect manual.

DEBRA M. KAMPS is a Senior Scientist with the University of Kansas at Juniper Gardens Children's Project. Her research has focused on improving the academic, social, and behavioral performance of children in elementary and middle school settings. She has completed multiple projects with children, teachers, and parents in urban, diverse communities and in general and special education classrooms. She has developed programs to support peer networks and social skills groups for students with behavioral and developmental disabilities, peer tutoring programs, and classroom management systems.

PAM KAY's research at the University of Vermont focuses on improving the relationship between parents and teachers. For the past 5 years, she has led the collaborative efforts of the researchers who contributed to this book to share their findings with principals, teachers, parents, and school board members. She is the parent of two sons who have significant disabilities, including emotional and behavioral issues; she was a founder of the Vermont Federation of Families for Children's Mental Health. She has also been an elementary school teacher and an executive in several community agencies.

PETER E. LEONE is a professor in the Department of Special Education at the University of Maryland. During his professional career he has been a teacher of adolescents with behavioral disorders, a teacher trainer, a researcher, and an advocate. During the past 15 years he has evaluated and monitored educational programs in many states, particularly in juvenile justice facilities. He currently directs EDJJ, The National Center on Education, Disability, and Juvenile Justice, jointly funded by the Office of Juvenile Justice and Delinquency Prevention and the Office of Special Education Programs.

STEPHANIE H. McCONAUGHY has served as a psychological consultant to Vermont school districts for 20 years and is a Vermont Practicing Psychologist and Nationally Certified School Psychologist. She is a Research Associate Professor in the UVM Department of Psychiatry and maintains a clinical practice at the Fletcher Allen Health Care Center for Children, Youth and Families. She collaborated on the research design and outcome evaluation of the ABC project described in Chapter 6.

MARY BETH MARR is Clinical Assistant Professor in the Department of Reading and Elementary Education at the University of North Carolina at Charlotte. Her research interests include children's early literacy development, strategy instruction, and classroom environments that promote literacy. Her 4-year role as project coordinator of a school-based primary prevention grant and subsequent 1-year return to the elementary classroom as a literacy teacher highlighted the urgent need to focus on both the quality of classroom instruction and the classroom learning environment.

MARY F. SINCLAIR is a Research Associate with the Institute on Community Integration in the College of Education and Human Development at the University of Minnesota. Her 14 years of applied research experience have focused on school engagement, dropout prevention, and support systems for youth placed at high risk for school failure, especially youth with disabilities. Currently, she is Principal Investigator for the OSEP-funded Persistence Plus study on the effectiveness of the Check & Connect school engagement model, targeting urban high school students with serious emotional and behavioral disabilities.

STEPHEN W. SMITH is a Professor in the Special Education Department at the University of Florida (UF). He is responsible for the teacher education program in emotional and behavioral disorders at UF and has conducted multiple investigations on behavior management techniques. His interests also include cognitive behavior training to reduce student aggression and the use of self-management procedures in classrooms. He is a trained mediator for the UF Center for Dispute Resolution. He spent 8 years as a teacher in special education.

MARTHA L. THURLOW is a Senior Research Associate, University of Minnesota, and Director of the National Center on Educational Outcomes. She has conducted research involving special education for the past 30 years in a variety of areas, including assessment, learning disabilities, early childhood education, dropout prevention, effective classroom instruction, and integration of students with disabilities in general education settings. She also is a coeditor of *Exceptional Children,* the research journal of the Council for Exceptional Children.

RICHARD WHITE is a Professor and Chair of the Department of Counseling, Special Education and Child Development in the College of Education at the University of North Carolina at Charlotte. He teaches courses in behavioral-emotional disabilities and focuses on the recruitment of special educators, especially those from ALANA populations. He is currently president of the North Carolina Council for Children with Behavior Disorders, and a member of the board of North Carolina's Exceptional Children's Assistance Parent Center. He has taught inner-city youth with behavioral disorders.

Promising Practices for Preventing Problem Behaviors

1

Bob Algozzine
Pam Kay

When I get up to go to school in the morning, I don't want to feel like I'm going to a correctional facility.
> —Students reporting on school violence
> (Brooks, Schiraldi, & Ziedenberg,
> 2000, pp. 3-4)

We've got to let the kids know who is in charge of the schools. And if that means infringing on somebody's individual freedom, so be it. There's been some criticism that, well, where does it end? And my point would be, I don't know where it ends, but it is sure going to begin with [mesh] book bags.
> —Chair of local school board
> (Brooks et al., 2000, pp. 3-4)

A child with behavioral problems becomes a healthy youth or a disturbed youth in response to a history of interactive patterns within her or his environment.
> —Osher and Hanley (1996)

The school's role in preventing problem behaviors has changed drastically in the past decade. Societal trends seem to promote violence as the solution to interpersonal conflicts. Increasing numbers of students bring to school the antisocial behaviors learned and reinforced in their out-of-school hours. Others turn their worries inward and withdraw from contact with peers. As a result, fewer students are fully available for learning. School administrators face daily and continuous challenges in their efforts to establish safe and orderly classroom environments, where teachers can teach and all students can learn (Nelson, Crabtree, Marchand-Martella, & Martella, 1998; Sugai, Sprague, Horner, & Walker, 2000). The challenge goes beyond their responsibility to create a safe haven where academic mastery can take place, however. Schools have a role to play in changing students' problem behaviors, and bringing together the elements and services that students need to cope with their out-of-school environments as well.

Administrators and teachers require the support of their communities to carry out this task. Excessive public pressure focused on improving academic results may eclipse the other role that schools have traditionally filled, that of socializing children and teaching them to behave in acceptable ways. Reactive and exclusively punitive responses to students' problem behaviors only move them from the school setting to the community, and too often to the nearest correctional facility. Communities need to acknowledge that the place to teach children positive and productive behaviors is the school, not the jail.

A school that adopts a comprehensive system of prevention strategies has the potential to reduce the development of both new and current cases, or the incidence and prevalence of school-related problems. A well-crafted approach to prevention improves the efficiency and effectiveness with which schoolwide, classroom, and individual behavior support systems operate. Without parent and community support, proactive models can be difficult to implement and maintain. Many students whose lives place them at risk for emotional and/or behavioral problems do not respond to generic discipline methods; their misbehavior can dominate the classroom. They respond slowly to even targeted interventions, and often demand intensive, ongoing, individualized behavior support (Sugai et al., 2000).

Schools need practical, proven methods for improving discipline and providing behavioral support. Teachers and school board members need to see how such methods will increase the time available for learning. Finally, administrators need ways of measuring their success in implementing prevention strategies, to ensure continued public support. This book will address these needs.

What We Know About Prevention

Professionals in special education designate three levels of prevention: primary, secondary, and tertiary (cf. Goldstein, Harootunian, & Conoley, 1994; Kamps & Tankersley, 1996; Kauffman, 1999; Simeonsson, 1991). Primary prevention, also called universal prevention, improves the environment of an entire population. Secondary prevention improves the lives of targeted individuals by either protecting them or improving their ability to function. Tertiary prevention improves people's lives by controlling further deterioration. Sugai and colleagues (2000) use these levels to describe an integrated model for preventing violent and destructive behavior in schools: Primary prevention interventions target the large group of students (80%-90%) who proceed through school exhibiting minor problem behaviors. Secondary prevention interventions address the needs of a small group (5%-15%) of students at risk for troubled and troubling behavior. Tertiary prevention interventions are reserved for students with chronic and severe problem behaviors.

Kamps and Tankersley (1996) described the following features regarding the prevention of emotional and/or behavioral disorders:

- ♦ Prevention means early intervention; the most effective and efficient treatment begins with young children.

- ♦ Prevention involves parents as key players.

- ♦ Prevention involves administrators, teachers, peers, and others; opportunities for success are maximized when key people are included.

- ♦ Prevention involves collaboration among families, schools, and service providers; improving behavior is not the sole responsibility of any caregiver.

- ♦ Prevention involves cross-setting, multiple, and proactive interventions; school provides a critical component in overall, effective treatment.

- ♦ Prevention involves self-management; students learn to maintain their positive behaviors and transfer their learning within their natural environments.

Effective prevention programs promote academic and behavioral success, mental and emotional wellness, and caring school environments that address three areas: classroom, school, and community. Classroom prevention approaches provide coordinated, comprehensive, intensive support designed to teach students appropriate behavior and problem-solving skills and to enhance academic instruction. Schoolwide prevention restructures schools and what goes on in them to create conditions that reduce inappropriate behavior; it creates environments where teachers can teach and students can learn. Community prevention interventions represent collaborative initiatives in which community members provide assistance to each other, especially parents and their children experiencing adjustment problems.

TABLE 1.1 Data-Based Prevention Practices

Location	Intervention Approach	Chapter
Classroom Interventions	Improving Behavior of Individual Students	2
	Total Quality Education	3
	Social Skills Instruction	4
	Unified Discipline	5
	Conflict Resolution	8
School Interventions	Total Quality Education	3
	Unified Discipline	5
	Peer Mediation	8
	Check & Connect	9
Community Interventions	Parent Partnerships	6
	Community Services	7
	Check & Connect	9

The effective prevention programs described in this book are based on the premise that early response to learning, behavior, and emotional problems can lead to better outcomes for students. The efforts are built into the school's foundation as part of the general education program. They are accessible to all students. They address three fundamental areas of need: improving student behaviors in individual classrooms, improving school-wide conditions, and improving family and community partnerships (see Table 1.1).

What We Need to Know About Prevention

Kamps and Tankersley (1996) identify the following needs for new knowledge about prevention: (a) applications including social, behavioral, and academic interventions, with teacher-, peer-, and parent-mediated programs that are implemented consistently; (b) continued investigation of teacher and parent support systems to carry out programs within natural environments and in a manner that meets the needs of all children in classrooms and other family members as well; (c) credible evaluation of long-term prevention including ecological assessment, multiple measures, and merging methodologies (e.g., qualitative measures, social validity); and (d) commitments to funding for prevention programs with acceptance of long-term interventions for more serious disorders and efficiency studies and dissemination to legislators and policymakers (p. 46).

Until recently, there has been little support for preventive interventions before a student shows serious signs of behavioral difficulties or emotional disturbance. In the 1990s, changes in the federal law known as the IDEA (Individuals with Disabilities Education Act) encouraged special education personnel to work with young students whose behavior indicated that they might be at risk of developing serious emotional and/or behavioral disorders. Federal funding initiated research projects that focused on prevention rather than remediation, encouraging the use of special education expertise in general education settings.

The information in this book is derived from the work of six research teams, each working toward improving knowledge about effective classroom, school, or community prevention practices. The funding came through the U.S. Office of Special Education Programs under the provisions of the IDEA. In the 1990 authorization of the program to address emotional and/or behavioral disorders, Congress specified that research projects might include

> developing and demonstrating innovative approaches to assist and prevent children with emotional and behavioral problems from developing serious emotional disturbances that require the provision of special education and related services. (20 U.S.C. 1426)

This book is one of the products of the funding initiative that resulted.[1]

In Chapter 2, Debra Kamps focuses on positive, proactive approaches to improving behavior for individual students. Providing these supports early in a child's life reduces the risk of more serious problems and improves the outcomes of schooling. Chapter 2 provides a blueprint for promoting supportive, structured, well-managed, educational environments for all children. The chapter includes information about antisocial behavior and tips for teaching rules and compliance, as well as procedures for using group contingencies to improve behavior, pointers for choosing rewards, and procedures for reducing inappropriate behaviors. It concludes with information about using functional assessment and intervention design procedures for children with chronic, more intensive needs for behavioral support.

Bob Audette and his colleagues address a model that focuses on improving classroom and overall school climate. The model is grounded in the principles of Total Quality Management that have transformed many of America's most successful businesses. The tools and skills of Total Quality

Management used by managers and employees in these companies help them continuously learn more about their customers and continuously improve the processes by which they produce quality products. These same tools and skills—group problem solving, process thinking, planning, data gathering, data analysis, listening, preventing and resolving conflict, and building cooperative relations—have been used to transform many of America's schools. The rhythm of learning in the classrooms in these schools is very different from that in traditional classrooms in traditional schools. Individual and group behavior responds to the atmosphere of thoughtful self-management. Children in these classrooms are well prepared to deal with and contribute to the ever-changing demands and challenges of a contemporary American education.

Social incompetence is a common characteristic of elementary school children at risk for referral for special education services. Behavioral excesses are identified by teachers as among the most difficult problems to deal with in general education classrooms. Shouting, arguing, and disrupting the group are typically part of the behavioral repertoires of these students. As children become older, violence, threats of violence, and other more aggressive forms of social problems create conditions that are not conducive to teaching or learning in middle and high schools. Teaching social skills is an important part of any prevention effort. Social skills curricula are designed to help students increase their awareness and understanding of personal emotions, values, attitudes, and appropriate ways to interact. In Chapter 4, Debra Kamps and Pam Kay address the importance of social skills instruction. They describe critical social skills, give examples of research-based curricula, outline effective instructional procedures and enhancements, and point out strategies to reinforce and maintain positive behaviors both inside and outside of the classroom.

The organization of orderly schools is characterized by commitment to appropriate student behavior and clear behavior expectations of students. Rules, expectations, and procedures are discussed, debated, and frequently formalized into school discipline plans and classroom management procedures. To balance this emphasis on formal procedure, the climate in these organizations conveys concern for students as individuals. This concern manifests itself in a variety of ways, including efforts to involve students in decision making, school goals that value student achievement, and classroom procedures that support order, respect, and learning. In Chapter 5, Bob Algozzine and Richard White address a schoolwide discipline model in which students are exposed to a united, caring, firm, loving, and very determined action plan. The objectives of Unified Discipline—unified attitudes, unified expectations, unified correction procedures, and unified team roles—are consistent with best practices. The outcomes of implementing the model provide strong support for the use of a schoolwide discipline plan.

Chapter 6 turns the focus to building effective partnerships between parents and teachers. Pam Kay, Martha Fitzgerald, and Stephanie McConaughy describe how Parent-Teacher Action Research (PTAR) provides a structure under which the parent(s) and the classroom teacher of children in the first and second grades work together. Under the guidance of a Parent Liaison, who is an experienced parent from the local community, the PTAR team assesses the child's strengths and needs, sets mutual goals, and follows a cycle of data collection and analysis. Using a process that is analogous to Functional Assessment, the parents and teachers create and carry out action plans that are designed to improve consistency between home and school, and begin the action research cycle again.

Many families need additional support from the community to meet their children's needs; this is especially true in schools where many families are recent immigrants. In Chapter 7, Peter Leone, Robert Evert, and Karen Friedman relate the experiences of Broad Acres Elementary School in Silver Spring, Maryland. In creating Linkages to Learning, the Montgomery County School District teamed with local public and private providers of health, mental health, and social work. The core elements for success included (a) stable and consistent funding, (b) a critical mass of resources, (c) cultural competence among staff, and (d) a collaborative program culture. These program features fostered effective partnerships between the Linkages staff and the local school staff.

In Chapter 8, Stephen Smith and Ann Daunic at the University of Florida address conflict resolution and peer mediation. Using the results of their long-term research project in three middle schools as a guide, they describe the components and function of conflict resolution and peer mediation programs and their rationale within a developmental framework, briefly reviewing some of the relevant research and providing recommendations about how to implement and maintain an effective program. The implications of their work for prevention of problem behaviors are clear: Helping students turn inevitable conflicts into opportunities for growth and learning reduces the need for punitive discipline and supports overall efforts to prevent more serious behavior problems.

The Check & Connect model, described by Mary Sinclair and colleagues in Chapter 9, is used to build connections with disenfranchised youth and families. The role of the person responsible for facilitating students' connection with school (the monitor) and the procedures monitors use to encourage school engagement (checking and connecting) are key components of the model. A caring adult works with disengaged students and their families over an extended period of time. This adult systematically checks student levels of engagement with school and provides timely individualized intervention to build and maintain connections to school and learning. As with the other models, Check & Connect is data based and grounded in research on resiliency and home-school collaboration.

Again, the implications are obvious: Keeping students in school prevents more serious problems from developing.

Until schools have the tools to measure and publicly discuss their prevention efforts, however, these proactive approaches will not become part of the true missions in public schools. Stephanie McConaughy and Peter Leone devote Chapter 10 to describing those tools so that administrators and school board members can choose and use them. They discuss each of the measures used in the research projects that are the bases of the preceding chapters. In addition, they recommend a strengths-based measure, the Behavioral and Emotional Rating Scale, or BERS (Epstein & Sharma, 1998), which was developed and published in the years since these projects began. This chapter provides solid information about the tools that researchers use to evaluate the success of their interventions, but avoids much of the technical language that can make these measures incomprehensible to educational leaders and the general public.

Today, most teachers will tell you that they spend an inordinate amount of time, energy, and effort managing problem behaviors. These same teachers will attest that time spent managing behavior seriously restricts the amount of time they spend teaching basic academic skills. Removing students who misbehave from the classroom only displaces the problem, and does nothing to address the school system's responsibility to educate them. Serious concern exists regarding problem behavior management at all levels of education.

The information in this book is drawn from the work of researchers at several universities who spent at least 4 years implementing and evaluating school-based prevention practices with their public school partners. Their focus was on students with (or at risk of being identified with) serious emotional disturbance as the result of unacceptable behavior in school. The research-based strategies varied across settings and were adapted and tested in urban, suburban, and rural schools in six states. This compilation of their work is designed to help parents, teachers, school board members, and administrators work together to create comprehensive systems that prevent problem behaviors.

NOTE _____

1. For other products and related research projects, see the Web site for *Prevention Practices That Work: What Administrators Can Do to Promote Positive Student Behavior.* The URL is www.air.org/cecp/preventionstrategies.

REFERENCES

Brooks, K., Schiraldi, V., & Ziedenberg, J. (2000). School house hype: Two years later. Washington, DC: Justice Policy Institute. Retrieved March 23, 2001 from the World Wide Web: www.cjcj.org/schoolhousehype/shh2.html

Epstein, M. H., & Sharma, J. M. (1998). *Behavioral and Emotional Rating Scale.* Austin, TX: PRO-ED.

Goldstein, A. P., Harootunian, B., & Conoley, J. C. (1994). *Student aggression: Prevention, management, and replacement training.* New York: Guilford.

Kamps, D. M., & Tankersley, M. (1996). Prevention of behavioral and conduct disorders: Trends and research issues. *Behavioral Disorders, 21*(1), 41-48.

Kauffman, J. M. (1999). How we prevent the prevention of emotional and behavioral disorders. *Exceptional Children, 65,* 448-468.

Nelson, J. R., Crabtree, M., Marchand-Martella, N., & Martella, R. (1998). Teaching behavior in the whole school. *Teaching Exceptional Children, 30*(4), 4-9.

Osher, D., & Hanley, T. V. (1996). Implications of the national agenda to improve results for children and youth with or at risk of serious emotional disturbance. In R. J. Illback & C. M. Nelson (Eds.), *Emerging school-based approaches for children with emotional and behavioral problems: Research and practice in services integration* (pp. 7-36). New York: Haworth.

Simeonsson, R. J. (1991). Primary, secondary, and tertiary prevention in early intervention. *Journal of Early Intervention, 15,* 124-134.

Sugai, G., Sprague, J. A., Horner, R. H., & Walker, H. M. (2000). Preventing school violence: The use of office discipline referrals to assess and monitor schoolwide discipline interventions. *Journal of Emotional and Behavioral Disorders, 8,* 94-101.

RESOURCES

Achenbach, T. M., & Howell, C. T. (1993). Are America's children's programs getting worse? A 13-year comparison. *Journal of the American Academy of Child and Adolescent Psychiatry, 32*(6), 1145-1154.

Algozzine, B., Audette, B., Ellis, E., Marr, M. B., & White, R. (2000). *Demography of disruptive behavior and the need for discipline.* Manuscript submitted for publication.

Algozzine, B., Audette, B., Ellis, E., Marr, M. B., & White, R. (2000). Supporting teachers, principals—and students—through unified discipline. *Teaching Exceptional Children, 33*(2), 42-47.

Brophy, J., & Good, T. L. (1986). Teacher behavior and student achievement. In M. C. Wittrock (Ed.), *Handbook of research on teaching* (pp. 328-375). New York: Macmillan.

Colvin, G., Kameenui, E. J., & Sugai, G. (1993). Reconceptualizng behavior management and school-wide discipline in general education. *Education and Treatment of Children, 16,* 361-381.

Gall, M. D., Borg, W. R., & Gall, J. P. (1996). *Educational research* (6th ed.). White Plains, NY: Longman.

Kauffman, J. M. (1996). Research to practice issues. *Behavioral Disorders, 21*(1), 55-60.

Kauffman, J. M. (1997). *Characteristics of emotional and behavioral disorders of children and youth.* Columbus, OH: Merrill.

Kerr, M. M., & Nelson, C. M. (1989). *Strategies for managing behavior problems in the classroom.* Columbus, OH: Merrill.

Marr, M. B., Audette, R., White, R., Ellis, E., & Algozzine, B. (in press). School-wide discipline and classroom ecology. *Special Services in the Schools.*

Sack, K. (1999, May 4). Schools add security and tighten dress, speech and civility rules. *New York Times.*

Stallings, J. (1975). Implementation and child effects of teaching practices in Follow Through classrooms. *Monographs of the Society for Research in Child Development, 40*(7-8, Serial No. 163).

Stallings, J. (1980). Allocated academic learning time revisited, or beyond time on task. *Educational Researcher, 8*(11), 11-16.

Sugai, G., & Horner, R. H. (1999). Discipline and behavior support: Preferred processes and practices. *Effective School Practice, 17*(4), 10-22.

Taylor-Greene, S., Brown, D., Nelson, L., Longton, J., Gassman, T., Cohen, J., Swartz, J., Horner, R. H., Sugai, G., & Hall, S. (1997). School-wide behavioral support: Starting the year off right. *Journal of Behavioral Support, 7,* 99-112.

White, R. (1996). Unified discipline. In B. Algozzine (Ed.), *Problem behavior management: An educator's resource service.* Gaithersburg, MD: Aspen Publishers.

White, R., Algozzine, B., Audette, B., Marr, M. B., & Ellis, E. (in press). Unified discipline: A school-wide approach for managing problem behavior. *Intervention in School and Clinic.*

White, R., Marr, M. B., Ellis, E., Audette, B., & Algozzine, B. (in press). Effects of school-wide discipline on office referrals. *Journal of At-Risk Issues.*

Preventing Problems by Improving Behavior

2

Debra M. Kamps

> *Toby comes to school every day eager to learn, but most days it just doesn't work out that way. Today, for example, he was sent to the principal's office because he had a fight with a student who accidentally bumped into him on the way to recess. Something like this happens almost every day, and his teacher is at a loss for what to do about it. Toby's parents have been told that if his antisocial behavior continues, he will be placed in a special class for students with emotional and behavioral disorders (E/BD), and they are not sure this is a good idea.*

At some point or another in growing up, nearly all children have behaviors considered problematic, challenging, or frustrating to parents and teachers. During normal development, it is common to observe behaviors that test adults as a way to learn the rules and to defy adult-determined limits as a means to exert control and independence. Half of all children exhibiting common behavior problems eventually progress on a normal developmental pathway, with appropriate communication and problem-solving skills replacing their early antisocial behaviors (Campbell, 1995). The frequency and intensity of problem behaviors are indicators that children may be at risk for continued problems of clinical significance. The behaviors may occur at a much higher rate than typically noted for children of the same developmental age. They may be much more intense in nature (e.g., self-injurious aggression), or continue to occur over a longer period than is considered normal (Kazdin, Mazurick, & Bass, 1993). Eventually these types of antisocial behaviors reduce the child's learning, and may result in the need for special education services.

This chapter focuses on positive, proactive approaches to improving behavior for individual students with antisocial tendencies. When these supports are provided early in a child's life, studies have shown that the risks can be reduced and the outcomes improved. The reader will find a blueprint for promoting supportive, structured, well-managed, educational environments for all children, including (a) information about antisocial behavior, (b) tips for teaching rules and compliance as well as procedures for using group contingencies to improve behavior, (c) tips for choosing rewards, (d) procedures for reducing inappropriate behaviors, and (e) information about using functional assessment and intervention design procedures for children with chronic, more intensive needs for behavioral support.

What We Know About Antisocial Behavior

Longitudinal research has provided a wealth of information regarding characteristics of antisocial behavior. Antisocial behavior can be either *overt* or *covert*. *Overt* involves acts against other people; *covert* involves acts against property and/or self-abuse. Consider these facts:

- The vast majority of children with antisocial behaviors are boys; antisocial behavior in girls is less evident and expressed differently (i.e., more often self-directed than outer-directed).

- Antisocial children can be identified very accurately at age 3 or 4. The idea that "He'll grow out of it" may deter early intervention efforts. Early starters are more at risk for long-term effects (e.g., delinquency, arrests) than children who begin antisocial patterns later.

- The more severe the antisocial behavior pattern, the greater the stability or persistence over time and settings with higher risk for negative developmental outcomes.

- If students do not change antisocial behavior patterns by the end of Grade 3, they should be considered to have a chronic condition, much like diabetes. Behaviors cannot be cured but can be managed with the appropriate supports and continuing interventions.

Early intervention in home, school, and community is the single best hope we have of diverting children from this path. Children who grow up with antisocial behaviors are at severe risk for a host of negative outcomes including school dropout, vocational adjustment problems, drug and alcohol abuse, relationship problems, and higher hospitalization and mortality rates (Patterson, 1982; Pettit, Bates, & Dodge, 1993; Walker, Colvin, & Ramsey, 1995). Loeber et al. (1993) describe three categories that indicate a developmental pathway to conduct disorders, or chronic patterns of antisocial behavior. Overt behaviors include aggression, coercion, bullying, manipulation of others, and escalated negative interactions with teachers, parents, and peers. Covert behaviors include stealing, lying, burglary, and drug/alcohol use. Disobedience is a third pathway, including noncompliance, oppositional-defiant behavior, and resistance to adults. These pathways are visible over time and can be interrupted by early preventive action.

Given the grim futures for students with antisocial behaviors, educators need to play a paramount role in teaching students how to behave appropriately, and correcting counter-productive habits. Carrying out this role becomes easier when teachers remember that students are typically not happy with their inappropriate behaviors. Half of all students with antisocial behaviors are clinically depressed, and many are rejected by peers and adults alike.

Why Do Inappropriate Behaviors Occur?

Inappropriate behaviors do not just happen. Biological conditions (e.g., organic problems, cognitive delays, neurological disorders) and environmental events (e.g., limited classroom structure, teacher inconsistency, non-nurturing home conditions, divorce) contribute to inappropriate behaviors. Similarly, consistent and fair discipline, nurturing homes, parental well-being, and organized school settings contribute to the occurrence of appropriate behaviors. Thus the origins of behaviors and conditions that trigger, maintain, or change behaviors rest both with the individual child and with teachers, parents, peers, and the community.

Research in child development shows that typically developing children learn appropriate behaviors via modeling and teaching by their parents. Success in building relationships and participating cooperatively with others is based upon early developmental progress within nurturing, safe environments. Adaptive behaviors include following directions from adults, following rules across different contexts, completing instructional tasks or chores, learning independence, requesting assistance appropriately, and interacting with peers in a cooperative manner. These developmental progressions result in appropriate behaviors, meaningful and productive relationships with others, school achievement, and acceptance by teachers and peers (Walker et al., 1995).

What Can We Do to Encourage Good Behaviors?

The most efficient way to eliminate inappropriate behaviors is to prevent their occurrence or escalation from the beginning. This philosophy implies a focus on proactive, positive, and instructive procedures, that is, a prevention approach. This further implies a shift away from reactive, punitive, and exclusionary practices. Proactive, not reactive, thinking is the principle to be followed. Schools that adhere to a prevention approach are highly effective. They can encourage resilience in children from environments that place them at a disadvantage (e.g., urban neighborhoods with high rates of violence, economically depressed communities, missing-parent families). Effective schools have the following characteristics:

♦ Productive academic instruction, high expectations, and structured classrooms with high engagement and efficient transitions

♦ Specialized curriculum to teach behaviors, including social skills, anger management, school safety, with schoolwide discipline plans

♦ Trained teachers who receive support for managing challenging behaviors

♦ Strong student-school bonding, with practices that connect children to adults, such as mentoring, and positive school climate with motivation systems

♦ Parent involvement and participation in behavior support

♦ Practices that encourage connections among students, such as tutoring and homework teams (Miller, Brehm, & Whitehouse, 1998; Rhode, Jenson, & Reavis, 1992)

These programs and procedures are considered "universal levels of prevention" and should be in place for all children, especially in environments that place children at an educational disadvantage. Studies have shown that universal prevention strategies, including effective instruction, implemented with moderate to high levels of fidelity, will work to promote academic and social development for most children and prevent many chronic behaviors (Kamps, Kravits, Rauch, Kamps, & Chung, 2000; Walker et al., 1995).

How Can We Effectively Teach Rules and Compliance?

Organized classrooms with enriching activities and predictable rules and schedules foster more productive children and thus greater learning. A primary task for supporting appropriate behaviors is to teach those behaviors.

Teaching Classroom Rules. Effective rules (a) are stated objectively so that compliance can be measured, (b) state positive or appropriate behavior (e.g., "Keep hands and feet to self," rather than "no hitting"), and (c) are kept to a minimum number, that is, five or six classroom rules. Classroom rules may be designed to create orderly routines, efficient work time, mannerly conduct, and successful transitions (Mayer, 1999; Rhode et al., 1992). The following examples illustrate practical rules:

A compliance rule: Follow the teacher's directions.

A preparation rule: Have books, pencils, and paper every day.

A talking rule: Raise your hand to talk.

An in-class behavior rule: Keep hands and feet to self.

A transition rule: Put materials away in three minutes, quiet voices.

An on-time rule: Be in your seat when the bell rings.

One critical strategy for improving student compliance to rules is *direct instruction.* That means treating behavior and social skills as curriculum areas to teach, similar to academic subject matter. A recommended sequence for teaching rules includes defining each rule, including why the rule is important, with examples and non-examples, and having students role-play effective rule following. In addition, teachers should explain the consequences for following and not following rules as specifically as possible (Babyak, Luze, & Kamps, 2000; Carpenter & McKee-Higgins, 1996; Rhode et al., 1992). Successful use of classroom rules includes the following five steps:

1. Teach rules using a direct instruction approach.

2. Post rules.

3. Post consequences for rule compliance and for noncompliance.

4. Carry out consequences consistently.

5. Use booster sessions as needed (re-teaching for individuals or the group when rule infractions occur at an unacceptable rate).

Nearly all classrooms have posted rules. However, posting of the rules is only one out of five steps, or a 20% level of implementation. In order for the rules to become a critical component in classroom management, and to increase the probability of student compliance and successful behaviors, teachers must follow all five steps.

Teaching Compliance. Many school staff and parents hold a traditional view that when teachers (or other adults) make a request or give a direction, students (children) should comply. For others, the term *compliance* has negative connotations. In school, as in any community, healthy compliance is critical to rule-following behavior. Learning compliance to the rules established by the school community leads children to recognize that appropriate behavior applies beyond the school walls as well. Noncompliance may be a problem for students with emotional and/or behavioral problems and those from disadvantaged backgrounds.

Some adult behavior shapes and reinforces noncompliance. For example, in *coercive* adult-child interaction patterns, adult requests increase in number without ensuring compliance (Patterson, 1982). The adult escalates to threatening, ridiculing, or yelling. Child behaviors similarly escalate from ignoring to delaying, arguing, or full-blown tantrums. Often the adult withdraws the initial request (e.g., walks away) so that the child will stop the aggressive behavior. This pattern, while it may temporarily relieve a difficult situation, reinforces the inappropriate behaviors of the child. Adult behaviors, such as yelling and ultimatums, signal a "coercive pattern" (Rhode et al., 1992). When students have a history of negative interaction patterns with parents and/or teachers, that negative attention often becomes reinforcing to them, and increases their inappropriate behaviors. The realistic conclusion is that it is better not to give a direction or request if you are unable to follow through with it or ensure a consequence.

Fortunately, many actions improve compliance. Teachers may stand close to and look at the student when issuing a request, use an unemotional voice with normal volume, give clear and short commands, allow a few seconds for compliance to begin, and praise compliance (Forehand & McMahon, 1981). Two common mistakes that inadvertently reinforce noncompliance are (a) issuing the command multiple times (thus teaching the child that she or he doesn't have to follow the direction the first time you give it), and (b) allowing a child to negotiate delaying compliance (e.g., giving 5 more minutes of free time after you have issued a clean-up instruction). Table 2.1 provides a brief overview of the strategies and how to use them.

TABLE 2.1 Strategies for Increasing Student Compliance

Strategy	*Procedures*
Precision requests— Making appropriate requests in a way that maximizes student compliance (Rhode, Jenson, & Reavis, 1992)	1. Teacher explains request and consequences simply and clearly. 2. Request is made up close with eye contact, using "please." 3. Teacher waits 5-10 seconds for compliance. 4. Specific verbal response is given for compliance. 5. For noncompliance a second request is given "I need . . ." 6. Continued noncompliance requires a preplanned consequence. RULE: Make more start/do requests than stop/don't commands. RULE: Minimum of 4:1 positive to negative teacher statements.
Precorrection— Instruction in appropriate behaviors, and reminders before setting/context occurs of expectations (Colvin, Sugai, Good, & Lee, 1997)	1. Identify the context and the predictable problem behavior. 2. Specify the expected behavior. 3. Modify the context. 4. Conduct behavior rehearsals. 5. Provide strong reinforcement. 6. Prompt expected behaviors. 7. Monitor the plan.
Differential attention— Ignoring behaviors that tend to be attention seeking, reinforcing alternative or appropriate behaviors (Rhode, Jenson, & Reavis, 1992; Forehand & McMahon, 1981)	1. Ignore inappropriate behavior (break eye contact, do not speak to student, walk away, engage with an appropriate student). 2. Differentially pay attention to appropriate behavior as soon as possible following misbehavior. 3. Reward appropriate behavior at a high rate. RULE: Ignoring behavior usually results in a quick increase or burst of behavior (student testing); teachers must be prepared to ignore all instances—intermittent attention will have a negative effect. RULE: Ignoring is more effective if peers ignore as well.
Behavioral momentum— Requesting 2-3 easy behaviors, immediately prior to difficult request to increase compliance (Davis & Reichle, 1996)	1. Identify multiple requests that student is highly likely to follow. 2. Give 2-3 requests with high probability for compliance. 3. Immediately follow high probability request with harder request. EXAMPLE: Pass these papers to your row. Please write numbers 1-10. Write your favorite movie for number 1. Please write the vocabulary words and definitions for numbers 2-10.
Compliance Games— Reinforcement systems designed to reward student compliance to teacher requests (Rhode, Jenson, & Reavis, 1992)	Sure I Will: 1. Students divided into teams. 2. Teams select specific/unique compliance phrase, e.g., "Sure I will." "Sure, anytime." "No problem." 3. Students receive points for their team for saying the phrase and complying with requests. 4. Teams earn rewards for reaching compliance goals. Compliance Matrix (Bingo game using compliance as markers).

What We Know
About Changing Behavior_____

Individual and group contingency programs, with a strong *reinforcement* component, are highly effective systems for encouraging appropriate student behaviors. Teachers and other adults need to understand the following principles, which are the basis of reinforcement systems:

Reinforcement and *punishment* are terms used to describe relationships between two environmental events (see Alberto & Troutman, 1999): a behavior (any observable action) and a consequence (a result of that action). When a behavior *increases* when a consequence (usually pleasant) is applied, positive reinforcement has occurred. Negative reinforcement has occurred when a behavior *increases* when a consequence (usually unpleasant) is removed or reduced in intensity. Punishment has occurred when consequences result in a *decrease* in behavior.

There are important reasons for choosing reinforcement over punishment. Currently there is a trend from *permissive* to *punishing* in child rearing and societal reactions to misbehavior. School research finds low rates of praise (e.g., once every 15 to 30 minutes) compared to criticism or negative remarks every 2 minutes (Walker et al., 1995). What many experts conclude is that we have to make changes in dealing with disruptive behaviors of students: The status quo (primarily punishment based) is not working! Changes include proactive, positive prevention programs, with schools as a primary setting and resource for early and continued intervention (Miller et al., 1998; Stage & Quiroz, 1997; Walker, 1998). Individual classrooms can be the starting point for positive practices and reinforcement of appropriate behavior. Reinforcement procedures in schools can be easily implemented with training, feedback, and supports. Further, classroom-based reinforcement systems are much less expensive than long-term alternative treatment/education. Consider these benefits to reinforcement-based intervention programs:

♦ Reinforcement and classroom management systems, if implemented properly, improve the daily behavior of the child. Payoffs include improved compliance and increases in appropriate behaviors.

♦ A reinforcement system helps teach appropriate behavior. It is a mandatory step to improved self-regulation. First, the teacher manages the behavior, then the child assumes the management (e.g., self-management, coping and survival skills).

♦ Reinforcement (social, tangible) helps make classrooms fun and motivating for students. Students using reinforcement systems report they like their teachers and school better.

♦ Reinforcement systems promote positive school climates, a key indicator or characteristic of successful schools.

♦ Reinforcement systems help increase students' acceptance of mild consequences for inappropriate behaviors.

♦ Starting a reinforcement system is much less stressful than reacting to bad behaviors or implementing consequences.

Reinforcement Systems Using Group Contingencies

Group motivational systems are designed to improve appropriate behaviors and decrease disruptive behaviors. Systems are often referred to as group contingencies because privileges and rewards, as well as negative consequences, are delivered to groups of students contingent upon their behaviors, rather than routinely or at random. Group contingencies can be incorporated into classroom business and routines, and are particularly helpful in the following four situations: (a) when starting the school year and creating a productive classroom climate; (b) when students' cooperation or on-task behaviors need improvement; (c) when the group is frequently disruptive to instruction; and (d) when peers contribute to misbehaviors through encouragement or attention. The following examples describe classroom group contingency programs. Selected examples are grounded in social learning theory principles and have a supportive research base.

Mystery Motivators (Rhode et al., 1992). The Mystery Motivator incentive program is simply a surprise reward for the group, contingent on appropriate behavior. To use the Mystery Motivator program, the teacher places an envelope bearing a question mark in view of the students. Written inside is a fun classroom activity that students may earn for accomplishing a predetermined goal (e.g., quick transitions without fights, increased compliance to classroom rules, improved recess behaviors, etc.). The teacher drops laminated yes/no cards or happy/sad face cards in a container for appropriate or selected inappropriate behaviors, commenting each time:

♦ "Carla raised her hand to talk. Thank you."

♦ "Duane kept his hands to himself walking down the hall."

♦ "Class, you got ready to begin math in three minutes. Great!"

At the end of the day, or more frequently if necessary, the teacher or a student draws a card from the jar. If a *yes* card is drawn, the class earns the activity written on the paper in the Mystery Motivator envelope. If a *no* card is drawn, they follow the regular routine. Increasing the initial likelihood of the students receiving the reward is important to reinforcement systems. The teacher may need to stock the container for the first few days with more *yes* cards. Students get the payoff activity, become excited, and are motivated to continue to behave well and earn rewards.

Teachers should not use *no* cards or other response cost measures for wrong academic answers. However, they may set up rewards and positive contingencies for meeting academic goals.

After students have learned and demonstrated appropriate behaviors, teachers may slowly fade the use of the Mystery Motivator program. Fading is the process of weaning students by decreasing the number of times they receive the reinforcement. This simultaneously increases the number (or periods) of good behaviors they must exhibit before receiving the payoff. Random and variable reinforcement is more powerful than continuous reinforcement. A suggestion from the *Tough Kid Book* (Rhode et al., 1992) is to have a card marked for Monday through Friday with an *M* marked in invisible ink on one day. At the end of each day, highlight the marked space to see if it is a "Mystery Motivator" day.

Contingencies for Learning Academic and Social Skills (Hops & Walker, 1988). An early, highly effective, group contingency model similar to the Mystery Motivator program is the *Contingencies of Learning Academic and Social Skills (CLASS)* program. Characteristics of the CLASS program include group reward contingency for the class or teams, goals that focus on clearly stated classroom rules, and a clocklight instrument that shows green when all are following the rules (or use of red/green signal cards). The clocklight records the total time in class that rules are followed with a contingent time for earning the group reward. An enhancement to the program is the *Musical Clocklight* (West et al., 1995). This program adds instruction of alternative behaviors to implementation, and music to the clocklight. Teachers teach, model classroom rules, and role-play with students using examples and non-examples of the behaviors. The developers stipulate that corrective interactions should require only 1 or 2 minutes. They further recommend teaching students how to gain the teachers' attention appropriately, and follow instructions. Data-based studies have demonstrated successful rule following, compliance, and appropriate attention-directed behaviors for elementary, secondary, and special education students, using the CLASS and Musical Clocklight procedures.

The *Good Behavior Game (Barrish, Saunders, & Wolf, 1969)*. A long-standing and powerful program illustrating successful implementation of group contingencies is the *Good Behavior Game* (Barrish et al., 1969; Tankersley, 1995). Similar to the Mystery Motivator system, this strategy centers on group compliance to rules, with an added element of team competition. The teacher follows these steps:

1. Divide the class into two or more teams.

2. Tally frequencies of inappropriate behavior (rule noncompliance) for each team.

3. Provide rewards for the teams with the fewest infractions and/or for all teams meeting a set criterion (e.g., less than 5 violations).

The *Good Behavior Game Plus Merit* (Darveaux, 1984) enhances the game by including attention for appropriate behaviors. Teams have a set criterion of five or fewer points to earn rewards. Students earn merits when they complete assignments at 75% accuracy and actively participate. One point is erased from the board for every five merits earned collectively by a team. This additional component reduced disruptive behaviors for students with E/BD and their peers in general education classrooms, while increasing on-task behavior and assignments completed.

Cooperative Behavior Management (Brigham, Bakken, Scruggs, & Mastropieri, 1992). This system uses the Good Behavior Game with several enhancements: (a) Both teams win rewards if point totals are low; (b) individual students, despite team membership, may earn rewards by exhibiting self-control over individual behavior; and (c) the teacher sets up an accommodation for children who are particularly noncompliant, with a prompting procedure (a warning and reminder to the individual before point loss for the team).

Occasionally an individual student refuses to participate or becomes disruptive when the team begins to lose. Other students may also have exceptionally high rates of behaviors (e.g., students with ADHD or conduct disorders). Their participation may cause friction with team members because they incur too many points for violations. These students can serve individually as their own team, with private goal setting and additional merits provided to the peer team for behavioral improvements (Rhode et al., 1992). Students who appear motivated by negative attention or engage in counter-control behaviors should also get individualized accommodations (Barrish et al., 1969; Kauffman, 1989).

FIGURE 2.1.   Sample Self-Management Form

Name: _____ Date: _____

I Am Doing My Work

	YES	NO
1		
2		
3		
4		
5		
6		
7		
8		
9		
10		

SIT   SILENT   WORK

Group Contingencies and Self-Management. Teachers in general education classrooms may also meet the needs of heterogeneous and culturally diverse groups through classwide self-management as a group contingency program. The *Good Student Game,* as an example, combines components from the Good Behavior Game with Merit and classwide self-management (Babyak et al., 2000; Landrum & Tankersley, 1997). The game includes the following processes:

- ◆ Teachers define and present good student behaviors.

- ◆ Students role-play appropriate work behavior, using multiple examples and non-examples.

- ◆ Students are trained in self-evaluation (scoring yes/no at the sound of the timer).

- ◆ Teacher assesses reinforcers for the class and selects rewards.

- ◆ Teacher starts the Good Student Game during independent seat work activities with 3- to 5-minute recording intervals (timer repeats and students score *yes* or *no*).

- ◆ Teacher assigns rows or small groups of students to teams (Note: Students with high rates of inappropriate behavior become individual teams).

Typically, reinforcement is provided for 80% or better (e.g., 8 out of 10 boxes are checked yes; see Figure 2.1), for individual teams or all teams meeting criteria. Fading of the reinforcement is done by requiring multiple sessions with 80% *yes* tallies or weekly reinforcement for meeting goals.

Improvements using the Good Student Game in elementary classes (Figure 2.2) have included (a) increased on-task behavior classwide and by highly disruptive target students, (b) improvements in gaining teacher attention appropriately, (c) decreases in disruptive behaviors, (d) improved teacher ratings of students' social competence, and (e) teacher comments on increased curriculum coverage with use of the procedure (Babyak et al., 2000; Mitchem, Young, West, & Benyo, in press). In addition, others have recommended the use of classwide self-management in conjunction with point systems, and with class teams (e.g., the class is divided into teams that compete for the highest numbers of points (Kern, Dunlap, Childs, & Clarke, 1994; Salend, Whittaker, & Reeder, 1992). Developers also recommend implementation of group self-management when student misbehavior appears to have a "contagious effect" on peers. It should also be used when attention from peers reinforces inappropriate behaviors of students with problems. Teacher reliability checks on student honesty may also be an important component to self-management (Mitchem et al., in press).

FIGURE 2.2. Improvements From Using the Good Student Game

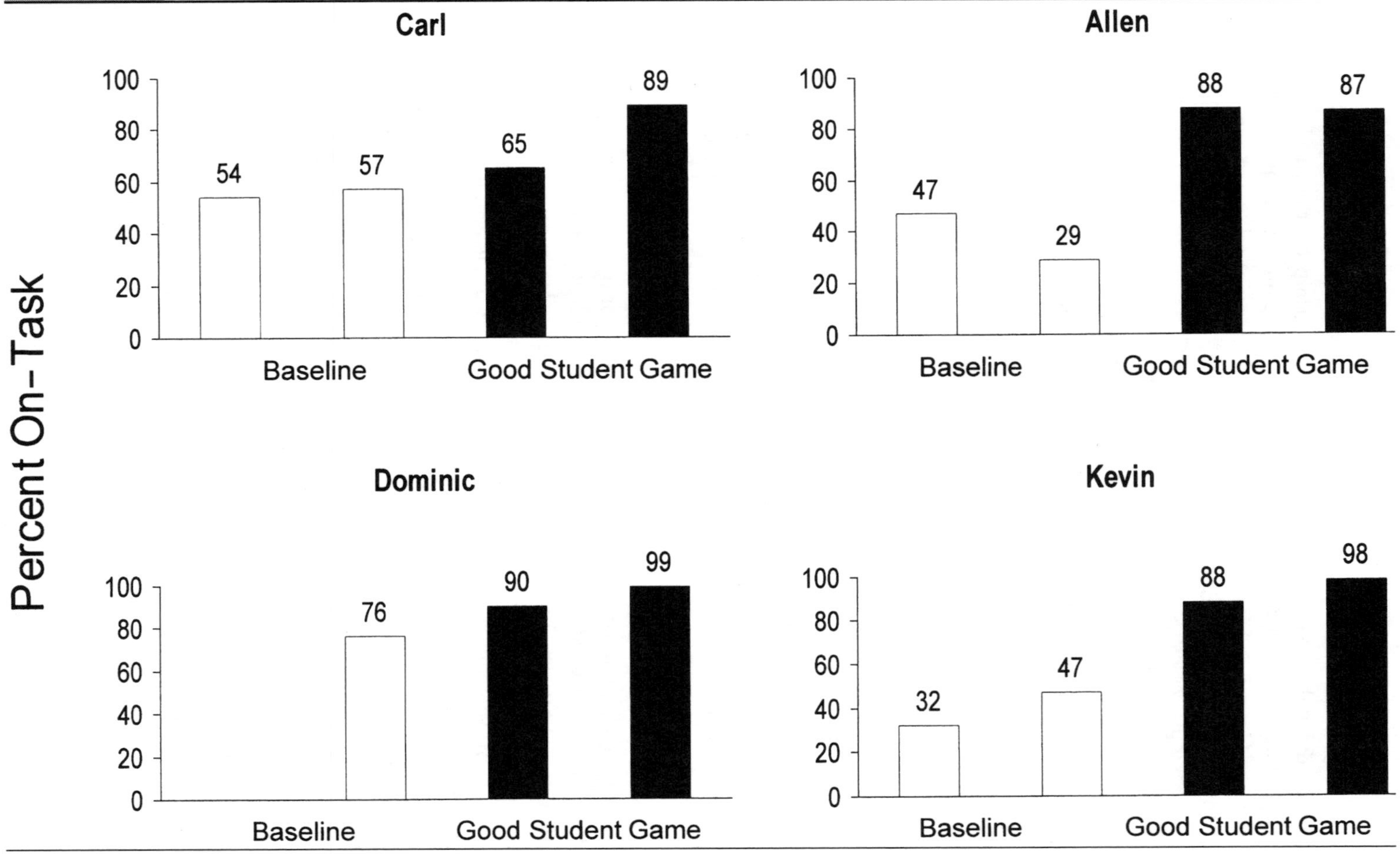

Steps in Choosing Reinforcers

By definition, reinforcement increases appropriate behaviors. All group contingency programs incorporate positive reinforcement of appropriate behaviors. Positive reinforcement has occurred when a behavior increases when a consequence has been applied. Researchers suggest the following guidelines to ensure that consequences (incentives or rewards) function as reinforcers:

- ♦ Immediate reinforcement is powerful, particularly when good behavior is initially being learned or in the acquisition stages.

- ♦ The reinforcement schedule must be frequent enough to improve behavior, and should be faded as behaviors improve (e.g., longer intervals or more work before payoffs).

- ♦ Frequent verbal praise with specific descriptors of the "positive behavior" may be effective social reinforcement, and may be a sufficient way to delay a tangible reinforcer.

- ♦ Tokens or points may be used to reinforce frequently while delaying tangible rewards.

- ♦ Enthusiastic, positive attitudes by adults as they deliver positive consequences help ensure that praise, tokens, and so on, are indeed reinforcing to students (Alberto & Troutman, 1999; Rhode et al., 1992).

In addition to these guidelines, student choice may enhance the effectiveness of the reinforcers. Ways for teachers to assess student preferences include (a) watching students to note their preferred activities and items, (b) tracking student requests and noticing favorites, (c) allowing students to sample a few items and soliciting comments on preferences, (d) asking students what they would like to earn, and (e) posting an agreed-upon reward for meeting goals, similar to a contract. It is important to note that desirability or preferences change, so frequent assessment is critical to reinforcement. Similarly, adults cannot assume that certain items will be truly reinforcing to all students. Input allows students to have appropriate control over this aspect of contingency programs, increases students' motivation to succeed (improve behaviors), and promotes cooperation between teachers and students.

Novelty and incorporating an element of surprise and chance into reinforcement may also be a powerful enhancement to the effectiveness of group contingency programs (Rhode et al., 1992). Lottery games are an example of this type of enhancement. In conjunction with a classwide self-management program, the teacher may pass out lottery tickets for predeter-

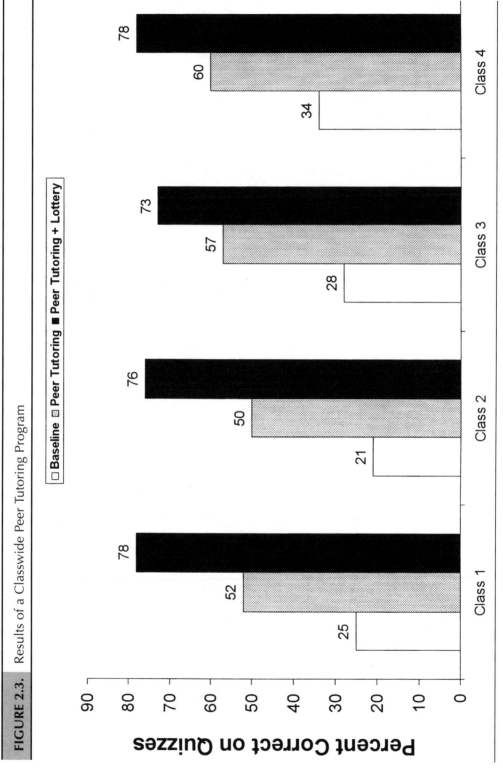

FIGURE 2.3. Results of a Classwide Peer Tutoring Program

mined appropriate behavior (staying in seat during work) or academic successes (e.g., 80% or better completion and/or accuracy on assignment, mastery of 10-12 multiplication facts). Drawings for prizes and special activities must then be frequent enough to provide the desired boost in performance in conjunction with the contingency, with fading of the schedule over time. As an example, in several middle school social studies classes during a classwide peer tutoring program, the teacher began using lottery tickets for appropriate on-task behaviors (listening to the partner read, tutor error corrections, answering comprehension questions). Four tickets were drawn on Fridays with prizes drawn from a grab bag, and surprise drawings occurred on occasion to maintain attention. Off-task behaviors decreased, and students' quiz scores increased as a result of improved engagement during tutoring (see Figure 2.3).

Negative Consequences and Reductive Procedures

The prior sections have described ways to teach appropriate behaviors and given examples of group contingency programs focusing on positive reinforcement procedures. Data, however, show that reinforcement of appropriate behavior may not always be enough to change very serious behaviors or very persistent behaviors such as aggression or ongoing disruptiveness (Bierman, Miller, & Stabb, 1987). Thus, for students with serious behavior problems such as those at risk for E/BD, the use of both positive and negative consequences may provide for maximum effectiveness for increasing appropriate and decreasing antisocial behaviors.

As with reinforcement choices, a key is to instruct students as to the consequences that will occur for rule infractions, disruptions, and so on, and to post those consequences along with the selected reinforcers/privileges for appropriate behaviors and meeting goals. The most effective consequences for inappropriate behaviors are mild punishment procedures that are consistently implemented. A definition of *punishment* is a consequence implemented following the behavior that decreases the frequency and/or probability of the behavior occurring in the future (Alberto & Troutman, 1999). Similar to reinforcement, a punisher can be identified only based on its effect for behaviors (decreases). As discussed earlier, some teacher behaviors such as reprimands or negative comments can be reinforcing to a student, rather than punishing.

Examples of mild punishment procedures that may be effective are response cost procedures and implementation of a brief time-out. *Response cost* is simply removal of something reinforcing. Examples of response cost include loss of 1 minute of recess, 5-minute delay in coming to fun activity, loss of lottery tickets, loss of points. *Time-out* is removal from the opportunity to earn positive reinforcement. Time-out procedures may be short periods within the same setting during which the opportunity to participate is withdrawn (e.g., lights out and heads down for 2 minutes, the student sits to the side in PE class for a few minutes following a disruptive behavior). Seclusionary time-out is use of a time-out room, secluding the child from the setting and activity. It is important to send a child to time-out as soon as behavior occurs, and not to talk to the child or attend in other ways, during the time-out period. Debriefing, or brief review of replacement behaviors may follow time-out. Time-out, particularly seclusionary time-out, should be implemented carefully and in adherence to school, district, and state policies (e.g., time away from instruction, frequency of use, preceding infraction). All punishment procedures should be carefully discussed with the administration and with parents. When student support team members are developing a punishment procedure for chronic behaviors, they will benefit from soliciting parental input and assistance. The following strategies for implementation of negative consequences will improve the accuracy and effectiveness of using mild punishment.

♦ Always use mild negative consequences. Do not start with a mild punisher and increase to more and more severe levels (this increases tolerance, or desensitizes the child and thus diminishes the effectiveness of punishment).

♦ When implementing a mild punisher (brief time-out, loss of 2 minutes of recess), verbally state the consequence, implement the consequence (if the correct time to do so), and move on with the regular routine. The key is not the severity of the consequence but the *consistency.*

♦ It is good to allow a 2-week trial period to determine if the system is working. Behaviors may increase for a short time as the student tests the system.

♦ In addition, it is important to remember that discussions regarding the problem behavior should occur after the consequence is implemented. It may be problematic to talk about behaviors immediately when they happen, in that this may inadvertently give attention for it (serving as reinforcement). The discussion may also be disruptive to the class routine and serve as peer entertainment. Debriefing happens later and is to plan for prevention in the future, and help the student determine how not to engage in the behavior next time.

It is important to start early in the behavior chain, that is, do not give repeated warnings and thus allow escalating behavior before implementing the consequence.

Functional Assessment and Analysis

A key to improving student behaviors is understanding the relationship of those behaviors to people and events within the students' environments. The technical terms for this process of understanding and planning for children exhibiting problem behavior are *functional assessment* and *functional analysis*. While some behavior problems may be a result of organic issues (e.g., hyperactivity, learning disability), other behaviors can be managed depending upon the responsiveness of others and environmental supports within a child's classroom or home setting. Understanding how such behavior is maintained or supported is a fundamental goal of functional assessment and analysis.

Common *functions* or *motivation* for individual children's inappropriate behavior to continue or escalate include attention, escape, access to tangibles or control, and stimulation (Dunlap et al., 1993).

♦ *Attention-motivated* behavior is exhibited to recruit a response (negative or positive) from teachers, parents, or peers.

♦ *Escape-motivated* behaviors occur when children are frustrated or bored with tasks and the behavior allows them to escape from that task, even if for a short period.

♦ *Access/control-motivated* behaviors occur when the child receives tangible items or access to an activity following the behavior (e.g., child hits a peer and the peer gives him the ball).

♦ *Sensory/stimulation-motivated* behavior provides a reinforcing physical condition for the child (e.g., rocking by a child with autism, fidgeting by a child with ADHD).

Functional assessment describes a range of techniques to seek information about the antecedents and consequences surrounding behaviors, and related conditions that may influence behavior. Examples of assessment procedures include rating scales, interviews, record searches, and observations of students under a variety of conditions (see Chapter 10 for more on measuring success of intervention programs). Assessment data are then reviewed by a student support team for hypothesis development: (a) The function or cause of the behavior is proposed, and (b) varying responses or consequences to behaviors are proposed as reinforcing or maintaining the behavior. *Functional analysis* refers to conducting "small experiments" or brief sessions during which conditions remain constant (hypothesis testing), and effects upon behaviors are observed. The final step then is to design assessment-based intervention resulting from the functional assessment procedures (Fox, Conroy, & Heckaman, 1998; Gresham, Quinn, & Restori, 1999).

While functional assessment and analysis procedures may seem time-consuming, research has shown that interventions designed from this process tend to be more effective. It is worth the time to be a "detective" to adapt more reliable, effective interventions. This approach has a better chance of truly helping students improve behavior and of preventing later more serious behaviors (Kamps et al., 1995). Thus more time up front is better for the students and teachers in eliminating wasted time as behavior escalates. Several publications provide detailed blueprints for using functional assessment and analysis procedures (Burke, 1992; Lohrmann-O'Rourke, Knoster, & Llewellyn, 1999; McEvoy, Davis, & Reichle, 1993; Symons, McDonald, & Wehby, 1998; Todd, Horner, Sugai, & Colvin, 1999; Umbreit, 1995; Witt, Daly, & Noell, 2000).

To summarize this process, functional assessment and analysis are critical for students with challenging behavior. Selection of the recommended intervention strategies described in prior sections (e.g., reinforcement systems and punishment procedures) are thus tied to functional assessment for individualized behavioral programming to support the student in developing appropriate behaviors and social skills. Generalized support tied to the functions of behaviors include the following strategies: (a) increase student control and choices, (b) increase opportunities for positive attention, (c) build positive relationships with students and build self-esteem, (d) teach adaptive behaviors to replace antisocial ones, and (e) use proactive, positive classroom management (Topper, Williams, Leo, Hamilton, & Fox, 1994). The most powerful interventions are tied to specific findings from functional assessment for individual children, and enacted in structured, consistent, nurturing environments. Samples of individualized interventions related to functions of behavior (e.g., escape, attention seeking, access/control, and stimulation) are provided in Table 2.2. Appendix 2.A provides an example of functional assessment for an individual child.

Token systems as well as student- or home-school contracts may also be enhanced through the functional analysis process. *Token systems* are motivational systems that use tokens (points, tickets) to bridge the delay between a desired behavior and a reward for that behavior. Tokens immediately follow the appropriate response and are later exchanged for items or privileges that are rewarding, thereby increasing the occurrence of desirable behaviors in the future (reinforcement; Alberto & Troutman, 1999; Rhode et al., 1992). *Student contracts* add reliability to contingency programs by clearly defining the behavior and the criteria for earning the reinforcer (80% of assignments turned in on time; Alberto & Troutman, 1999; Rhode et al., 1992). Parent involvement in contracts may increase the likelihood for success, provide a means for parents to assist in reinforcement, and

TABLE 2.2 Interventions to Address Behavioral Function

Function	Possible Intervention
Escape/Avoidance	Reinforce compliance
	Reinforce on-task behavior at 3- to 5-minute intervals (self-management)
	Teach how to ask for help appropriately (always respond)
	Provide additional assistance, monitor performance frequently
	Increase motivating and hands-on activities
	Intersperse easy parts of task with difficult parts/problems
	Allow student choice in task selection or order of completion
	Have written model of task problems/solutions at student's desk
	Initially decrease task volume, gradually increase as behaviors improve and productivity increases
	Reinforce absence of disruptive behaviors
	AVOID: Ignoring, time-out
Attention Seeking	Reinforce immediate compliance
	Reinforce appropriate behaviors at 3- to 5-minute intervals (self-management)
	Teach appropriate attention-seeking behavior (social skills)
	Allow low number of requests/attention per session with visual tallies, use penalty for additional attention seeking
	Reinforce absence of problem behavior
	Ignore low-level attention-seeking behavior
	Use specific praise and privileges for on-task peers
	Allow peer tutoring and cooperative activities
	Use time-out as last resort
	AVOID: Verbal reprimands, response interruption/redirection
Access to Tangibles/Control	Do not allow access following misbehavior
	Teach acceptable ways to request access, anger management
	Teach and reward appropriate social interaction with peers
	Use contract or work requirement in exchange for access
	Provide some noncontingent access
	AVOID: Access to materials, activity, etc., following misbehavior
Sensory Stimulation	Interrupt and redirect behavior
	Reinforce alternative, appropriate behaviors frequently
	Increase access to other sources of stimulation
	Use sensory powerful rewards for appropriate work (koosh balls, vibrating toys/pens, music, kaleidoscopes)
	AVOID: Time-out, withholding attention

SOURCE: Adapted from Mayer, 1999; Scott & Nelson, 1999; Todd et al., 1999.

increase communication between home and school. A caution with all contingency programs is to make sure the reward/exchange period is short enough to succeed. The more frequent the inappropriate behavior, the more frequent the time period (or less required behavior) for reinforcement, to ensure student buy-in and success.

Perspective on Promoting Success for Individual Students

This chapter has outlined procedures and strategies for promoting success for individual students exhibiting problem behavior. A key is to implement interventions that are the least intrusive yet have the highest chance for success (best practices). A recent review of data-based studies found that group contingencies, self-management, and differential reinforcement programs are the most powerful and effective interventions (Stage & Quiroz, 1997). Walker et al. (1995) further suggest several critical variables that impact the magnitude or effectiveness of interventions. *Comprehensive interventions* include teachers, parents, and peers as active social agents, and procedures address multiple needs of students (e.g., academic tutoring, group contingency for reducing disruptive behaviors). *Fidelity of interventions* includes skillful delivery and best practice strategies. *Length of intervention* implies that interventions are in place for a sufficient duration to be effective and to enable maintenance of improved behaviors. Monitoring/assessment occurs to note when "booster sessions" (reteaching) and revision are needed. Schoolwide discipline programs (see Chapter 5), positive behavior support models (Todd et al., 1999), and technical assistance teams (McEvoy et al., 1993) are all additional support strategies to maintain effective prevention and intervention.

Improving appropriate student behavior and growth is hard work. This chapter has provided some tools for establishing effective, well-managed classrooms focusing on a positive, proactive approach to improving behaviors for students with antisocial tendencies. Put simply: Make a plan using team resources, and implement the plan; then assess the effectiveness of the plan (see Chapter 10), regroup, and revise. These methods provide a framework for positive individual interventions. Consistent, quality implementation and data-based decision making can greatly support improved performance and behaviors for students with antisocial behaviors and contribute greatly to efforts to prevent more serious problems.

APPENDIX 2.A

Samuel—A Case Study in Functional Assessment

Samuel had some behavior problems in first grade, and his behavior continued to deteriorate after he began second grade. He often cried, refused to complete his work, and sometimes destroyed property. Samuel's teacher noticed that his behavior seemed to get worse when the class was working on math. The teacher believed that math was a weak area for Samuel, and academic records from first grade confirmed this. An objective observer noticed that there were no accommodations being made for Samuel in math. The teacher used examples on the overhead projector, followed by 20-minute independent work time. Samuel was often warned by the teacher to get his work done, and he responded by pouting and crying. When Samuel's behavior escalated, he was removed to the study carrel in the back of the room.

Using this information, the student support team hypothesized that Samuel's behaviors were triggered by his difficulty in math, and exacerbated by the fact that he wasn't getting individual help. Because Samuel's behavior often resulted in removal from the group, the team theorized that he was misbehaving to escape from having to complete difficult tasks.

The team tested this theory over a 1-week period, comparing two different instructional strategies. On 2 days, the teacher stayed with his original teaching style. During three math sessions, the teacher and a class assistant gave a 10-minute tutorial in problem solving, working with small groups of students before independent work time. Samuel was given a card he could use to ask for more help when he felt frustrated. Observations confirmed the team's hypothesis: Samuel made only a few verbal protests during the 3 days when additional assistance was provided. On the other 2 days he spent more time off task. A data-based intervention was developed, with intensive instruction for several students during math periods, older tutors three times per week to boost basic skills, and a reward for 75% completion during each math session.

REFERENCES

Alberto, P., & Troutman, A. (1999). *Applied behavior analysis for teachers*. Upper Saddle River, NJ: Prentice Hall.

Babyak, A., Luze, G., & Kamps, D. (2000). The Good Student Game: Behavior management for diverse classrooms. *Intervention in School and Clinic, 35,* 216-223.

Barrish, H., Saunders, M., & Wolf, M. (1969). Good Behavior Game: Effects of individual contingencies for group consequences on disruptive behavior in a classroom. *Journal of Applied Behavior Analysis, 2,* 119-124.

Bierman, K., Miller, C., & Stabb, S. (1987). Improving the social behavior and peer acceptance of rejected boys: Effects of social skill training with instructions and prohibitions. *Journal of Consulting and Clinical Psychology, 55,* 194-200.

Brigham, F., Bakken, J., Scruggs, T., & Mastropieri, M. (1992). Cooperative behavior management: Strategies for promoting a positive classroom environment. *Education and Training in Mental Retardation, 27,* 3-12.

Burke, J. (1992). *Decreasing classroom behavior problems: Practical guidelines for teachers*. San Diego, CA: Singular.

Campbell, S. (1995). Behavior problems in preschool children: A review of recent research. *Journal of Child Psychology and Psychiatry, 36,* 113-149.

Carpenter, S., & McKee-Higgins, E. (1996). Behavior management in inclusive classrooms. *Remedial and Special Education, 17,* 195-203.

Colvin, G., Sugai, G., Good, R., & Lee, Y. (1997). Using active supervision and precorrection to improve transition behavior in an elementary school. *School Psychology Quarterly, 12,* 344-363.

Darveaux, D. (1984). The Good Behavior Game plus merit: Controlling disruptive behavior and improving student motivation. *School Psychology Review, 13,* 510-514.

Davis, C., & Reichle, J. (1996). Invariant and variant high-probability requests: Increasing appropriate behaviors in children with emotional behavior disorders. *Journal of Applied Behavior Analysis, 29,* 471-482.

Dunlap, G., Kern, L., dePerczel, M., Clarke, S., Wilson, D., Childs, K., White, R., & Falk, G. (1993). Functional analysis of classroom variables for students with emotional and behavioral disorders. *Behavioral Disorders, 18,* 275-291.

Forehand, R., & McMahon, R. (1981). *Helping the noncompliant child*. New York: Guilford.

Fox, J., Conroy, M., & Heckaman, K. (1998). Research issues in functional assessment of the challenging behaviors of students with emotional and behavioral disorders. *Behavioral Disorders, 24,* 26-33.

Gresham, F., Quinn, M., & Restori, A. (1999). Methodological issues in functional analysis: Generalizability to other disability groups. *Behavioral Disorders, 24,* 180-182.

Hops, H., & Walker, H. (1988). *CLASS: Contingencies for Learning Academic and Social Skills*. Seattle, WA: Educational Achievement Systems.

Kamps, D., Ellis, C., Mancina, C., Wyble, J., Greene, L., & Harvey, D. (1995). Case studies using functional analysis for young children with behavior risks. *Education and Treatment of Children, 18,* 243-260.

Kamps, D., Kravits, T., Rauch, J., Kamps, J., & Chung, N. (2000). A prevention program for students with or at risk for ED: Moderating effects of variation in treatment and classroom structure. *Journal of Emotional and Behavioral Disorders, 8,* 141-154.

Kauffman, J. (1989). *Characteristics of children's behavior disorders.* Columbus, OH: Merrill.

Kazdin, A., Mazurick, J., & Bass, D. (1993). Risk for attrition in treatment of antisocial children and families. *Journal of Clinical Child Psychology, 22,* 2-16.

Kern, L., Dunlap, G., Childs, K., & Clarke, S. (1994). Use of a classwide self-management program to improve the behavior of students with emotional and behavioral disorders. *Education and Treatment of Children, 17,* 445-458.

Landrum, T., & Tankersley, M. (1997, February). *Implementing effective self-management for students with behavioral disorders.* Paper presented at the Midwest Symposium for Leadership in Behavior Disorders, Kansas City, MO.

Loeber, R., Wung, P., Keenan, K., Giroux, B., Stouthamer-Loeber, M., Van Kammen, W., & Maughan, B. (1993). Developmental pathways in disruptive child behavior. *Development and Psychopathology, 5,* 103-134.

Lohrmann-O'Rourke, S., Knoster, T., & Llewellyn, G. (1999). Screening for understanding: An initial line of inquiry for school-based settings. *Journal of Positive Behavior Interventions, 1,* 35-42.

Mayer, G. R. (1999). Constructive discipline for school personnel. *Education and Treatment of Children, 22,* 36-54.

McEvoy, M., Davis, C., & Reichle, J. (1993). District-wide technical assistance teams: Designing intervention strategies for young children with challenging behaviors. *Behavioral Disorders, 19,* 27-33.

Miller, G., Brehm, K., & Whitehouse, S. (1998). Reconceptualizing school-based prevention for antisocial behavior within a resiliency framework. *School Psychology Reviews, 27,* 364-379.

Mitchem, K., Young, K. R., West, R., & Benyo, J. (in press). CWPASM: A classwide peer-assisted self-management program for general education classrooms. *Education and Treatment of Children, 24.*

Patterson, G. R. (1982). *A social learning approach: Coercive family process.* Eugene, OR: Castalia.

Pettit, G. S., Bates, J., & Dodge, K. (1993). Family interaction patterns and children's conduct problems at home and school: A longitudinal perspective. *School Psychology Review, 22,* 403-420.

Rhode, G., Jenson, W., & Reavis, H. K. (1992). *The tough kid book: Practical classroom management strategies.* Longmont, CO: Sopris West.

Salend, S., Whittaker, C., & Reeder, E. (1992). Group evaluation: A collaborative, peer-mediated behavior management system. *Exceptional Children, 59,* 203-209.

Scott, T., & Nelson, C. M. (1999). Using functional behavioral assessment to develop effective intervention plans: Practical classroom applications. *Journal of Positive Behavior Interventions, 1,* 242-251.

Stage, S., & Quiroz, D. (1997). A meta-analysis of interventions to decrease disruptive classroom behavior in public education settings. *School Psychology Review, 26,* 333-368.

Symons, F., McDonald, L., & Wehby, J. (1998). Functional assessment and teacher collected data. *Education and Treatment of Children, 21,* 135-159.

Tankersley, M. (1995). A group-oriented contingency management program: A review of research on the Good Behavior Game and implications for teachers. *Preventing School Failure, 40,* 19-24.

Todd, A., Horner, R., Sugai, G., & Colvin, G. (1999). Individualizing school-wide discipline for students with chronic problem behaviors: A team approach. *Effective School Practices, 17,* 72-82.

Topper, K., Williams, W., Leo, K., Hamilton, R., & Fox, T. (1994). *A positive approach to understanding and addressing challenging behaviors: Supporting educators and families to include students with emotional and behavioral difficulties in regular education.* Burlington, VT: University of Vermont, University Affiliated Program.

Umbreit, J. (1995). Functional assessment and intervention in a regular classroom setting for the disruptive behavior of a student with attention deficit hyperactivity disorder. *Behavioral Disorders, 20,* 267-278.

Walker, H. (1998). First steps to prevention of antisocial behavior. *Teaching Exceptional Children, 30,* 16-19.

Walker, H., Colvin, G., & Ramsey, E. (1995). *Antisocial behavior in school: Strategies and best practices.* Pacific Grove, CA: Brooks/Cole.

West, R., Young, K., Callahan, K., Fister, S., Kemp, K., Freston, J., & Lovitt, T. (1995). The musical clocklight: Encouraging positive classroom behavior. *Teaching Exceptional Children, 28,* 46-51.

Witt, J., Daly, E., & Noell, G. (2000). *Functional assessments: A step-by-step guide to solving academic and behavior problems.* Longmont, CO: Sopris West.

RESOURCES

Algozzine, B., Ysseldyke, J., & Elliott, J. (1997). *Strategies and tactics for effective instruction.* Longmont, CO: Sopris West.

O'Neill, R., Horner, R., Albin, R., Sprague, J., Storey, K., & Newton, J. (1997). *Functional assessment and program development for problem behavior: A practical handbook.* Boston: Brooks/Cole.

Preventing Learning Problems Using Total Quality Principles

3

Bob Audette
Bob Algozzine
Mary Beth Marr
Edward D. Ellis, Jr.
Richard White

Imagine a classroom where children are eagerly raising their hands to give an answer or express an opinion. Imagine a classroom where students are quietly listening when a peer is talking. Imagine a classroom where teachers spend time teaching and supporting student learning rather than policing student behavior—where students are policing their own behavior. That's what we see when we look in classrooms where Total Quality Education principles are being used.

The application of quality principles has significantly improved the effectiveness and profitability of some of the nation's most successful businesses. Improving processes to produce higher-quality work has also taken hold in efforts to change America's schools. The principles of Total Quality provide a framework for more actively engaging students in responsibly managing and improving their own learning and achievement. A shift in the role of teachers from directors to facilitators of learning is also a by-product of implementing Total Quality principles in educational environments. Active engagement of students and shifting roles for teachers are key aspects of preventing learning problems that are gained in using Total Quality Education principles in the classroom.

The patterns and rhythms of learning and teaching that have emerged from applying the organizational principles of Total Quality Management to classrooms provide a framework for understanding how Total Quality Education benefits all children. The essence of Total Quality is recognizing that quality of products and outcomes is the direct result of the processes or systems that produce them. From this perspective, in order to change or improve a product or outcome, one must change or improve the process or system that produced it. Furthermore, the criteria for defining quality are determined by the needs and expectations of the customers of products and outcomes.

The concept of quality has been around for a very long time. Skills and the quality of work have been described throughout history. Typically the quality of a product was described by some of its attributes, such as strength, beauty, or finish. It was not until the introduction of mass production that the reproducibility of the size or shape of a product became a quality issue. Recently, concern for managing quality processes has taken center stage as a business improvement practice. Throughout this chapter, classrooms that are not explicitly applying the principles of Total Quality Management are represented as "traditional," whereas those actively applying the principles of Total Quality are referred to as "quality" classrooms. The use of the term *quality* is integral to any description of the organizational principles of Total Quality Management. There is no assumption that schools, classrooms, or teachers that are not explicitly applying these principles are not doing work that is of good educational value.

Total Quality Education

Since the conclusion of World War II, there has been a growing worldwide movement to understand, define, and apply organizational principles associated with the production of high-quality work. In the postwar era, Japanese industrial leaders translated the theory of Total Quality Management into what has now become the way of doing business in most leading corporations around the world. In the 1980s, the organizational principles of Total Quality began to take hold in service and health-related industries. Since then, the adoption of these organizational principles has taken place in government services and most recently in schools and classrooms. Every day, in every school, teachers and students engage in processes of teaching and learning. In some schools, classroom processes contribute to a culture of active inquiry in which the natural curiosity of students is nurtured. Students in these schools are encouraged in their self-directed pursuit of solutions to problems that affect them inside and outside of their classrooms. Prior to the recent interest in the principles of Total Quality Management, there was already considerable evidence that students' active participation in the processes of planning and assessing their own learning enhances their love for learning. Students' involvement in planning and assessing their own learning makes it more concrete and clarifies for them the processes they use to acquire knowledge and skills. In other schools, classroom processes (e.g., worksheet drills) may actually reduce students' educational experiences to instructional routines in which they do "stuff" without any sense of relevance or personal benefit. In some cases, the resultant lack of accomplishment not only promotes students' apathy toward school learning, it also contributes to an outright dislike of school and exhibition of behavior problems.

A rapidly increasing number of school districts across the country have begun implementing the paradigm-shifting reform initiative grounded in the principles of Total Quality Management. The focus of their implementation has been the use of Total Quality principles in the learning environments of their classrooms. The initiative usually begins with the recruitment of "demonstration" or "volunteer" teachers in every school building across the entire school system. Working with university and corporate partners, these teachers plan, receive training, and pilot the first applications of quality principles in their classrooms. The success of their early experiences evokes considerable interest from their teaching colleagues and a commitment of the district's leadership. These pilot efforts have provided a unique opportunity to experience, observe, identify, document, and describe the processes of learning and teaching that are grounded in the organizational principles of Total Quality Management. For the purposes of this chapter, we will compare and contrast the fledgling Total Quality processes with the processes used in more traditional classrooms. These comparisons are drawn from the direct experiences of teachers and administrators, including formal discussions, systematic classroom observations, and countless hours of informal experiences in classrooms ranging from those where quality principles are being explicitly implemented to more traditional classes where some quality principles are actually present but not explicitly understood or expressed, and finally, to classrooms where there is no evidence of Total Quality principles being applied.

It All Begins With a Mission

The processes of learning and teaching in traditional classrooms are almost always related to the purposes imposed upon teachers to "cover the curriculum" and to "raise their students' test scores." Many schools have published formal mission statements describing public purposes such as "preparing contributing citizens" or "being the premier, integrated school district in the . . . region." There is rarely any reference in these documents to students' responsibilities for learning and development.

Formal and Actual School Missions. Often, formal missions in traditional schools are simply mottoes for public consumption, developed for the purpose of rallying support and enthusiasm. There is little evidence that such formal mission statements have much impact in traditional K-12 classrooms. For example, in most schools, formal mission statements are seldom posted in classrooms. Similarly, students and teachers cannot provide an accurate description of the formal mission for their school. The formal school mission statement is usually irrelevant to daily instruction.

In contrast to formal published missions, the actual missions in most public schools are based on what is most publicly measured and most widely recognized. It is the actual mission that determines teachers' priorities and the processes of learning and teaching associated with their classrooms. There seems to be little doubt that in the traditional American public school, curriculum coverage and high scores on tests constitute the actual mission of public education. Instead of the problem of the means (end-of-grade testing) justifying the end, this seems to be a case where the means have actually become the end.

Roles Aligned With Missions. The roles of teachers and students are typically derived from their perceptions of the actual missions in their schools. The current emphasis on attaining high scores on end-of-grade tests causes many teachers to shift their role from that of teaching students the knowledge, skills, and attitudes that they can apply in pursuit of their careers to coaching and preparing students to pass end-of-year tests. Teachers and students race through the curriculum, hoping most of the content sticks before moving on to subsequent sections of the curriculum regardless of whether students have actually learned or can apply what they have learned.

Based on observations in traditional classrooms under the pressure of end-of-grade-test accountability, it would be reasonable to conclude that the teacher's role is to tell students what to do and the student's role is to do what the teacher says. Teachers and students consistently report that it is the teachers who "are responsible for what students do in classrooms." In typical interviews in traditional schools, teachers are described by students as "in charge," "*making* us learn," "telling us what to do," and "getting our test scores up," while students' roles were described by teachers as "listening to the teacher," "following directions," and "working hard." Clearly, in schools driven by high-stakes accountability missions, students with learning and behavior problems present significant concerns.

Quality School Missions and Teachers' Roles. In contrast to traditional schools, schools using Total Quality practices are driven by their learning missions. Those missions have been developed with the active participation of students and teachers, and with the consultation and support of many parents. While the specific wording and themes vary somewhat from school to school and from classroom to classroom, the message is clear. The consistent priorities in the mission statements of quality schools are (a) the learning and development of students and every member of the school community; and (b) the development of the attitude and skills associated with personal responsibility as expressed in purposeful, self-directed learning and behavior. In these schools, learning missions are not merely paper documents. They represent the actual values and priorities of the school communities that have discovered their core purpose.

Missions Are Active. The single most important difference between traditional schools and quality schools is that in the latter, learning missions dominate every aspect of life. Class mission statements are not only displayed prominently, but they are frequently referenced by students and teachers. It is usual in quality classrooms for teachers and students to praise each other frequently for actions and work products that move them toward achievement of their learning mission. Conversely, it is not unusual for them to caution each other about activities that distract from their learning goals. Classroom management is geared to the class mission. In correcting students, teachers ask, "Will this behavior help us to reach our goals?" Students readily concede that certain behavior is not helping them and more readily revert to positive behavior designed to support goal achievement. Likewise, they celebrate the success of students who have completed good work because "it helps us to reach our mission."

Students and teachers use their learning mission as the critical context within which they make individual and classroom decisions. For example, one fourth-grade class made the decision not to request a specific field trip because it was the consensus of the students that this particular field trip (a dinosaur exhibit), while interesting, would not contribute to their attainment of their learning goals for the next few months. In addition, they concluded that the field trip would cost them valuable learning time.

Missions and Monitoring. The class mission in quality classrooms is the basis for all assessment and evaluation. It establishes a learning focus that is detailed in students' goals and objectives. While standardized tests are still used to summatively assess some elements of student achievement, the emphasis in quality classrooms is on continuous, authentic performance assessment and evaluation of learning in the form of work products that are presented in projects and portfolios. Assessment of progress and quality of work is not only continuous, but much of it is implemented by the students, who daily monitor and self-assess the manner in which they have managed their time as well as their progress toward meeting and exceeding the quality standards for their work.

It is not our intention to convey the impression that teachers and students in quality schools are unconcerned about standardized tests. In quality schools, the emerging attitude of most teachers and students is analogous to the old adage, "Take care of the pennies and the dollars will take care of themselves." The emphasis, therefore, is on formative daily assessment of students' work products and behavior. Teachers and students in quality schools believe that if "the curriculum is learned, applied, and assessed daily, standardized tests will take care of themselves." The early evidence bears out that belief. The schools applying Total Quality principles described in this chapter have steadily improved their test scores over the past 8 years.

Quality Schools and Students' Roles. In quality schools, there is a consensus that students are the primary learners. Consequently, everyone recognizes that teachers cannot make students learn nor can they learn for them. Rather, teachers and students work together to study and understand their respective roles in the learning processes. The general role of teachers is to lead the class in achieving its learning mission. The specific role of teachers is to help students learn. Through their active participation, students are increasingly able to identify the support they need from teachers and others in order to become better learners and achieve their learning goals. After almost every learning activity, teachers elicit students' descriptions of which processes "worked for me" and which "need to be improved." A concern for preventing problems is embodied in quality classrooms.

Missions Translate to Actions (or Inaction)

The difference in the missions' impact on the roles and actions of teachers and students in traditional and quality schools is profound. In schools with a curriculum coverage/higher test score mission, teachers are responsible for exposing students to every segment of the curriculum and preparing them to be successful in taking their tests. In schools with a learning mission, teachers are responsible for helping students continuously improve their learning and demonstrate that they can apply what they have learned in the curriculum.

Observations and discussions with teachers and students in both traditional and quality public schools have identified distinct and repetitive patterns of teaching and learning activities that describe the roles and activities of teachers and students. These classroom processes have direct connections to the missions of these schools and are reflected in the roles and duties of teachers as well as in the nature of students' responses.

Teacher Roles and Duties in Traditional Schools. The iterations of teaching and learning in traditional schools are characterized by teachers' roles that

FIGURE 3.1. First-Grade Teacher's Flowchart of the Teaching/Learning Process in a Traditional School

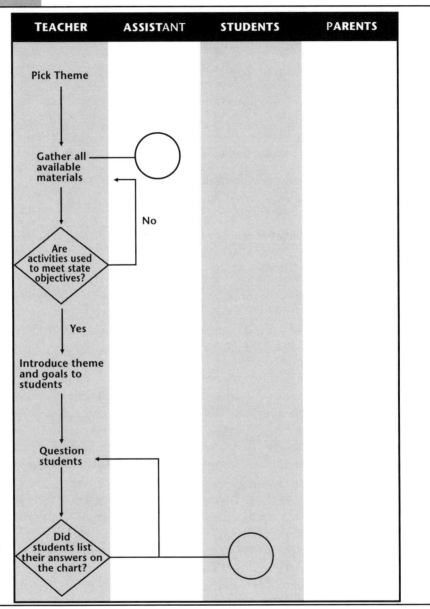

are controlling of students while placing complete responsibility on teachers for every facet of classroom activity. With some minimal variation, teaching and learning in traditional classrooms can be understood from the steps and flowchart (see Figure 3.1) produced by a first-grade teacher in a traditional school:

1. The teacher consults the curriculum and pacing guide.

2. The teacher plans instruction (lessons and units) to address the curriculum objectives.

3. The teacher carries out the instruction.

4. The teacher tests the students.

5. The teacher analyzes the test results.

6. The teacher reteaches and remediates where necessary.

7. The teacher retests where necessary.

8. The teacher self-evaluates the instruction.

9. The teacher reports students' progress.

10. The teacher moves on to the next objectives in the curriculum.

As similar processes are repeated day after day by teachers from kindergarten through high school, a generalized rhythm of teaching and learning emerges that is depicted in Figure 3.3.

While they typically follow a rhythm similar to this pattern, teachers in all schools carry out many additional duties related to their instructional roles. They strive to individualize instruction to meet students' needs; they assign and review homework; they evaluate and grade students' assignments; they prepare students to take standardized tests; they communicate with and involve parents; and they complete a myriad of other assigned duties.

In order to survive as they carry out so many important roles, responsibilities, and duties, many teachers, especially those in traditional schools, find themselves "needing to control my students." Some of the more popular teachers are subtle in their use of power. They control their classes with "smiles and a light touch." Some cleverly "entertain my students using my enthusiasm, manipulation, and even guile to direct them."

Other teachers feel too much of a "time constraint," and "can't waste time with such (artifices)." They openly leverage their power by making commands and delivering consequences for misbehavior in an attempt to maintain control. There is little questioning or problem solving involved in the correction of student behavior. It is a "great" year for most teachers when they are blessed with a class of students who are dutifully obedient.

Students' Roles. Students can also be quite busy in traditional classrooms. However, their roles are limited to following teachers' directions and orders without much thought or reason. Interviews with students in traditional

FIGURE 3.2. Fifth-Grade Teacher's Flowchart of the Teaching/Learning Process in a Quality School

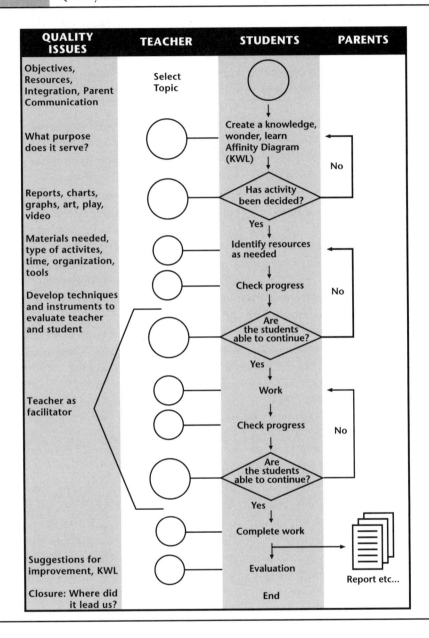

classrooms typically reveal that very few of them (less than 5%) can articulate meaningful reasons for their current class work or homework activities.

It is important to note that the few students who can express a rationale for their work usually are of high school age and have developed adult-like learning goals, the genesis of which generally is their "parents' example and encouragement." High percentages of the students who are interviewed in traditional schools (primary grades through high school) produce responses to questions about the relevance of their classroom and homework activities that range from shoulder shrugs, implying that they have no idea, to comments such as, "The teacher said to do it." Often, appropriately inquisitive students who would innocently ask, "Why are we doing this?" are inappropriately treated as disobedient or disrespectful.

Quality School Differences. The processes employed in quality classrooms emphasize learning the curriculum and applying what has been learned in some concrete and relevant form. The learning focus, in conjunction with the application of quality principles, dramatically restructures the roles of teachers and students. Like their counterparts in traditional settings, teachers in quality schools are responsible for contributing to the achievement of their schools' missions. Unlike traditional schools, teachers in quality schools study and apply Total Quality principles in seven critical areas: leadership, customer focus, systemic thinking, management by fact, continuous improvement, teamwork, and long-term commitment.

Leadership is a Total Quality principle that requires that teachers be completely committed to the attainment of the learning mission for *every* student in their class. As leaders, they keep the learning mission in the forefront of their interactions with students and parents. They frequently refer to it in their discussions, and they are constantly seeking ways to facilitate its attainment. The following types of comments are frequently heard in quality schools: "How is your progress toward your learning goal?" "How will this goal help you reach your learning mission?" "What is your learning strategy?" "Why did you pick that strategy?" "Does it seem to be working well for you?" "What isn't working so well?" "How can you improve it?" "What would help you?"

Another aspect of leadership is removing or reducing systemic barriers to the learning mission. As the leaders of their classrooms, teachers have the authority and ability to change the ways that learning and teaching occur. Teachers are frequently heard to say, "How can I help you?" "Did it help you when I demonstrated how to do it?" "How could I improve my demonstration to help you more?" "Should I do it more slowly?" "What other things have really helped you in the past?" This type of leadership promotes a developmentally appropriate assumption of responsibilities by students for their own learning and for the activities and functions within the classroom. It also illustrates the growth of teachers in their leadership role and is a clear indication of the importance of preventing learning problems in quality classrooms. Teachers who truly understand leadership are more disposed to respond in a positive manner to students' suggestions about improving instructional methods.

Everyone in a quality school learns to apply the Total Quality principle of *customer focus*. A customer is defined as any person who uses or inherits the results of another's work. The primary customers in a quality school are the students. "Did students learn what we said we wanted them to learn? If not, what were the barriers that kept them from learning?" "Does students' work meet our quality criteria?" "If students had difficulty, are there some better ways for them to learn this?" These key questions, squarely focused on the students' learning, are asked by students and teachers together after each learning activity. Students and teachers continue to explore strategic options until students are successful in their learning efforts. This approach contrasts with the curriculum coverage approach in which teachers move along irrespective of student mastery. Likewise, when teachers ask students for feedback about the helpfulness of their instructional activities, they are attending to their customers' needs.

Teachers in a quality school employ and model the Total Quality principle of *systemic thinking*. Systemic thinking is the process of incorporating cause-and-effect reasoning into the planning, implementation, and assessment of learning. Students and teachers employ systemic thinking when they engage in discussions such as, "When we do things this way, we don't seem to finish our work on time. How can we change the way we are doing this?" "When I do it this new way, it comes out better than when I used the old way." "When they got angry with each other, neither one of them got what he wanted." "Whenever we break a class rule, we are responsible for making it right. That means, we have to face the consequences of what we do. That way, we are responsible."

Systemic thinking is also applied when teachers sensitively and responsively promote the development of their students' emerging awareness and ability to understand their own learning needs. "You did this much better than the last time. What was different about how you went about doing it?" "You seem to work better when you are with this group." "What do you think you do in this group that is different from what you do in the other groups?"

The Total Quality principle of *management by fact* is modeled by teachers every day when they use process and outcome data to think aloud with their students and make decisions in pursuit of their goals. By constantly organizing, displaying, and referring to their data, teachers model and involve students in using data to better understand how they are doing. "Let's see, when you used this new strategy, you met all of the quality criteria and you finished in twenty-three minutes. When you used the old strategy, you finished in nineteen minutes, but you missed three of the six criteria.

What did you do in the new strategy that made the difference? What do you think you should do next time?" "What do your completion data tell you about this strategy?" "According to our graph, most of our discipline problems occur after lunch. What do you think is happening? How can we improve this?" Similarly, when students become accustomed to collecting and using data to make decisions and monitor their work, they are developing some of the most essential abilities of responsible persons. They are managing their learning and behavior. In one school, a group of fourth-grade students collected and charted data on learning interruptions caused by announcements on the school loudspeaker. They presented their data to the principal and recommended a change of policy regarding the use of the loudspeaker during class time. After reviewing their data, he adopted their recommendation that loudspeaker announcements would occur only in circumstances that "are a matter of life or death."

Teachers apply the Total Quality principle of *continuous improvement* when they empower students to monitor their own work and use their data to make improvements. In addition, teacher feedback to students is always couched in terms of "ways of improving this work." When students' work does not meet expectations (quality criteria agreed to by teacher and students), they are encouraged by their teachers and classmates to take some risks and try new approaches. "I can see that your work is OK—but it isn't as good as you had wanted it to be." "What could you try that might improve it and meet your goal?" "Have you ever tried doing it this way?" "Some students in the next class did it another way. Do you want to ask them about it?"

Teachers also encourage students to become personally involved in continuously improving classroom processes. "Some of you have said that you think we should do our reading work earlier in the day. Why do you think this might help us meet our reading goals?" "Would this hurt our progress on our math goals? What other ways can we make this a better classroom and reach our learning mission?"

The Total Quality principle of *teamwork* is integral to the learning mission that is the collective reason for being "a class." Teachers model teamwork in their cooperation with colleagues and parents, but especially with their participation in class activities. Teachers are not only leaders of their classes, but they are very important members of their classes. Their verbal contributions model respect for the ideas of others and the responsibility to be meaningfully involved. "That is an interesting idea. It shows that you are thinking about this." "Everyone's ideas have value in our class. After all, we have a great mission and if we help each other, we will make it." "It is probably too late to try your idea now, but let's write it down so that we can think about it before our next unit."

Students' sense of team membership begins with their participation in developing a class mission and ground rules. Their sense of team membership is strengthened each day as they collectively monitor class progress toward the mission. The sense of team membership creates incentives to help each other learn and succeed in achieving their shared mission. Teamwork is best exemplified when students are highly motivated to help each other. The sense of team was powerfully demonstrated in a second-grade classroom where the students had set very ambitious goals for their math achievement. Most of the students were working hard and progressing well enough to reach their goals. One boy, however, was really struggling. Two other students, a boy and a girl, came to the teacher and asked if the struggling student could be assigned to their group because "we can help him to reach his goals." The teacher agreed, and after 2 weeks the struggling student indeed reached his goal. The entire class celebrated their success.

The Total Quality principle of *long-term commitment* brings everything back to the learning mission. Teachers and students not only attend to the more immediate learning goals of their current academic year, but they also think about the ongoing educational processes within the school and view their work relative to their long-term educational dreams. The long-term view encourages and strengthens the hopes and dreams of students in terms of careers and lifestyles. "You are making progress in learning your multiplication tables. Pretty soon, you won't need to look at your tables to solve problems." "Gosh, you are doing so well in your reading! This will help you later if you decide to go to law school. Lawyers have to read lots of cases." "Your writing is getting neater every day. If you do have your own store, that will be important so that all your workers can read and understand your instructions." "You have such good work habits, you will be excellent at whatever you decide to do."

Quality Teaching and Learning—How It Works

Teachers' applications of Total Quality principles briefly described above have produced processes of learning and teaching typified by the flowchart of a fifth-grade teacher in a quality school (see Figure 3.2). This view of learning and teaching processes in a quality class contrasts sharply with the process displayed by the first-grade teacher in the traditional school (see Figure 3.1). The clear emergence of student engagement in all aspects of planning, implementing, and assessing learning is one of the most important features of a quality class. When the process is repeated each day in quality schools, the rhythm of teaching and learning is quite different (see Figure 3.4).

To further illustrate, in quality classrooms:

1. Teachers *and* students discuss the relevance of upcoming curricular goals to their learning mission.

FIGURE 3.3. Rhythms of Traditional Teaching/Learning Processes

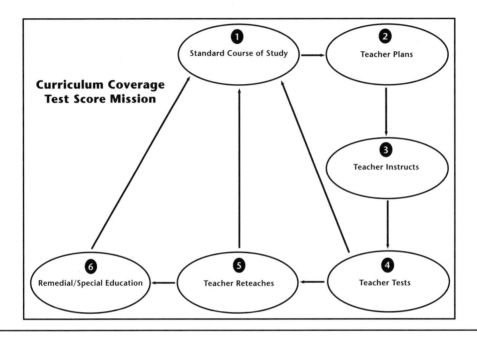

FIGURE 3.4. Rhythms of Quality Teaching/Learning Processes

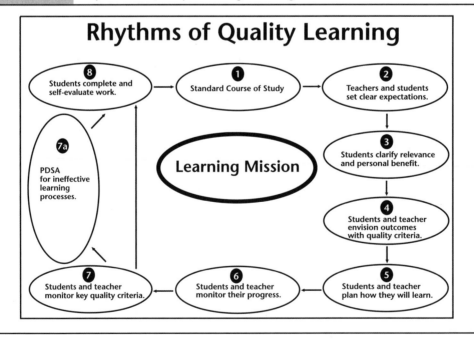

2. Teachers *and* students highlight the curricular goals they are preparing to learn and apply.

3. Teachers *and* students clarify what they will know, and what skills they will be able to apply when the curricular goals have been met.

4. *Students,* with teacher support, clarify the relevance of the curricular goals and identify how they will personally benefit from their achievement.

5. *Students and* teachers identify methods by which students can demonstrate their achievement of curricular goals and the quality criteria by which their work will be evaluated upon its completion.

6. *Students and* teachers plan strategies so that everyone can achieve their curricular goals by meeting their quality criteria.

7. *Students and* teachers daily monitor their progress in meeting their curricular goals.

8. *Students and* teachers use their criteria to monitor the quality of their "work in progress."

9. *Students* submit their completed work with a self-evaluation of its content and the learning strategy they employed.

10. *Students,* with support from their teacher, lead conferences with their parents in which they review their own progress, identify what is working well for them, describe what they need to improve upon, identify areas where they need support, and establish goals for the next reporting period.

How to Prevent Learning Problems Using Total Quality Education

Clearly, the teaching and learning that take place within any classroom are part of a complex process. The intended outcome of the process is students' learning. Contributing members to the process are the teacher and the student, but often others also participate, including parents, principals, teachers, librarians, students, and other school personnel. The communities served are also important because they help to identify relevant learning material. Maintenance and custodial personnel are contributors because they affect the quality of the learning environment.

School administrators face daily and continuous challenges in efforts to establish and maintain safe and orderly classrooms where teachers can teach and students can learn. Prevention strategies are valued because of the potential to reduce the development of problems. A well-crafted approach to prevention improves the efficiency and effectiveness with which school, classroom, and individual behavior support systems operate. When considering prevention, teachers in quality classrooms consider alternatives to many current educational practices. For example, they

♦ Adopt the philosophy that all students do learn and their goal is to develop teaching/learning processes that will maximize students' learning successes and will eliminate failures

♦ Believe that intelligence reflects a rate of learning with natural variability that can be accounted for in the teaching/learning process

♦ Examine school policies and practices that inhibit learning, and create opportunities to change them

♦ Change current grading practices to reflect the opportunity for continuous improvement

♦ Rethink traditional ideas about teaching and learning and apply principles of process improvement in their classrooms

Improving Classroom Process

In classrooms engaging in traditional management methods, teachers are expected to act like supervisors or bosses and students are expected to follow directions and do as they are told. Rules are the framework for law and order, and the teacher's role is to enforce them. Often, the policing role detracts from more important roles like teacher, mentor, guide, counselor, and collaborator.

Three stages are part of the Total Quality Education classroom improvement process: readiness, revision, and realization. During the readiness phase, processes that are working and those that need to be improved are identified and next steps are defined. In the revision phase, quality principles are studied and applied to the conditions identified in the readiness phase. At the end of the second phase, a clear vision and detailed plans for continuous improvement are developed. In the third phase, realization begins, and teaching and learning systems are then continuously improved using Total Quality Management concepts and tools adapted for classrooms.

For each quality principle there are a myriad of methods and tools that can be applied in the classroom. Many of these methods are currently found in traditional schools. The problem is that they are applied without any theoretical or principle connection. For example, there are many teachers who involve students in assessing their own work. However, they do not connect the self-assessment to students' learning nor to long-term goals and dreams. In order for students to derive the maximum benefit from self-assessment, they need to have articulated personal goals and they need to understand the relevance and connection of those goals to their dreams. If this has not occurred, self-assessment becomes "just one more thing we do because the teacher said we should do it." When the connection has occurred, students truly become stakeholders in the learning activities in their classrooms and the value of self-assessment is powerfully amplified. Self-assessment becomes a means for students to achieve their own goals and dreams by monitoring and managing their own progress. "I know how I am doing all the time."

When teachers manage classroom behavior by linking behavior to progress in achieving personal learning goals, the emphasis shifts from blaming, punishing, and designating "good students" and/or "bad students" to the power of systemic thinking whereby students recognize that "what I was doing wasn't working for me. I needed to change what I was doing so that I can get what I really want." The linkage of principles to practice helps teachers and students to continuously monitor and improve the processes in their classrooms so that there is a clear alignment between learning missions, students' goals, students' and teachers' roles, instructional strategies and practices, students' learning activities, parents' expectations, and procedures for evaluating outcomes.

Perspectives on Quality

Most situations requiring discipline do not occur because there are no rules in the classroom. Typically, teachers have plenty of rules to direct students' behavior. What they do not have is shared agreement and/or shared commitment with regard to the importance of the rules and their effects on behavior. Total Quality Principles are linked to a set of tools (see Table 3.1 for examples) that creates processes and conditions of shared learning. These processes form the foundation for a rhythm of learning (see Figure 3.4) that is very different than the one in traditional classrooms (see Figure 3.2). They also define a clear process for preventing behavior problems. For example, posting an issue bin and responding to items in it on a regular basis enables students to resolve conflicts before they become serious problems and to open channels of communication in positive and constructive ways. Similarly, using the plus/delta process taps the energy of the entire

TABLE 3.1 Total Quality Tools

Tool	Purpose	Use
Issue Bin	• To capture ideas that require discussion or investigation. • To identify concerns that prevent positive learning outcomes. • To open channels of communication in positive and constructive ways.	1. Explain purpose of issue bin; explain to students what types of ideas or concerns are appropriate for inclusion. 2. Determine form (flip chart, shoe box) and location for issue bin. 3. Establish issue bin process (e.g., How will items be recorded? By whom? At what times? Under what conditions?). 4. Review and update items in the issue bin regularly.
Plus/Delta	• To provide a process for open sharing of ideas. • To encourage students to identify what worked well and what did not work well in a process or learning activity. • To encourage active participation of all students in solving classroom problems.	1. Explain purpose of the plus/delta process. 2. Write + and Δ at the top of a flip chart or chalk board. 3. Have students identify what worked well (+) and what could be changed (Δ) to improve a process. Record responses in appropriate column on the plus/delta chart. 4. Review the information in the chart. Discuss what made items successful and identify opportunities for improvement.
Light Voting	• To provide opportunities for all students to participate in decision making. • To encourage teamwork and valuing the opinions of others. • To encourage collaboration in solving problems.	1. Introduce the tool to the class and identify its purpose. 2. Post a list of ideas. 3. Divide number of items on list by 3 and assign that number of votes to each student (e.g., 15 items divided by 3 means each student can vote for 5 items). 4. Assign points (i.e., First choice = 4 points, Second choice = 3 points, etc.) to reflect importance and have each student post points for selected items. 5. Tally total points and discuss results to arrive at final decision.

class in solving problems and offers opportunities for active participation in generating positive learning outcomes before a concern becomes a problem and inappropriate behavior becomes a solution.

The role of teachers in guiding the processes described above requires the thoughtful exercise of developmentally sensitive leadership. While their responsibilities are substantial, teachers in quality schools seem to avoid the stress associated with worrying about things they cannot control. Instead, teachers and students work together on processes that they can control and improve. They support each other with the full confidence that comes from having a shared purpose. They encourage each other when they have problems, look for ways to improve their processes, and celebrate their successes.

Teachers establish a culture of prevention and quality in their classrooms by championing the learning mission and clarifying for students and parents their respective roles in its attainment. They promote students' natural motivation to learn by leading them in visioning exercises that "picture" their successful lives when they have met their learning goals. They use a variety of Total Quality tools and methods to lead their students through a variety of processes for thinking together as learning organizations. With their mission and their ground rules, students have clear boundaries within which they can be actively engaged in learning and applying what they have learned.

To an outside observer, the most dramatic difference in quality classrooms is in the roles and behavior of students. In contrast to many of their counterparts in traditional schools, students in quality classrooms seem to be much more purposeful and engaged, and to take far more responsibility for their own learning and behavior. They are respectful and appreciative of their teachers, but they also expect reasons for requests that are made of them. They can tell you what they are doing; they can tell you why they are doing it; they develop data that show how they are doing; and they have a clear picture in their minds of what their work will "look like" when it is finished.

The early attempts to implement quality principles in classrooms provide a solid basis for further and more extensive application and study. Teachers who are applying quality principles consistently report that they want "to go much deeper in their understanding and application of quality principles," and that "the potential for unleashing students' untapped abilities to learn is staggering."

Students in quality schools are learning which activities are most helpful in preventing learning problems and promoting successful learning processes. They demonstrate that students are a great and relatively untapped resource in achieving the learning missions of public schools. They are proud of their work and they seek greater challenges. They love learning and they love their schools.

RESOURCES

Aguayo, R. (1990). *Dr. Deming: The man who taught the Japanese about quality.* New York: Carol Publishing Group.

Andrade, A., & Hakim, D. (1995). Letting children take the lead in class. *Educational Leadership, 53*(1), 22-24.

Audette, B., & Algozzine, B. (1992). Free and appropriate education for all students: Total quality and the transformation of American public education. *Remedial and Special Education, 13*(6), 8-18.

Candy, P. (1991). *Self-direction for lifelong learning.* San Francisco: Jossey-Bass.

Cohen, D. (1991). Overcoming student apathy and bewilderment: Setting an example of responsibility and attentiveness. *Proteus, 8*(1), 27-29.

Deming, W. (1986). *Out of the crisis.* Boston: MIT Center for Advanced Engineering Studies.

Dewey, J. (1902). *The child and the curriculum.* Chicago: University of Chicago Press.

Downey, C., Frase, L., & Peters, J. (1994). *The quality education challenge.* Thousand Oaks, CA: Corwin Press.

Flantzer, H. (1993). What we say and what we do. *Phi Delta Kappan, 75*(1), 75-76.

Juran, J. (1988). *Juran on planning for quality.* New York: Free Press.

Juran, J. (1989). *Juran on leadership for quality.* New York: Free Press.

Kohn, A. (1993). Turning learning into a business: Concerns about total quality. *Educational Leadership, 51*(1), 58-61.

McClanahan, E., & Wicks, C. (1994). *Future force: A teacher's handbook for using TQM in the classroom.* Glendale, CA: Griffin Publishing.

Moses, M., & Whitaker, K. (1990). Ten components for restructuring schools. *School Administrator, 47*(8), 32-34.

Scherkenbach, W. (1991). *The Deming route to quality and productivity: Road maps and road blocks.* Washington, DC: CEAP Press.

Shewhart, W. (1986). *Statistical method from the viewpoint of quality control.* Washington, DC: Dover.

Preventing Problems Through Social Skills Instruction

4

Debra M. Kamps
Pam Kay

"If I were a principal, that would probably be one of my top priorities . . . a social skills program, starting in kindergarten." The teacher paused, then said, "Sometimes I think I'm hitting my head against a wall because these things aren't followed through in third and fourth grade. But I just read some research that said first grade is the place to make a lot of this happen. Next year I'm going to do it even more in-depth than I have."

The first-grade teacher quoted above had been quite skeptical when she was asked to attend a workshop to learn the new social skills curriculum that her school had agreed to adopt in the first and second grades. "I already teach social skills," she said, indignantly. After 2 years of using the curriculum, however, she was thoroughly convinced, and ready to persuade her colleagues to extend its use into the upper grades.

Some parents and teachers question whether students who *do* come to school with appropriate social skills should be spending valuable classroom time relearning them. As this teacher pointed out, social skills lessons in the classroom give these students the language and tools to use in communicating with their less-skilled peers. "The other day, I heard one student reminding another 'The behavior you pay attention to is the behavior you get!' . . . and she sounded just like me."

Changes in society at the beginning of the 21st century make social skills instruction an essential part of the course of study in public schools.

Employers require skills in teamwork, communication, and problem solving, yet more students come to school with significant deficits in those abilities. Economic and social pressures leave families less time to teach their children how to get along with others. At the same time, developmental theorists like Vygotsky and Bronfenbrenner have expanded educators' awareness of the impact of relationship on intellectual growth. Learning takes place best in a healthy social environment. The school classroom needs to become a community where students and teachers encourage one another to grow. As John Dewey (1916) wrote, "Education is not preparation for life, education is life itself."

Children who exhibit emotional and behavioral problems in the classroom hamper the development of the learning community within that class. Those who have internalizing behaviors, who are extremely shy, cry frequently, or refuse to participate in group activities, are gradually neglected or rejected by others. These students do not contribute to the work of the group, and their withdrawal is frustrating to the teacher and to those children who try to include them. Others have overt antisocial behaviors. Their aggressive style of social interaction results in behavioral excesses such as arguing, shouting, teasing, blaming, and fighting. They have behavioral deficits in such areas as self-control, cooperating, problem solving, following rules, helping, sharing, making good decisions, and accepting consequences.

Students with antisocial behaviors may think about interactions differently from typical students. They may blame others for their problems, believe that others want bad things to happen to them, and generally have difficulty reading social situations. They seem unable to determine cause and effect from their behaviors. Conversely, socially appropriate students are well liked, play often with friends, treat friends kindly, share, defend friends, show empathy, and help friends when they are hurt. They are more likely to settle problems with a compromise and take time to give explanations. They are often puzzled and frightened by peers' antisocial actions (Sheridan, 1995). Without intervention, effects from these behavioral differences have long-lasting consequences. Antisocial behaviors have repercussions across environments (school, home, community) and social groups (peers, teachers, and family members). For example, peer rejection due to aggressive behavior can result in delinquency and the creation of antisocial peer groups. More than 25 years ago, Bronfenbrenner (1974) warned that schools were becoming "one of the most potent breeding grounds for alienation in American society" (p. 60).

Effective teaching of social skills in the natural setting of school can result in increasing social competence across peer groups, and decreases in inappropriate interactions. For example, studies of resilient people who grew up in unfavorable environments often cite the following as key variables in their resiliency: adaptive social behaviors, problem-solving skills, positive social orientation including close peer friendships, warm relationships with family members, and supportive positive social networks (Doll & Lyon, 1998; Masten & Coatsworth, 1998).

Social skills instruction in general education classrooms is an important prevention strategy. This chapter will define social skills, give examples of research-based curricula, outline effective instructional procedures and enhancements, and describe strategies to reinforce and maintain positive behaviors both inside and outside of the classroom.

_____ **Social Skills, Competences, and Curricula**

Social competence is a very complex area of child development. A broad array of behaviors is relevant to any given social situation, appropriate responses vary according to context and persons therein, and behaviors considered appropriate in one circumstance may be punished or viewed as "uncool" in another. In this chapter, social skills are defined as behaviors that *significant* others consider to be appropriate for the setting and situation. In school, teachers, administrators, ancillary staff, and peers all have expectations for students' behavior; all are significant to the student. However, agreement, consistency, and modeling among the adults should establish the norms for that setting. In home and community settings, parents, siblings, and the public may have differing expectations. Students need to learn how to adapt their skills from one setting to another in order to be considered socially competent.

McGinnis and Goldstein (1997) carried out a behavioral task analysis to identify 60 social skills, shown in Table 4.1. These vary from basic classroom skills, such as "listening," to skills for dealing with stress, such as "reacting to failure." Although this list may seem lengthy, its specificity allows teachers and other professionals to hone in on the exact set of skills that a student or class may need.

To acquire competence in a complex skill, students may first need to learn several component skills. For example, in the survival skill of *following instructions,* students must demonstrate listening to or reading the instructions, mentally rehearsing the required steps, carrying out the instructions, and monitoring their own progress. Students may have deficits in learning the skills, in using them, once learned, or in transferring the training to apply the skills in different settings. A student's problem behaviors may also impede his or her acquisition or performance of skills (DuPaul & Eckert, 1994; Gresham, 1995). The dual purpose of teaching social skills should be to increase competent performance and to decrease problem behaviors.

TABLE 4.1 Sixty Social Skills for Elementary Students

Group I: Classroom Survival Skills

1. Listening
2. Asking for Help
3. Saying Thank You
4. Bringing Materials to Class
5. Following Instructions
6. Completing Assignments
7. Contributing to Discussions
8. Offering Help to an Adult
9. Asking a Question
10. Ignoring Distractions
11. Making Corrections
12. Deciding on Something to Do
13. Setting a Goal

Group II: Friendship-Making Skills

14. Introducing Yourself
15. Beginning a Conversation
16. Ending a Conversation
17. Joining In
18. Playing a Game
19. Asking a Favor
20. Offering Help to a Classmate
21. Giving a Compliment
22. Accepting a Compliment
23. Suggesting an Activity
24. Sharing
25. Apologizing

Group III: Skills for Dealing With Feelings

26. Knowing Your Feelings
27. Expressing Your Feelings
28. Recognizing Another's Feelings
29. Showing Understanding of Another's Feelings
30. Expressing Concern for Another
31. Dealing With Your Anger
32. Dealing With Another's Anger
33. Expressing Affection
34. Dealing With Fear
35. Rewarding Yourself

Group IV: Skill Alternatives to Aggression

36. Using Self-Control
37. Asking Permission
38. Responding to Teasing
39. Avoiding Trouble
40. Staying Out of Fights
41. Problem Solving
42. Accepting Consequences
43. Dealing With an Accusation
44. Negotiating

Group V: Skills for Dealing With Stress

45. Dealing With Boredom
46. Deciding What Caused a Problem
47. Making a Complaint
48. Answering a Complaint
49. Dealing With Losing
50. Being a Good Sport
51. Dealing With Being Left Out
52. Dealing With Embarrassment
53. Reacting to Failure
54. Accepting No
55. Saying No
56. Relaxing
57. Dealing With Group Pressure
58. Dealing With Wanting Something That Isn't Yours
59. Making a Decision
60. Being Honest

SOURCE: Reprinted with permission from the *Social skills planning guide* (Alberg, Petry [Tashjian], & Eller, 1994).

Choosing a Curriculum

Social skills are taught both formally and informally in the classroom. Teachers in the elementary grades frequently remind students about appropriate behaviors, and use teachable moments to help the class develop greater interpersonal skills. This informal approach was sufficient when most of the students learned the skills from their families and the community. However, practitioners and researchers alike agree that schools now must be in the business of directly teaching appropriate social skills.

Administrators who want to begin preventive social skills teaching in their schools can choose a curriculum from among the many available from commercial publishers. The most effective approach is to use one curriculum schoolwide. Adults and children will then develop a common language for each skill. A schoolwide approach increases the opportunities for all adults, custodians and food service personnel as well as teachers and administrators, to reinforce appropriate behaviors. A common curriculum can also clarify home and school expectations, and provide tools for home-school communications around social skills. Continued use of the curriculum can result in greater consistency between home and school, and smoother transitions for students with emotional and/or behavioral issues.

A five-step decision-making process for choosing a curriculum is outlined in Figure 4.1. The first step, identifying and prioritizing the needs, requires honest input from teachers and administrators about the needs of both students and teachers. Ideally, parents and other members of the community would be involved as well. This assessment of needs can be based on formal or informal observations, a review of the reasons for office referrals, or a simple checklist, among other methods. Teachers may need encouragement to identify the specific social problems they are encountering in the classroom, and may prefer to complete anonymous questionnaires. Cultural differences in the student population must be taken into account, and this needs assessment should avoid stereotyping or labeling any groups or students. Appendix 4.A, which may be copied, provides a checklist with which to match needs and local criteria to commercially available programs.[1]

Step 2 is similar to the process for adopting any course of study. Among the other criteria an administrator would consider would be the developmental level of the students, the type of skills most needed (communication skills, interpersonal skills, personal skills, or response skills), and the size of student groups in which the program will be delivered. Preparation, Step 3, consists of many activities: setting goals, informing families, providing training for teachers and other school personnel, planning time for practice, generalization, and maintenance of skills, and creating a plan for evaluation. Step 4 is implementing the program, and Step 5 is evaluat-

FIGURE 4.1. Decision-Making Process for Selecting Social Skills Programs

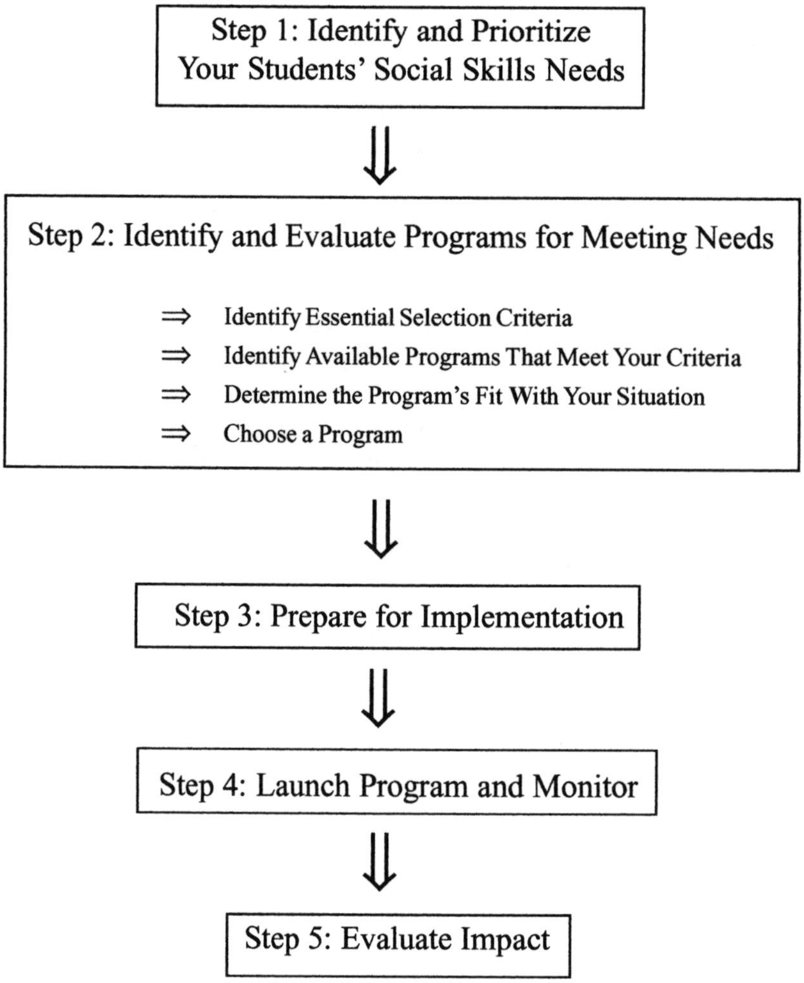

Step 1: Identify and Prioritize
Your Students' Social Skills Needs

Step 2: Identify and Evaluate Programs for Meeting Needs

⇒ Identify Essential Selection Criteria
⇒ Identify Available Programs That Meet Your Criteria
⇒ Determine the Program's Fit With Your Situation
⇒ Choose a Program

Step 3: Prepare for Implementation

Step 4: Launch Program and Monitor

Step 5: Evaluate Impact

ing its impact. For more information on evaluation of prevention programs, please see Chapter 10.

Current concerns about safety in the schools have brought the need for training in social skills to the forefront. In response, some programs have been rushed into print without sufficient research to test their success. The examples used in this chapter have been selected because they are grounded in social learning principles and have a supportive research base. This short list is intended only to illustrate the variety of curricula available. The first three mentioned focus on teaching and maintaining specific social skills. The next three highlight building healthy relationships as a part of the classroom and school climate. Most also include training in anger management. Check the Resources at the end of this chapter for more detail.

Skillstreaming. There are three versions of this popular and easy-to-use curriculum available, to address needs from preschool through high school. There are 60 separate skills outlined in the Elementary edition, making this curriculum appropriate for schools with a high proportion of students lacking basic social skills (see Table 4.1). The structured learning approach breaks each skill down into simple steps, reducing the amount of training time required for teachers before beginning the curriculum. The program provides materials for self-management, group self-report, and parent communication around homework.[2]

ASSIST: Affective/Social Skills: Instructional Strategies and Techniques. The ASSIST Program was developed and validated in elementary schools in the state of Washington. Some manuals focus a specific set of lessons on social skills such as handling anger, learning friendship and cooperation skills, and avoiding sexual abuse. Others, such as Creating a Caring Classroom and Building Self-Esteem, are a broader form of affective education, with lessons that can be used in the classroom as needed.[3]

The Tough Kid Social Skills Book. This program focuses on 10 social skills that are often difficult for students in groups that have a high level of aggressive behaviors. The 10 skills include recognizing and expressing feelings; using self-control; having a conversation; solving arguments; playing cooperatively; dealing with teasing; solving problems; dealing with being left out; joining in; and accepting "No." The manual guides teachers through assessing students' skills, planning for implementation, teaching the lessons, and connecting with families.[4]

Bully-Proofing Your School. Teaching social skills is not enough in a school where bullying behavior is prevalent. Often students are well aware of incidents of bullying long before the adults in the school tune in to bullying, but lack the skills to stop it without adult support. The *Bully-Proofing* series allows the entire student body to participate in the development of a caring climate within the school.[5] Sample lessons include strategies for victims and changing bullying behavior (e.g., correct social thinking, problem solving, anger management). In addition, the program provides ideas for schoolwide implementation and parent involvement.

Second Step. This *violence-prevention* program was developed by the Committee for Children in Seattle, Washington, and has proven itself in numerous studies. It expands anger management by using modeling, role playing, and generalization strategies to reduce aggressive and antisocial behaviors. It builds a core of social competences including problem solving, anger management, impulse control, and empathy. Socially responsible decision making becomes the basis for students adopting appropriate social behaviors. Lessons are designed for classroom teachers, and all the materials are provided.[6] Recent studies including more than 500 students observed in classrooms, lunchrooms, and playgrounds have shown decreases in aggression and verbal hostility with implementation of Second Step.

Responsive Classroom. The Northeast Foundation for Children considers this program to be a "social curriculum," or a way for teachers to conduct the daily routines of their classrooms and for administrators to manage their schools. Components of the Responsive Classroom program are Morning Meeting, Cooperative Learning, Role Playing, Rules With Logical Consequences, and Guided Discovery. The purpose of the program is to create an instructional environment where (a) the way children and teachers treat each other is as important as facts and skills; (b) feelings, thoughts, dreams, values, friendships, and conflicts are fundamental elements of the curriculum; and (c) children learn the tools to confront new problems, and demonstrate a responsible investment in their learning.[7]

Effective Teaching of Social Skills

The first objective in a social skills lesson is that students *overlearn* the steps in the skill. The models must be provided frequently enough that all students can repeat the steps to the teacher or a peer. Overlearning happens through repetition and review, observing the steps from different models (teachers and peers), and visual reminders such as posters or individual student cue cards. Lessons should be presented a *minimum* of two times per week, for 15 to 20 minutes. Most programs recommend greater frequency, while the length of the lesson depends on the grade level of the students. The second objective of a social skills lesson is that students will *transfer their learning*, remembering the lesson and performing the skills in natural settings.

Effective teaching principles must be used in teaching social skills, just as they would in teaching academic content. The teaching procedures for a social learning model involve demonstrating and modeling the skill using examples and non-examples of the social behavior, practice and self-management by students, feedback and reinforcement from the teacher, and a plan for use of the skill in school and home settings with peers and adults. A complete social skills curriculum will have detailed or scripted lessons that include the effective instructional components listed in Table 4.2.[8]

TABLE 4.2 Steps in Teaching Social Skills

- Define the skill for students.

- Model the skill.
  - Use this sequence—example/non-example/example.
  - Include students in the modeling.

- Using role plays, have students rehearse the behavior.
  - Rehearse a few in front of the whole group, and a few by twos, with each student in the class having a peer partner.

- Review the skill.
  - Have students practice in small groups during a natural social activity (academic game, free-time activities).
  - Monitor and supervise during the social activity, giving feedback to individuals on their performance.

- Summarize the group's performance.
  - Select partners to demonstrate successful examples of skill use.

- Assign homework.
  - Include suggestions for using the skill in natural settings.
  - Provide a visual prompt card with steps in using the skill.
  - Provide a process for families to report success.

- Continue incidental teaching and reinforcement of skills throughout the school day.

- Use group contingency to maximize attainment and maintenance of skills.

- Use individual contracting for students with severe antisocial behaviors.

SOURCE: Adapted from lessons in published curricula (Jackson, Jackson, & Monroe, 1983; McGinnis & Goldstein, 1997; Sheridan, 1995; Walker, Stiller, Golly, Kavanagh, & Feil, 1998).

Modeling Skills

A critical component in social skills instruction is *modeling*, which may promote skill usage beyond the lessons. McGinnis and Goldstein (1997), in the *Skillstreaming* curriculum, describe several key variables for effective modeling:

Use at least two examples for each skill demonstration. If a skill is used in more than one group session, develop two new modeling displays.

Select situations relevant to students' real-life circumstances.

The model (i.e., the person enacting the behavioral steps of the skill) should be portrayed as a youngster reasonably similar in age, socio-economic background, verbal ability, and other characteristics salient to the youngsters in the Skillstreaming group.

Modeling displays should depict positive outcomes. In addition, the model who is using the skill well should always be reinforced.

Modeling displays should depict all the behavioral steps of the skill in the correct sequence.

Modeling displays should depict only one skill at a time, with no extraneous content. (McGinnis & Goldstein, 1997, p. 62)

To enhance modeling, teachers need to use models who are (a) highly skilled or expert in good social skills, (b) high-status peers, (c) friendly and helpful toward the students, and (d) in control of the rewards for appropriate social behaviors. Research clearly shows that good peer models, who are valued as high-status peers, can greatly influence students toward using appropriate behaviors. Examples include school athletes with appropriate social skills, students who have multiple friends and appropriate social networks, and community mentors, who might be successful high school students and adults.

Practice and Self-Management

Besides effective modeling and instruction, a key enhancement to social skills instruction is the use of *practice time, self-management,* and *self-regulation strategies.* Overactive students, particularly younger students, have a hard time attending to verbal instructions, the typical format for skill presentation and modeling. Thus less time in formal instruction and more time in skill practice may be a key. The practice time needs to include structured, yet novel, stimulating activities.

Charlebois, Normandeau, Vitaro, and Berneche (1999) incorporated four critical components of effective teaching of social skills: formal lessons in problem solving, self-regulation training, hands-on activities to practice skills, and frequent individual contact with participants during small group practice. Participants included 30 six-year-old males described as inattentive, overactive, and aggressive. The self-regulation training groups required approximately 30% listening to skill instruction, 70% practice in small peer groups, and self-regulation of skill use. Steps in self-regulation included:

1. Define what the problem is or what the objective of the task is.

2. Suggest some possible plans or operations needed to complete the task.

3. Decide what is the best plan or operation.

4. Execute the plan or operation.

5. Evaluate whether or not the plan or operation worked. (p. 141)

The authors of this study suggest that allowing the students to self-evaluate their use of the steps in problem solving may be more effective than high rates of role playing. The final critical component is that the teacher reduces instruction during student practice. This time is child centered and activity based, creating a closer resemblance to children's natural social settings. The teacher's role is performance feedback for social skills, positive interaction, and effective problem solving. The researchers found much less problem behavior (e.g., disobedience, bullying, inattention, being out of seat, fidgeting) during this format of instruction. There are two messages here for teachers: (a) Social skills lessons must include active student engagement in activities for practicing social skills, and (b) students must be able to evaluate their use of the skills along with the teacher's feedback.

Students with aggressive and antisocial behaviors may need to learn frequent self-management to use in natural settings as well as in the classroom. Kern and colleagues (1995) provided a model program for using self-evaluation for students with emotional and behavioral disorders. The setting included a typical social activity: playing games with peers. Students initially exhibited high rates of inappropriate peer interaction (100+ per hour), and equal or lower rates of appropriate interactions. The teacher made 5-minute videotapes during the game activities, then watched them with the students. For each 30-second segment of the tape, students scored a *yes* on their score sheet ("I got along with my classmates.") or a *no*. For each *no* rating, the student announced what the inappropriate behavior was and what an acceptable replacement behavior would be. Students received points for each accurate rating and more points for *yes* agreements with the teacher. Negative peer interactions decreased significantly and appropriate comments increased dramatically. The self-evaluation was faded to every other day and eventually rewards alone maintained the appropriate behaviors. Clearly, the use of self-evaluation or self-management of behaviors by students may be a necessary component to social skills instruction for changing high rates of antisocial behaviors.

Improving Social Skills at Recess

Recess and other social activities in school settings are perfect opportunities for building social relationships. On the other hand, *unsupervised recess* settings, with limited instruction and guidance from teachers, parents, and peers, can have very negative results. Antisocial behaviors, the growth of deviant peer groups, and rejection of aggressive students by students who might otherwise provide critical appropriate modeling all occur. Researchers suggest that several key skills are difficult for children with antisocial, aggressive behaviors: (a) joining, maintaining, or keeping appropriate interaction going, (b) responding to teasing and bullying, (c) anger management, and (d) complying with commands and requests from teachers and peers.

Walker, Colvin, and Ramsey (1995) provide a summary of appropriate behaviors to teach students for *joining existing activities*, including:

♦ Select a game that you know the rules to join.

♦ Stay close and wait for a natural break to initiate contact.

♦ Help others and make group-oriented, positive statements while waiting.

♦ Ask politely, "Can I play?"

♦ Respond promptly if accepted, and take any offer, even if a small role (referee).

♦ Get someone to quickly teach you the rules if necessary.

♦ If refused, go look for someone who has few friends, or play by yourself as an alternative.

Teachers should also confirm that students understand what *not* to do, empowering them to prevent problems. Behavior non-examples include: Ask frequent questions or interrupt the group, talk about yourself or brag, seek attention, disagree with the group or try to instruct them in the game, be overly persistent (excessive tagging along), barge in to play or make threats to play (e.g., "Let me play or I'll steal the ball").

Walker and colleagues also report that *teasing* is more likely to occur on the playground. Teasing is a behavior that appears to be easily ignored when done among socially appropriate friends. Children with antisocial attitudes and beliefs often respond to teasing with intense anger, threats, and sometimes tantrums. They may need additional social skills instruction to respond appropriately to teasing on the playground. *Adaptive responses* to teasing include ignoring, asking the persons to stop, leaving the situation, and walking toward an adult, followed by reporting to the adult if it doesn't stop. *Maladaptive responses* to teasing include teasing back, name calling, getting angry, crying or acting hurt, hitting or threatening harm, having tantrums, and leaving but later retaliating with a friend (Walker et al., 1995).

In addition to students being able to join groups at recess, they need to *maintain their participation* through appropriate engagement and behaviors. As an example, the following steps were implemented as a recess program encompassing social skills instruction.

- ♦ 15-minute social skills lessons are taught immediately prior to recess, including how to join groups, examples of appropriate/ inappropriate statements, and appropriate use of hands and feet during recess.

- ♦ From a visual menu, students identify an activity they want to do during recess.

- ♦ An adult coaches individual students during recess, with prompts at 2- or 3-minute intervals if students are unengaged with peers, and signals (e.g., thumbs up, smiles) when students are playing appropriately.

- ♦ Students evaluate their own behavior immediately following recess by completing a *recess buddies form* with yes/no checks for specific social skills.

- ♦ The adult provides performance feedback following recess, offering and soliciting from students specific examples of appropriate and inappropriate behaviors.

The self-management form used for this program is provided in Appendix 4.B. Students increased their appropriate play with peers using the program (see Figure 4.2). In addition, students' negative behaviors and alone time decreased during recess.

An additional model program for improving recess behaviors for highly aggressive students is called RECESS. The RECESS program consists of four components:

1. Scripted training in cooperative, positive social behavior for the aggressive student and all classmates

2. A response-cost point system with loss of points for inappropriate social behavior and rule infractions

3. Praise and bonus points by the consultant, teacher, and supervisor for appropriate social behavior

FIGURE 4.2. Increases in Appropriate Play Using Recess Buddies

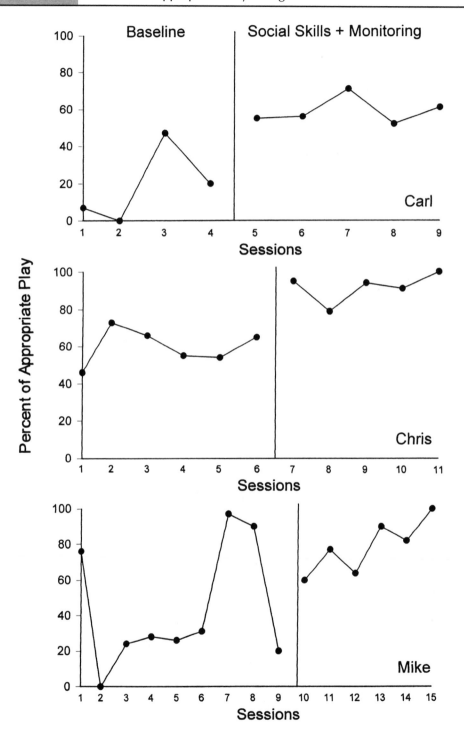

4. Concurrent group and individual reinforcement contingencies

The authors report that the RECESS program is a powerful, yet intensive intervention for severely aggressive youth in grades K-3. A consultant spends approximately 40 hours over a 2- to 3-month period assisting in implementation. Maintenance procedures ensure continued success for the students. While this appears labor intensive, one might consider the consequences of no intervention or use of ineffective procedures: (a) continued serious aggression with potential student injury, (b) predictable delinquent behaviors by students for whom schools do not invest support for effective intervention, (c) a general school trend of increasing playground aggression and an unsafe school environment (Walker, Hops, & Greenwood, 1993).

Reinforcement and Transfer of Social Skills Training

The practice known as *reinforcement* applies to social skills instruction as well as to teaching academic content. Reinforcement is any action that strengthens the child's motivation to continue the behavior. Adults must provide reinforcement during both the instruction and the maintenance phases of social skills training if students are to transfer their skills to natural settings. Verbal praise should be specific to the behavior, delivered as immediately as possible, frequent enough to make a difference, and with enthusiasm and eye contact. For example, on the way back to the classroom from recess, the teacher might comment to a small group of students, "That was great that your team let Tom join the soccer game!" In addition, tangible and frequent *social rewards* are necessary for reversing antisocial patterns. Examples of these would be extra recess, free time, time with a peer partner for study, and positive notes to parents.

The *Play Time/Social Time: Organizing Your Classroom to Build Interaction Skills* curriculum provides a model for delivering reinforcement during social skills practice. In this program, primary skills are taught using scripted lessons. These include sharing, agreeing, play-organizing behaviors, and helping. Following the structured teaching, students practice for approximately 10 minutes in a small group with appropriate peer models. The teacher marks happy faces on a chart by each student's name for appropriate skills and interactions (6-8 times). At the end of sessions, the teacher provides verbal feedback and praise and stickers or grab bag rewards for appropriate social skills. This program was used in one study for approximately 40 children in Head Start and kindergarten classes. Only with reinforcement were students with antisocial behaviors able to approximate the levels of appropriate interaction demonstrated by peer models.

In this study, the authors also tested two ways to promote generalization. In the Head Start classes, five or six students wore colored necklace tags during social activities throughout the day. The student group rotated randomly but always included students with antisocial behaviors. Teachers drew happy faces or put small stickers on the tags for appropriate use of the social skills during sessions (4-5 times). In the kindergarten classes, teachers made posters that corresponded to the social skills the students had learned. A small bag was attached to the poster for the week. The teacher placed tokens in the bag when individual students were "caught" using appropriate social skills. A minimum of 20 tokens per week was used as a prompt to teachers to reinforce skills in natural settings (Kamps, Ellis, Mancina, & Greene, 1995).

The Tough Kid Social Skills Book suggests having students set social skills goals, with reinforcement delivered based upon meeting individual goals. The book recommends the following in setting goals for students with antisocial behaviors:

♦ Help students choose goals that they will probably be successful in meeting (e.g., skills that they sometimes exhibit, with small steps as goals for new behaviors).

♦ Encourage students to make specific goals including information on what, when, where, with whom, and how the behavior is accomplished (e.g., "I will play with a friend at morning recess").

♦ Ensure that children choose goals over which they have control (e.g., they can access the person and activity without adult assistance such as transportation).

♦ Help students select goals that tell them what to do, rather than what not to do ("I will play soccer at recess" is better than "I will not play alone").

♦ Use homework assignments from social skills lessons as a mechanism for working on goals.

♦ Decide with students how to keep track and evaluate attainment of goals, and deliver reinforcement (see Sheridan, 1995, pp. 87-88).

Generalization or Transfer of Learning

Teachers can increase the impact of their classroom social skills training by encouraging their students to use their new skills in other settings. There are many strategies that improve transfer of training or *generalization* (see Scott & Nelson, 1998). Teachers can (a) design a plan to promote generalization, (b) reinforce students verbally when they attempt or actually use the skills in natural contexts, (c) cue students and give them an appropriate model when an opportunity occurs and they do not use their skills, and (d) reward them for meeting a predetermined goal for their use of skills in social contexts (recess, lunchroom, free time).

Additional strategies for promoting generalization are:

♦ Individual and group contracts and contingency programs (see Chapter 2)

♦ Booster sessions to reteach skills periodically

♦ Peers as reinforcers and prompters during recess (see Dougherty, Fowler, & Paine, 1985)

♦ Mild punishment for antisocial behaviors coupled with reinforcement for prosocial skills

♦ Pre-correction, or reminders of appropriate social behaviors immediately prior to social activity, followed by active supervision of social time by adults

♦ Environmental assessment and alteration of consequences in settings to improve social skills performance (see Lewis & Sugai, 1996)

Multicomponent Interventions. In the introduction to the chapter, we presented information regarding antisocial characteristics of children with emotional and behavioral problems, and the magnitude of the effects of aggressive behaviors over time and with significant others, such as peers, teachers, and family members. Many propose that a problem of this significance requires a solution that encompasses multiple persons and settings and begins at an early age. Individual students who show signs of emotional or behavioral problems at preschool or kindergarten age can make large gains in their social skills when parents, peers, and teachers are involved as key players.

The *First Step to Success: Helping Young Children Overcome Antisocial Behavior* is an exemplary model of school and home intervention for teaching social skills and appropriate behaviors. Three modules make up the program: (a) screening of all kindergartners to determine the students most at risk, (b) a consultant-based school intervention involving the target child, peers, and teachers, and (c) parent training in caregiver skills to promote positive school adjustment and appropriate behaviors. In the CLASS program, first the consultant, then the teacher and peers, monitor the student's behavior and give him or her feedback. The Home Base component consists of six lessons provided by the consultant during home visits. Parents learn how to teach their children the following skills: (a) communication and sharing in school, (b) cooperation, (c) limits setting, (d) problem solving, (e) friendship making, and (f) development of confidence. Data-based studies show important gains in appropriate behaviors for participants. These gains persist into the primary grades. Clearly the use of multiple persons to deliver the social skills intervention increased the benefits to participants. Chapter 6 outlines another approach to involving parents and teachers in early prevention activities.

Why Social Skills Programs Sometimes Fail

Social skills as an intervention can be very powerful. Program failures, however, may occur and are typically related to poor instruction, limited reinforcement, and negative modeling. Instructional issues include poor teaching (lecturing vs. active student practice), too few lessons in social skills, and not targeting critical skills for the individual or group (see Figure 4.1). Reinforcement issues include not establishing student goals and a reinforcement plan for improved social skills in natural settings, or not reinforcing at a high enough level to motivate students to change. In addition, negative modeling by adults and peers may diminish the effects of social skills and reinforce antisocial behaviors. Grouping students with antisocial behaviors together (as sometimes occurs for social skills groups) may actually increase problem behavior through negative peer modeling. In 1999, researchers reported three experimental studies of adolescents with antisocial behavior. Guided group counseling, including social skills training, was delivered with small groups. Results actually showed an increase in problem behavior (initiation of substance use, self-reported delinquency, and violent behavior) for the intervention groups when compared to control groups. The authors suggest that high-risk peers support or reinforce one another's deviant behavior; thus group intervention with exclusively deviant peers should be avoided. They describe this phenomenon as *deviancy training* (Dishion, McCord, & Poulin, 1999; Feldman, 1992; Kamps et al., 1995; Kamps, Tankersley, & Ellis, 2000). Antisocial peers react positively to deviant talk in the groups, a powerful reinforcement for deviancy. Nondelinquent students ignore deviant talk in favor of typical discussions. The message for conducting group social skills intervention is clear. Students with antisocial behaviors should be separated as much as possible. Small groups for practice should be at a minimum ratio of three or four good peer models for every student who has antisocial behaviors.

Administrators who institute social skills training in their schools have a special responsibility to monitor the behavior of the adults in the school toward each other and toward the students. One principal suggested that her first step might need to be social skills training for the staff. The most powerful modeling takes place when students observe the casual social interactions that take place in their school on an everyday basis. Students will benefit from a school setting where adults model appropriate social skills and respect, other students understand and reinforce appropriate behaviors, and all adults use the same language in their reminders and reinforcements.

A final caution: It is important to note that social skills instruction is only one component of an effective behavior support plan for students identified as having emotional and behavioral disorders. Kamps and colleagues, as an example, found that the most effective prevention program included social skills, classroom management and group contingencies, and academic tutoring. Thus implementation of social skills as a single prevention strategy is going to be limited in its effectiveness without other supportive programs.

Gaining Community Support for Social Skills Training

Mayer (1995) emphasized the pivotal role of schools in society in either preventing or promoting antisocial behaviors. Schools have opportunities to intervene around *motivational variables* such as low student involvement, poor attendance and poor participation in class, lack of homework completion, and limited involvement in after-school activities. Schools can address *variables related to individual differences* with effective instructional practices, active student engagement, academic remediation, and behavioral/social support for students with problems. Schools can fail at *support variables,* including weak or inconsistent administrative support for staff in carrying out student discipline and follow-through, staff disagreement with discipline policies, and a heavy reliance on punitive procedures.

As we begin the new century, schools can find themselves at odds with a punishment-oriented society. Zero-tolerance policies can tie administrators' hands and limit their abilities to use mild misbehavior as a learning opportunity. Community and state systems may seem to value the results of standardized tests over breadth, depth, and self-direction in student learning. However, teaching *socially valid* skills in the classrooms will be supported if the community has been a part of the decision-making process in choosing the curriculum. Even when an area has great cultural diversity in its population, families can understand and appreciate the behavioral expectations of the school's culture, as long as they are explained with respect for the family's culture. The effort required to choose and use a good social skills program should eventually pay off in student achievement. As one teacher stated, "How can you teach anything else until you teach social skills?"

NOTES

1. Figure 4.1 and the checklist in Appendix 4.A are used with permission from the authors of the *Social Skills Planning Guide,* which is no longer in print. However, it can be accessed on microfiche through ERIC (ED386892).

2. The *Skillstreaming* series includes versions for early childhood and adolescence. See the Research Press Web site at www.researchpress.com.

3. For more information on the ASSIST Program, see the Sopris West Web site at www.sopriswest.com.

4. This book is part of a series that includes classroom management strategies, positive behavior management with individual students, and a six-tape set of staff development videos. For more information, see the Sopris West Web site at www.sopriswest.com.

5. The Bully-Proofing series includes a parent's guide titled *Bully-Proofing Your Child.* For more information, see the Sopris West Web site at www.sopriswest.com.

6. For more information on *Second Step,* please see the Web site of the Committee for Children, www.cfchildren.org; see Frey, Hirshstein, and Guzzo, 2000; Grossman et al., 1997.

7. Elliott found an increase in social skills, a decrease in problem behaviors, and improved academic competence for students in an urban elementary school using the Responsive Classroom model. For the report from this study, titled *Caring to Learn: A Report on the Positive Impact of a Social Curriculum,* by S. N. Elliott, contact the Northeast Foundation for Children, 71 Montague City Road, Greenfield, MA 01301.

8. For example, *Skillstreaming, The Tough Kid Social Skills Book,* and *First Step to Success.*

APPENDIX 4.A

Comparison Summary Checklist
(adapted with permission from the
Social Skills Planning Guide)

	Essential Criteria for Program Selection *(Check all that apply.)*				
Identify needs of your student(s): **Program Characteristics**	Program Title:	Program Title:	Program Title:	Program Title:	Program Title:
GRADE LEVELS					
Preschool (3- and 4-year-olds)					
Elementary (K-5)					
Middle/Junior (6-8)					
Secondary (9-12)					
Postsecondary					
INSTRUCTIONAL GROUPING					
Whole Class					
Small Group					
One-on-One					

(continued)

	Essential Criteria for Program Selection (Check all that apply.)				
Identify needs of your student(s): **Program Characteristics**	Program Title:	Program Title:	Program Title:	Program Title:	Program Title:
INTENDED STUDENT OUTCOMES					
COMMUNICATION SKILLS (giving feedback, listening, using a quiet voice, negotiating, apologizing, conversing, speaking, seeking and giving help)					
INTERPERSONAL SKILLS (asserting oneself, making friends, dating, negotiating, being aware of and understanding others, dealing with authority figures, initiating interactions, interacting with strangers, interacting with adults, interacting with peers, interacting with co-workers, showing consideration of others, sharing, cooperating)					
PERSONAL SKILLS (being self-aware, maintaining a positive self-concept/personal identity, accepting responsibility for self-care and hygiene, dealing with feelings, using manners, setting goals)					
RESPONSE SKILLS (receiving feedback, following directions, dealing with criticism, dealing with frustration, controlling aggression, accepting consequences of behavior, responding to peer pressure, resolving conflicts, solving problems dealing with stress, empathizing)					

	Essential Criteria for Program Selection (Check all that apply.)				
Identify needs of your student(s): **Program Characteristics**	Program Title:	Program Title:	Program Title:	Program Title:	Program Title:
INSTRUCTIONAL MATERIALS					
Text for Trainer(s)					
Student Assessment Instrument(s)					
Maintenance/Generalization Procedures					
Outcome Evaluation Component					
Consumable Student Materials					
Nonconsumable Student Materials					
Audio/Video Technology					
Computers					
Visuals/Manipulatives					
Total Cost					
INSTRUCTIONAL TIME REQUIREMENTS					
Write in Frequency/Length of Intervention					
NOTES:					

Self-Management Form
for Recess Buddies

Name_____ Week of_____

		Play Games		Nice Talk		Ok Hands & Feet	
		Start	Cont.	Start	Cont.	Start	Cont.
Monday	A.M.	Yes No	Yes No	Yes No	Yes No	Yes No	Yes No
	P.M.	Yes No	Yes No	Yes No	Yes No	Yes No	Yes No
Tuesday	A.M.	Yes No	Yes No	Yes No	Yes No	Yes No	Yes No
	P.M.	Yes No	Yes No	Yes No	Yes No	Yes No	Yes No
Wednesday	A.M.	Yes No	Yes No	Yes No	Yes No	Yes No	Yes No
	P.M.	Yes No	Yes No	Yes No	Yes No	Yes No	Yes No
Thursday	A.M.	Yes No	Yes No	Yes No	Yes No	Yes No	Yes No
	P.M.	Yes No	Yes No	Yes No	Yes No	Yes No	Yes No
Friday	A.M.	Yes No	Yes No	Yes No	Yes No	Yes No	Yes No
	P.M.	Yes No	Yes No	Yes No	Yes No	Yes No	Yes No

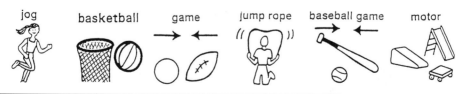

jog   basketball   game   jump rope   baseball game   motor

_____ REFERENCES

Alberg, J., Petry (Tashjian), C., & Eller, S. (1994). *The social skills planning guide.* Longmont, CO: Sopris West.

Bronfenbrenner, U. (1974). The origins of alienation. *Scientific American, 231,* 53-61.

Charlebois, P., Normandeau, S., Vitaro, F., & Berneche, F. (1999). Skills training for inattentive, overactive, aggressive boys: Differential effects of content and delivery method. *Behavioral Disorders, 24*(2), 137-150.

Dewey, J. (1916). *Democracy and education: An introduction to the philosophy of education.* New York: Macmillan.

Dishion, T. J., McCord, J., & Poulin, F. (1999). When interventions harm: Peer groups and problem behavior. *American Psychologist, 54*(9), 755-764.

Dodge, K., Coie, J., & Brakke, N. (1982). Behavior patterns of socially rejected and neglected adolescents: The roles of social approach and aggression. *Journal of Abnormal Child Psychology, 10,* 389-410.

Doll, B., & Lyon, M. A. (1998). Risk and resilience: Implications for the delivery of educational and mental health services in schools. *School Psychology Review, 27*(3), 348-363.

Dougherty, B. S., Fowler, S. A., & Paine, S. (1985). The use of peer monitors to reduce negative interactions during recess. *Journal of Applied Behavior Analysis, 18,* 141-153.

DuPaul, G., & Eckert, T. (1994). The effects of social skills curricula: Now you see them, now you don't. *School Psychology Quarterly, 9,* 113-132.

Feldman, R. A. (1992). The St. Louis experiment: Effective treatment of antisocial youths in prosocial peer groups. In J. McCord & R. E. Tremblay (Eds.), *Preventing antisocial behavior: Interventions from birth through adolescence* (pp. 233-252). New York: Guilford.

Frey, K., Hirshstein, M., & Guzzo, B. (2000). Second step: Preventing aggression by promoting social competence. *Journal of Emotional and Behavioral Disorders, 8,* 102-112.

Gresham, F. M. (1995). Best practices in social skills training. In A. Thomas & J. Grimes (Eds.), *Best practices in school psychology—III* (pp. 1021-1030). Washington, DC: National Association of School Psychologists.

Grossman, D., Neckerman, H., Koepsell, T., Liu, P., Asher, K., Beland, K., Frey, K., & Rivara, F. (1997). Effectiveness of a violence prevention curriculum among children in elementary school: A randomized controlled trial. *Journal of the American Medical Association, 277,* 1605-1611.

Jackson, N. F., Jackson, D. A., & Monroe, C. (1983). *Skill lessons and activities: Getting along with others: Teaching social effectiveness to children.* Champaign, IL: Research Press.

Kamps, D. M., Ellis, C., Mancina, C., & Greene, L. (1995). Peer-inclusive social skills groups for young children with behavioral risks. *Preventing School Failure, 39*, 10-15.

Kamps, D., Tankersley, M., & Ellis, C. (2000). Social skills intervention for young at-risk students: A 2-year follow-up study. *Behavioral Disorders, 25*, 310-324.

Kern, L., Wacker, D. P., Mace, F. C., Falk, G. D., Dunlap, G., & Kromrey, J. D. (1995). Improving the peer interactions of students with emotional and behavioral disorders through self-evaluation procedures: A component analysis and group application. *Journal of Applied Behavior Analysis, 28*(1), 47-59.

Lewis, T., & Sugai, G. (1996). Descriptive and experimental analysis of teacher and peer attention and the use of assessment-based intervention to improve pro-social behavior. *Journal of Behavior Education, 6*, 7-24.

Masten, A. S., & Coatsworth, J. D. (1998). The development of competence in favorable and unfavorable environments: Lessons from research on successful children. *American Psychologist, 53*(2), 205-220.

Mayer, G. R. (1995). Preventing antisocial behavior in the schools. *Journal of Applied Behavior Analysis, 28*(4), 467-478.

McGinnis, E., & Goldstein, A. P. (1997). *Skillstreaming the elementary school child: New strategies and perspectives for teaching prosocial skills.* Champaign, IL: Research Press.

Scott, T. M., & Nelson, C. M. (1998). Confusion and failure in facilitating generalized social responding in the school setting: Sometimes 2 + 2 = 5. *Behavioral Disorders, 23*, 264-275.

Sheridan, S. M. (1995). *The tough kid social skills book.* Longmont, CO: Sopris West.

Walker, H. M., Colvin, G., & Ramsey, E. (1995). *Antisocial behavior in school: Strategies and best practices.* Pacific Grove, CA: Brooks/Cole.

Walker, H. M., Hops, H., & Greenwood, C. (1993). *RECESS: Research and development of a behavior management package for remediating social aggression in the school setting.* Seattle, WA: Educational Achievement Systems.

Walker, H. M., Kavanagh, K., Stiller, B., Golly, A., Stevenson, H. H., & Feil, E. G. (1998). First step to success: An early intervention approach for preventing school antisocial behavior. *Journal of Emotional and Behavioral Disorders, 6*(2), 66-80.

Walker, H. M., Stiller, B., Golly, A., Kavanagh, K., & Feil, E. G. (1998). *First step to success: Helping young children overcome antisocial behavior.* Longmont, CO: Sopris West.

RESOURCES

Charney, R. (1992). *Teaching children to care*. Greenfield, MA: Northeast Foundation for Children.

Colvin, G. (1993). *Managing acting-out behavior*. Eugene, OR: Lane Educational Service District.

Colvin, G., Sugai, G., Good, R., & Lee, Y.-Y. (1997). Using precorrection and active supervision to improve transition behaviors in an elementary school. *School Psychology Quarterly, 12*(4), 344-363.

Colvin, G., Tobin, T., Beard, K., Hagan, S., & Sprague, J. (1998). The school bully: Assessing the problem, developing interventions, and future research directions. *Journal of Behavioral Education, 8*(3), 293-319.

Committee for Children. (1990). *Second step: A violence prevention curriculum committee for children*. Available: 172 20th Avenue, Seattle, WA 98122-5862.

Doll, B., Sheridan, S. M., & Law, M. (1990). *Friendship group: Parents manual*. Unpublished manual, University of Wisconsin—Madison, Department of Educational Psychology.

Fowler, S., Dougherty, B., Kirby, K., & Kohler, F. (1986). Role reversals: An analysis of therapeutic effects achieved with disruptive boys during their appointments as peer monitors. *Journal of Applied Behavior Analysis, 19*, 437-444.

Garrity, C., Jens, K., Porter, W., Sager, N., & Short-Camilli, C. (1994). *Bully-proofing your school: A comprehensive approach for elementary schools*. Longmont, CO: Sopris West.

Goldstein, A., & Glick, B. (1997). *Aggression replacement training: A comprehensive intervention for aggressive youth*. Champaign, IL: Research Press.

Gresham, F. M., & Elliott, S. N. (1990). *Social Skills Rating System*. Circle Pines, MN: American Guidance Service.

Gumpel, T. (1994). Social competence and social skills training for persons with mental retardation: An expansion of a behavioral paradigm. *Education and Training in Mental Retardation and Developmental Disabilities, 29*(3), 194-201.

Gumpel, T. P., & David, S. (2000). Exploring the efficacy of self-regulatory training as a possible alternative to social skills training. *Behavioral Disorders, 25*(2), 131-141.

Gumpel, T. P., & Frank, R. (1999). An expansion of the peer-tutoring paradigm: Cross-age peer tutoring of social skills among socially rejected boys. *Journal of Applied Behavior Analysis, 32*(1), 115-118.

Huggins, P. (1995). *Helping kids handle anger: Teaching self-control.* Longmont, CO: Sopris West.

Langland, S., Lewis-Palmer, T., & Sugai, G. (1998). Teaching respect in the classroom: An instructional approach. *Journal of Behavioral Education, 8*(2), 245-262.

Lewis, T. J., Sugai, G., & Colvin, G. (1998). Reducing problem behavior through a school-wide system of effective behavioral support: Investigation of a school-wide social skills training program and contextual interventions. *School Psychology Review, 26*(3), 446-459.

Odom, S. L., & McConnell, S. R. (1997). *Play time/social time: Organizing your classroom to build interaction skills.* Minneapolis: University of Minnesota, Institute on Community Integration.

Salend, S. J., Whittaker, C. R., & Reeder, E. (1992). Group evaluation: A collaborative, peer-mediated behavior management system. *Exceptional Children, 59,* 203-209.

Sheridan, S. M., Dee, C. C., Morgan, J. C., McCormick, M. E., & Walker, D. (1996). A multi method intervention for social skills deficits in children with ADD and their parents. *School Psychology Review, 25,* 57-76.

Sugai, G., & Fuller, M. (1991). A decision model for social skills curriculum analysis. *Remedial and Special Education, 12*(4), 33-42.

Tankersley, M., Kamps, D., Mancina, C., & Weidinger, D. (1996). Social interventions for Head Start children with behavioral risks: Implementation and outcomes. *Journal of Emotional and Behavioral Disorders, 4*(3), 171-181.

Tremula, R. E., Pagan-Kurtz, L., Masse, L. C., Vitaro, F., & Phil, R. O. (1995). A bimodal preventive intervention for disruptive kindergarten boys: Its impact through mid-adolescence. *Journal of Consulting and Clinical Psychology, 63,* 560-568.

Vygotsky, L. S., & Luria, A. (1994). Tool and symbol in child development. In R. van der Veer & J. Valsiner (Eds.), *The Vygotsky reader* (pp. 94-174). Cambridge, MA: Blackwell.

Walker, H. M., McConnell, S., Holmes, D., Todus, B., Walker, J., & Golden, N. (1983). *The Walker social skills curriculum: The ACCEPTS program* (A Curriculum for Children's Effective Peer and Teachers Skills). Austin, TX: PRO-ED.

Zaragoza, N., Vaughan, S., & McIntosh, R. (1991). Social skills interventions and children with behavior problems: A review. *Behavior Disorders, 16,* 260-275.

Preventing Problem Behaviors Using Schoolwide Discipline 5

Bob Algozzine
Richard White

*Jamarian sits in the hall beside the classroom door. When asked what happened, he replies: "Nothing!! That *$&%# just doesn't like me!! I hate this school!!" His teacher has a different view: "How do you expect me to teach when students don't want to learn? Kids like Jamarian should be in special classes so the rest of the class can learn!"*

Every day, school personnel face continuing and important behavioral challenges in efforts to establish and maintain safe, orderly classroom environments where teachers can teach and students can learn. Preventing problem behaviors is important because of its role in reducing serious school problems. Primary interventions keep more serious disorders from occurring and target the large group of students (80%-90%) who proceed through school exhibiting minor problem behaviors. Secondary interventions slow down the progress of disorders and, if possible, reverse or correct them. Tertiary interventions target serious problems in efforts to keep disorders from becoming more severe. A well-functioning schoolwide discipline system improves the efficiency and effectiveness of group and individual management efforts (primary, secondary, and tertiary interventions).

Unified Discipline

The three most important student behaviors that must be taught the first days of school are these:

Discipline

Procedures

Routines (Wong & Wong, 1998)

Improving discipline is central to prevention efforts designed to improve the lives of children, those with behavior problems and the peers who share their classrooms. Unified Discipline takes the guesswork out of management and behavioral instruction.

Components of the Model

In schools where Unified Discipline is practiced, students are exposed to a united, caring, firm, loving, and very determined action plan. Four interrelated objectives drive efforts to implement Unified Discipline: unified attitudes, unified expectations, unified correction procedures, and unified team roles.

Attitudes. An effective discipline program requires action that is firm and caring without overly emotional responses. Interacting with misbehaving students without responding in kind and without becoming emotionally upset is the key attitude that is being shared by those who practice Unified Discipline. These unified *attitudes* stem from the following widely accepted beliefs: Successful learning activities can improve behavior; learning to manage one's own behavior is an important part of an education; behavioral instruction is part of teaching; personalizing or becoming tangled up in student misbehavior makes matters worse; and teachers' mental and emotional poise and firmness make discipline methods work.

Expectations. Consistency and positive, unified *expectations* for successful behavioral instruction are a hallmark of an effective discipline plan. Schools using Unified Discipline have clearly described school and classroom rules, procedures, and consequences that define the expectations for success. Having clear-cut expectations does not mean every school practicing Unified Discipline looks the same. Administrators and teachers in each school define their particular expectations based on architectural arrangements, prior history, and staff and community concerns. Regardless, some considerations are fundamental.

First, rules are set without equivocation. Rules form the basis for describing expectations; following rules is the major objective of behavioral instruction. Correctly used rules depersonalize conflict and protect teachers and administrators (i.e., conflict is between student and an expectation, not a teacher or administrator). Rules provide a basis for establishing and maintaining a consistent, safe, and orderly environment. Rules are a way to work together to accomplish learning goals.

Three clear, specific, and reasonable expectations are evident: school rules, classroom rules, and classroom procedures. School rules apply across all locations and activities within the school, at all times and with all personnel. Major school rules describe actions that threaten the safety and well-being of people in the school (e.g., "Verbal or physical threats are prohibited in this school."); minor school rules describe actions that disrupt the orderly flow of the learning processes (e.g., "Walk in the hallways at all times."). Classroom rules apply across all activities, at all times, regardless of the adult in charge. Areas typically addressed by classroom rules are teacher-student talk, student-student talk, student movement, and student work. Classroom procedures apply to specific activities, at all times and with all personnel (e.g., where to turn in work, where to find free-time activities, where to find transition activities, how to prepare work for credit).

Correction. When a student violates expectations (i.e., school rules, classroom rules, classroom procedures), professionals practicing Unified Discipline respond similarly and consistently with correction procedures. When everyone handles infractions with unified *correction procedures,* students learn that what happens when they misbehave is procedural, not personal. Teachers gain competence ("I know what to do") and confidence ("I know that what I do is respected and practiced by my colleagues"). Inconsistent consequences represent broken promises. Nonassertive behaviors by adults create opportunities for student distrust and invitations for rule infractions. Consistent correction procedures build trust, provide opportunities for change over time, and represent consistent consequences. They illustrate a commitment to students and colleagues within the school.

Unified correction procedures involve actively monitoring student behavior and applying consequences consistently, in a warm, assertive, firm voice. Four steps are used: State the behavior, state the violated rule, state the unified consequence, and offer encouragement to prevent future violations (see Table 5.1). In Unified Discipline, faculty act as referees. They "call the fouls" every time. They maintain their poise and composure. If players get upset, they remind them that rules are part of the game and they deliver the promised consequences.

The particular consequences applied vary by school. At the upper school levels, teachers often carry a clipboard and note infractions as they

TABLE 5.1 Four-Step Error Correction Procedure

Action	Example
State the behavior.	John, you are out of your seat.
State the rule violated.	John, you are violating the "Stay in your assigned area" rule.
State the unified consequence.	John, my job is to give you a verbal warning for this first violation.
Offer encouragement.	I want you to be successful today, John. Let's work to avoid a second violation.
	Other examples: You can beat that rule, don't let it beat you; Get on top of the rule; You can do the rule right; Alright, you are doing a good job of dogging the rule, now!

occur. At lower school levels, teachers pull colored tickets, change colors on a stoplight, or turn happy faces on a board to unhappy faces. Often, the faculty unify on a system currently used by one of their respected and effective colleagues (see Table 5.2).

Roles. In a school where Unified Discipline is practiced, clear team *roles* and responsibilities are set for all school personnel. Faculty support administrators and administrators support faculty. Unified roles eliminate second-guessing when disciplinary and classroom actions are taken. Unified roles also develop collegial participation in Unified Discipline programs. For example, the principal's role is to acknowledge and recognize teachers when they follow the Unified Discipline procedures correctly. Respect and recognition are based on teacher performance, not student response to correction or improvement. When the procedures are followed correctly, second-guessing is not allowed regardless of a student's response to them. Principals are also expected to make flexible and individualized decisions about discipline. This means principals make decisions on student needs and reinforcement history, not on a "one size fits all," inflexible policy. For example, "Students who violate a major school rule will receive three days out-of-school suspension" is inflexible policy that puts principals in a straightjacket. There really is no decision making. The principal is forced to suspend, even if suspension is reinforcing to the student ("Thank you. I want to go home!!"). Under Unified Discipline, the principal does what is

TABLE 5.2 Illustration of Unified Consequences

If (Violation)	Then (Consequence)
Major School Rule	Office Referral
	(John, my job is to send you to the office immediately when a major rule is violated.)
Minor School Rule	Verbal Reprimand (1st offense)
	(John, my job is to give you a warning for this first violation of a school rule.)
	Office Referral (2nd offense)
	(John, my job is to send you to the office on a second violation. "On your wagon!")
Classroom Rule	Verbal Reprimand (1st offense)
	(John, my job is to give you a warning for this first violation of a classroom rule.)
	Roster Mark (✓ or dot on a clipboard) (2nd offense)
	(John, this is your second violation of a classroom rule. The roster is marked.)
	Classroom Pass (3rd offense)
	(John, my job is to pass you to Ms. Smith for this third violation of a classroom rule. Let's work together to get it right when you return.)
Classroom Procedure	Student Correction
	(John, your job is to head your paper on the right side, not the left. Please correct the paper. Thanks.)
	OR
	Possible Point Loss
	(John, your job is to head your paper on the right side, not the left. One point off the paper for this error.)

best for the student, and is assured of faculty support, no matter what action is taken. Similarly, the faculty's role is to follow the procedures as a job requirement. Each teacher should expect support for a correction done accurately. Support is no longer defined as the principal providing harsh punishment for a student offense. Second-guessing of principal decisions for office referrals is not allowed regardless of student response. An "I do my job and you do your job" attitude is encouraged.

Implementing the Model

Implementation of Unified Discipline involves several steps, including developing inservice procedures and materials, preparing staff (demonstrations, practice, and follow-up), establishing unified expectations (e.g., school rules), specifying start dates, implementing intervention, and conducting review, revision, and update sessions at regularly scheduled and unscheduled staff meetings. Treatment fidelity refers to the extent to which intervention conditions conform to specifications and plans. Fall and spring treatment fidelity checks determine the nature and extent of using the system. Treatment fidelity is maximized by carefully administered training included as part of implementation of Unified Discipline. Implementing Unified Discipline involves three observable sets of behaviors: actively monitoring student behavior, using appropriate voice tones, and using unified correction procedures. The extent to which teachers implementing this intervention do each of these activities should be observed on three separate occasions during the fall and spring semesters of the school year. Data from these observations should be used as feedback for participating teachers throughout the course of the school year. For additional general information on evaluation, see Chapter 10.

Evidence Supporting Effectiveness

Overton Elementary is a motel-style school with few internal corridors and classroom doors that open to outside walkways. Space for displaying student work outside the classroom is unavailable. Interior bulletin boards and glass cases providing space for student work and displays are limited. Teachers supervise their classes as they move to various areas and activities throughout the buildings. Prior to using Unified Discipline, several behavior programs were in effect schoolwide to encourage good behavior during unstructured times. A behavior manager and teacher assistants supervised time-out programs with students needing to be removed from the general classroom.

Overton students (a) came from backgrounds of poverty as indicated by high rates of free or reduced lunch, (b) lived in neighborhoods with high rates of violent crime, (c) were likely to drop out of school based on past school records, and (d) were likely to develop high rates of school-recorded behavior problems. These characteristics were all viewed as the foundation for serious emotional disturbance based on records of past students.

As a result of busing and a related pupil assignment plan, 16% of students at Overton were classified as needing special education. Because Overton was the "home school" for three self-contained special classes, many students (approximately twice the number as in most other schools within the district) were classified with emotional disturbance. Greater numbers of students in Overton participated in free or reduced lunch programs, came from families with incomes below $25,000, and were absent 18 or more days during the school year. Fewer students lived with families in which both parents were living at home. Fewer students at Overton participated in gifted and talented programs offered by the school district. Overton was among the lowest schools in terms of school achievement and among the highest schools in numbers of students participating in special education programs for students with emotional and social problems. In addition, students leaving this school and participating in middle and high school programs had high rates of teen pregnancy and dropout. Again, the picture here was one of children whose academic careers and lives were in serious need of improvement.

Implementation and Evaluation

Efforts to evaluate Unified Discipline in Overton Elementary School focused on improvements in office referrals (including suspensions and expulsions), classroom climate and instructional ecologies, student behavior, and academic achievement.

To assess violations of school rules, classroom rules, and classroom procedures, *discipline referrals* were monitored on a daily basis using a standardized form (see Figure 5.1) and computerized tracking system. The form provided categories for major and minor school rule infractions that represent misbehaviors for which an office referral was appropriate; each infraction was cross-referenced with those in the computerized tracking system. Numbers and types of referrals for different groups of students were compared within and across participating classrooms as a measure of the effectiveness of the project interventions.

Classroom *climate and ecology* were assessed using the Stallings Observation System (SOS). Each teacher was observed for three 1-hour periods before, during, and after participation in the project interventions. The SOS is a complex, low-inference observation system sensitive to different instructional methods, teaching styles, and classroom environments. Using the SOS, an observer alternatively gathers data on the teacher and his or her immediate environment and on the entire class. The SOS has been a major process data gathering instrument in a variety of instructional and teacher effectiveness studies. The Classroom Snapshot (CS) of the SOS yields data on the activities of each adult and student in a classroom at a given time; sizes of groups, types of materials, and several aggregated activities (e.g., Interactive Teaching and Organizing/Off-Task). Positive predictors of student achievement, such as reading aloud, instruction and explanation of new materials, review and discussion, and drill and practice, are

FIGURE 5.1. Standardized Office Referral Form

Student's name:		ID #
Date	Time	Teacher
CMS Student Code of Conduct **Major Offenses**		
❑ Threatening	❑ Throwing objects at someone	❑ Shoving or kicking
❑ Profanity/obscenity directed toward someone	❑ Lying or cheating	❑ Refusal of authorized direction/insubordination
❑ Trespassing	❑ Hitting, biting, or spitting	❑ Fighting
❑ Sexual offense	❑ Gambling	❑ Vandalism
❑ Extortion	❑ Burglary, robbery, or theft	❑ Initiating a riot
❑ Drug or alcohol offense	❑ Leaving school without permission	❑ Tobacco offense
❑ Assault and battery: Staff	❑ Assault and battery: Student	❑ Arson/false alarms
❑ Firearms violation	❑ Weapons/dangerous instruments	❑ Gang activity
Other Offenses		
❑ Chronic disruption (2nd Classroom Pass Grade 2-6 Plan)		
For major offenses, describe specifically what the student did or said. For the 2nd classroom pass, list the rule violated most often.		
Handled by:_____		

included in Interactive Teaching activities that are observed. Passing out papers and lining up students for recess are examples of Organizing activities, and negative social interactions and discipline are examples of Off-task activities that are observed. CS data (i.e., number of times behaviors were observed) were compared across classrooms using a pretest/posttest design.

To address questions related to effects on classroom *behavior*, 30 randomly selected students were periodically monitored using a time sampling procedure with 10-second intervals observed for a period of 30 minutes on at least 10 different occasions during the fall and spring semesters of the school year. On-task categories included writing, reading, answering questions, asking questions, talking academically, playing an academic game, paying attention (eyes on teacher in designated area), raising hand, looking at materials, and moving or playing appropriately. Disrupting class, looking around, talking inappropriately, and doing an inappropriate task were coded as off-task behavior. Percentages were calculated by dividing the total number of intervals into the number of intervals the observed students were on-task or off-task and multiplying by 100. These observational data were compared across groups of students as additional evidence of effectiveness.

Standardized *achievement* tests routinely administered at the end of each school year in the Charlotte-Mecklenburg Schools were used to address additional questions about school and classroom behavior improvements. Communication and mathematics scores from these assessments were compared across groups of students.

Attitudes of teachers, students, and parents regarding school climate and *other aspects of schooling* were routinely assessed with end-of-the-year attitude surveys. A 75-item questionnaire addressed opinions about the school administration, management of school resources, instructional leadership, student outcomes and staff morale, school discipline and behavior, and overall satisfaction of parents and teachers. Students responded to items about their school, the school climate, and their opinions about their education. Comparisons of these available data were completed for groups of students participating and were used to address additional evaluation questions related to effects of the schoolwide discipline program.

Unified Discipline Outcomes

Participating teachers implemented Unified Discipline (UD) to varying degrees in their classrooms. This occurred as a result of new teachers entering the system and staged-implementation phases for instituting the intervention within Overton. Treatment fidelity was evaluated using observations of expected behaviors over time. Discipline demography (i.e., nature and number of office referrals) was documented using teacher checklists, standardized forms (see Figure 5.1), and an electronic database system. School, classroom, and student improvements were monitored using data-based comparisons, behavior observations, and analyses of rule violations. For example, to evaluate the effectiveness of this intervention, a comparison was completed for teachers using UD for at least 2 years and teachers using UD for less than 1 year. Classroom behavior was periodically monitored using a time sampling procedure with 10-second intervals observed for a period of 30 minutes on at least 10 different occasions during the fall and spring semesters of the school year. In addition, SOS student-teacher interactions and classroom rule violations were also compared. Office referrals were monitored on a weekly basis, and reductions in nature and extent of problems provided evidence of effectiveness (e.g., minor rule violations were being handled by the system; serious rule violations were coming to the office infrequently).

Using the System. The following behaviors were observed as evidence of use of Unified Discipline:

> *Teacher monitors:* Teacher actively watches and corrects at least 80% of infractions.
>
> *Voice tone:* Voice tone is firm and direct without any demonstration of personalization or entanglement in the verbal correction sequence.
>
> *Correction procedure:*
>> *State behavior.* Behavior is verbally identified.
>> *State rule.* Correct rule is identified in the verbal correction procedure.
>> *State unified consequence.* Correct consequence is delivered in the verbal correction procedure.
>> *Offer encouragement.* Praise and support is delivered intermittently.

High rates of monitoring (M = 94%, range = 86%-100%) and using appropriate voice tone (M = 85%, range = 55%-100%) were observed. Use of correction procedures was somewhat lower. These outcomes suggest that teachers understood and implemented the basic principles of Unified Discipline and that there was room for improvement in their levels of implementation of all aspects of the procedures (except Teacher Monitoring, which was at a very high level already).

After reviewing the outcomes of the initial classroom observations, individual feedback sessions were provided for teachers. Levels of implementation of each expected behavior of the Unified Discipline procedure were discussed with each teacher; no judgments were offered regarding the quality of an individual teacher's use of Unified Discipline. Any questions a teacher had about the procedure were answered and additional inservice was provided individually on an as-needed, as-requested basis. Teachers were informed of plans to conduct follow-up observations.

At the end of the school year, high rates of monitoring ($M = 95\%$, range = 88%-100%) and using appropriate voice tone ($M = 97\%$, range = 92%-100%) were evident. With regard to the initial observations, teachers' use of correction procedures was greatly improved. Teachers were observed to appropriately state the behavior and the rule violated by it in about two thirds of the observations; they stated consequences appropriately in about half of the observations. Their use of encouragement remained low but higher than in the earlier observation; in fact, significant improvements were evident in all areas except teacher monitoring. Similar rates of behavior were evident in subsequent years of the project and these outcomes suggested that teachers understood and implemented the basic principles of Unified Discipline.

Identifying Problems. Teachers were asked to nominate students at risk of failure and continued school problems in their classrooms, and complete a rating scale describing their behavior. These data served two purposes. First, they established a baseline reflective of levels of need within the classroom context of the participating teachers and students. They also served as a basis for identifying comparison groups (i.e., at risk vs. not at risk) for subsequent analyses of the effectiveness of selected project interventions.

Initially, eight teachers referred 27 students: One teacher referred 1 student, two teachers referred 2 students, one teacher referred 3 students, three teachers referred 4 students, and one teacher referred 7 students. Twenty (74%) boys and 7 (26%) girls were referred. Their behaviors were typical of those of students experiencing difficulties in school (e.g., not attending school, not asking for help, not completing work, misbehaving in and out of the classroom, interrupting). These data reaffirmed the high levels of discipline, management, and instructional need evident in Overton classrooms.

Additional urgency was illustrated in teachers' apparent use of office referrals as disciplinary measures. More than 500 office referrals were received prior to the initial year of the project; these infractions were analyzed as evidence of the extant, baseline discipline demography of the school. One hundred sixty-one (161) students (27% of 598) accounted for the 501 office referrals. Seventy-three percent of students did not receive an office referral during the school year.

Thirty-eight teachers and other staff members (100% of those employed, excluding central office personnel) referred at least one student. Nine teachers were responsible for single referrals and the three top-referring teachers were responsible for 35 (20%) referrals. Eight people were responsible for about half, and 30 people were responsible for slightly more than half of the referrals. Clearly, office referrals were used by some teachers as part of their classroom discipline program; others used them infrequently.

About 4% of the school population (26 students) accounted for almost half (48%) of the referrals. Overall, more than 70% of the referrals involved black students; specifically, 59% of the referred students were black males, 26% were white males, 13% were black females, and 2% were white females. Fighting, being disruptive in classroom behavior, being noncompliant in classroom behavior, making inappropriate physical contact, using bad language, making other inappropriate, loud noises, talking inappropriately, and being disrespectful toward others accounted for about 85% of the office referrals.

School Improvements. Numbers of office referrals steadily declined for the duration of the project. An initial decrease of 20% was observed from the first full year of systematic data collection; decreases of 50% to 59% were evident in subsequent project years. Rate of office referrals remained consistently low after the first year of the project. High numbers of referrals were evident in the beginning and at the end of the school year. Numbers of referrals each project year were somewhat higher in upper elementary grades (i.e., 49%-92%). Trends were also evident in student cohorts (e.g., 1994-1995 kindergarten, 1995-1996 first grade, 1996-1997 second grade, and 1997-1998 third grade). For example, high referral rates for students in second grade during the first year of the project were consistently lower during the third-, fourth-, and fifth-grade school years for these same students. Similarly, referral rates steadily decreased for Associates and Special Area Teachers, providing additional evidence supporting the effectiveness of the schoolwide discipline program. During the second and third project years (with lowest rates), unacceptable physical contact, classroom disruptions, and fighting accounted for most of the office referrals. All other problem areas accounted for small (i.e., less than 10%) proportions of overall problems referred to school administrators.

Classroom Improvements. Classroom behavior cards were collected periodically in efforts to monitor the implementation of Unified Discipline. Results were shared with teachers after each data collection. Random samples of these records were compared in the fall and spring to evaluate the effectiveness of the intervention. Means and standard deviations for weekly classroom rule violations in randomly selected classrooms were compared; significant differences were indicated for following directions, staying on task, and talking in turn as well as for the weekly totals across classrooms. Total weekly rule violations were significantly less at the end of the school year than at the beginning of the school year. Significant individual rule differences were also noted in following directions promptly, staying on task, and talking in turn. The "respecting the rights and property of others" and the "keeping hands, feet, and objects to self" rules were seldom violated in any of the classrooms.

Student Improvements. With the exception of reading, students in project classrooms demonstrated more positive on-task behavior and less negative off-task behavior than students in comparison classrooms. Total on-task behavior was significantly higher in project classrooms than in comparison classrooms. Similarly, off-task behavior was significantly lower in project classrooms than in comparison classrooms. Significant specific on-task differences were indicated in question-answering and hand-raising behaviors as well as in paying attention. Few students were observed disrupting their classes; students in comparison classrooms were not more disruptive than their peers in project classrooms. Significant off-task differences were indicated in time spent looking around, talking inappropriately, and engaging in appropriate tasks.

During the initial implementation year, nine teachers were judged to have "model" classrooms (i.e., Unified Discipline was in use to a high degree). An additional effectiveness comparison was completed using SOS summary observational data from these and other classrooms in comparisons of behaviors over time. At the beginning of the project, on-task behavior was significantly lower in model classrooms than in other rooms. Significant improvements in on-task behavior were evident in the spring observations conducted in the model classrooms, while fall and spring on-task observations were similar in comparison classrooms. At the beginning of the project, off-task behavior was significantly higher in model classrooms than in other rooms. Significant improvements in off-task behavior were evident in the spring observations conducted in the model classrooms, while fall and spring off-task observations were similar in comparison classrooms.

End-of-grade (EOG) assessments were completed as part of school district evaluation practices. EOG performance improved for all three grades assessed at Overton. Improvements in third and fifth grade resulted in overall performance at or above criterion set for "exemplary performance" within the school system. Scores in half the classes at Overton were at or above the same criterion levels.

The system for managing special education referrals was well established at Overton. First-level referrals were managed by Teacher Assistance Teams composed of special and general education personnel concerned with gathering data and managing problems within the context of the student's classroom. Unsuccessful management by Teacher Assistance Teams resulted in second-level referrals to School-Based Committees for more formal assessments and determination of eligibility or ineligibility for special services. Upward trends evident in referrals during the first 2 years were reversed during the final year of the project.

At the end of each school year, district personnel surveyed teachers at Overton Elementary School. The questionnaire requested opinions about the school's administration, instructional leadership, discipline, student behavior, morale, and general outcomes. Responses were provided on a Likert-type agreement scale. Data were typically used by central administration as a reflection of areas of satisfactory performance as well as those needing improvement within the local school district. Overall, opinions of faculty and staff at Overton improved and general levels of support were evident. Agreements increased by at least 10% in all areas. The changes were evident across multiple categories (e.g., school administration and discipline) and multiple items (e.g., principal gives teachers authority, principal is truly the instructional leader, not too much time is spent on discipline, and staff morale is good).

Lessons Learned and Challenges for the Future

School administrators and their faculty have many options for how to make classrooms safer, more disciplined environments. Universal interventions target the large group of students (80%-90%) who proceed through school exhibiting minor problem behaviors. Specialized group interventions address the needs of a small group (5%-15%) of students at risk for problem behavior. Specialized individual interventions are reserved for students with chronic and severe problem behaviors. According to Sugai, Sprague, Horner, and Walker (2000),

> Universal interventions focus on improving the overall level of appropriate behavior of most students but will have limited impact on the 10% to 15% of students with chronic patterns of problem behavior. Selected interventions that deliver more intense procedures, but are packaged for efficiency and implemented similarly across many students, are designed to address the needs of many of these students but will not prove effective for the 3% to 5% of students with the most intense and chronic patterns of problem behavior and for whom highly individualized, targeted interventions are needed. The challenge faced by schools is not to identify the one perfect strategy for improving school discipline. Rather, all schools need at least three different discipline efforts: universal, selected, and targeted. (p. 95)

| **FIGURE 5.2.** | Theory Reflected in Practice |

The discipline challenge for schools is meeting the needs of three groups of students: Those without serious behavior problems, those at risk for problem behavior, and those with intense and chronic problems (Sugai, Sprague, Horner, & Walker, 2000). Unified Discipline represents a primary prevention strategy for students (80%-90%) without serious behavior problems and a secondary prevention strategy for students (5%-15%) at risk for problem behavior. As illustrated in the following field notes, the system also provides a consistent framework within which to implement individualized interventions for students with intense and chronic problems (tertiary prevention).

Morgan (Observation and Intervention)

Discipline Principle:	Instruction can improve behavior.
Application:	Improving behavior begins with assessment driven to identify needed teaching and learning improvements.
Principle in Practice:	**Observational Running Record**
9:05 AM	Morgan entered the room from speech with a good sticker on his hand and without any disruption. He sat with you as you described the headband activity at that table and he began the required coloring and cutting. He was engaged quite well. He told a few other students, "No, go away" when they tried to help, but basically he worked consistently. He accepted the assistant's help stapling his headband and then went to the computer. He was very successful playing the counting game (up to 6). Then he sat on the carpet with another group of students listening to a female student point to pictures in a book and telling a story. He took part with the other students quite well. He followed your direction to get his book bag, and returned a sheet to you. You starred his sheet.
9:20 AM	You called the students to the rug for whole group, using a count-to-3 prompt. Morgan successfully sat by you in a timely manner. He took part very well, calling out responses to the words and charts correctly with the other children. He sang the money song with another child upon your direction and with the whole group quite nicely. Transitioning from the rug back to the tables, he got into a push-and-shove with Justin, but Justin was the instigator. Both students were required to put a ticket in their pockets for not keeping hands to self, and Justin had to sit out. (This is correct teaching; both the inappropriate instigator and responder must be consequented.)

(continued)

FIGURE 5.2. Continued

Morgan (Observation and Intervention)

Principle in Practice: | **Observational Running Record**

9:40 AM | Morgan walked over to your table and began to use the stencil to make shapes, color them, and then cut the shapes. He sings to himself quietly as he uses the glue stick to paste his cutouts. He takes the work to you and shows it to you. You tell him good job. He walks from the table and pretends to shoot rubber bands. He walks into the housekeeping area and is called out by the assistant to sit at a table. He sits on a roller chair and rolls between the tables. He walks over to our table and begins jumping up and down. You call him to you and direct him to put another ticket into his slot for failure to follow direction. He crosses his arms and refuses to go. He is angry at this point. You begin to count and he heads to his pocket, puts a ticket in, and slaps the board. He returns to the table frowning and arms crossed. Do your work or go to time out, you tell him. He talks back in baby talk; "I want another table." You talk to him and he says, "Get away from me." You leave him alone. He sits with lip out and pouting. He walks over to the closet doors, and bangs on them. He returns to the table and sits scowling. You are directing the students to clean up. Where is your paper, you ask, and he refuses to answer. You direct him to leave the class and he refuses with a loud "No." You ask if he wants to go by himself or have someone come to take him. "I hate this class," he says as he leaves.

Conclusions and Recommendations

Morgan has good strengths. He clearly has ability. He can attend for good periods of time when he wants to do so. He has clear leadership ability. If we can help him control his misbehavior, Morgan could grow into a stellar student and leader.

Morgan is rambunctious and headstrong. He wants to do what he wants to do, when he wants to do it. He does not take direction well. He needs to learn to follow direction, even when asked to do a non-preferred activity. He refuses direction too frequently.

When corrected for failure to follow direction, he gets angry and has tantrums. He takes correction badly. He needs to learn to take correction without losing his temper. When he loses his temper, it builds to a tantrum, and then it takes him too long to recover.

FIGURE 5.2.	Continued

What do we need to do?

We would recommend more structure during center time. In particular, we would recommend clear procedures for going from table to table and from table to individual activity.

Morgan must know that we mean business. I understand the team has discussed the importance of holding high expectations for the student's behavior and of being firm and consistent. He must learn that refusals and tantrums do not get him out of work, or make us leave him alone. He must learn we are very stubborn about him acting correctly and being successful. So, I concur with this new initiative to hold the student very accountable.

We need to teach the student that refusals and temper tantrums only cause trouble. If the student refuses a direction, say, "Morgan, refusing keeps us from learning. I know you can follow this direction. (Encouragement). I am going to repeat the direction." Then repeat it. If he complies, "Good job following direction. Good job controlling your temper." If he does not comply, consequent consistently using the plan.

Some individual instruction for the student on anger control makes sense. I talked to Mr. W and he too felt that a little role playing with the student on what to do when angry would help. We discussed Mr. W giving the student choices on what he wants to do, and then directing him to do what he did not choose! Then if the student gets angry, he can talk about better ways of dealing with anger than refusing or throwing tantrums.

These are not major problems to us. We do not think that Morgan has any kind of deep problem behavior. He just has picked up a few bad habits and disruptive behaviors. We need to help him get a handle on these before they become major issues. If we can teach him to forgo his tantrums and refusals, he can really become one of our stronger students with all his leadership.

Unified Discipline has demonstrated effectiveness with students with minor behavior problems and those at risk for problem behavior in school (see Figure 5.2).

Despite considerable evidence for feasibility, effectiveness, and sustainability, several caveats remain. First, although significant improvements are evident across grade levels and groups of students, problems of some students remain resistant to change, perhaps intractable without specialized individual intervention. As Kamps and Tankersley (1996) indicate, school variables (such as crowded classrooms, minimal resources, and negative teacher-student interaction styles) may contribute to behavioral and emotional disorders. What is not clear is whether intractable behavior is due to such school factors or to characteristics of particular students (e.g., low self-esteem, delinquent lifestyle, rejection by peers and teachers). Clearly, the problems of some students require direct, targeted intervention (see Chapter 2 for more information).

Second, the foundation of all effective schoolwide discipline efforts remains in systematic attention to universal preparation of administrators, faculty, and staff; continuous monitoring of progress grounded in establishing and maintaining treatment fidelity; and universal recognition and support. This attention ultimately is incorporated into the daily life of schools implementing Unified Discipline; however, administrators should not assume it will occur without internal or external support.

Third, teacher turnover creates conditions of constant flux within a system designed to eliminate inconsistencies in how problem behaviors are managed and more broadly in how discipline is delivered. Once in place, the culture of the school needs to sustain it. Again, this is a target of administrator concern.

REFERENCES

Kamps, D. M., & Tankersley, M. (1996). Prevention of behavioral and conduct disorders: Trends and research issues. *Behavioral Disorders, 21*(1), 41-48.

Sugai, G., Sprague, J. A., Horner, R. H., & Walker, H. M. (2000). Preventing school violence: The use of office discipline referrals to assess and monitor school-wide discipline interventions. *Journal of Emotional and Behavioral Disorders, 8,* 94-101.

Wong, H. K., & Wong, R. T. (1998). *The first days of school.* Mountain View, CA: Harry K. Wong Publications.

RESOURCES

Algozzine, B., Audette, B., Ellis, E., Marr, M. B., & White, R. (2000). Supporting teachers, principals, and students through unified discipline. *Teaching Exceptional Children, 33*(2), 42-47.

Brophy, J., & Good, T. L. (1986). Teacher behavior and student achievement. In M. C. Wittrock (Ed.), *Handbook of research on teaching* (pp. 328-375). New York: Macmillan.

Colvin, G., Kameenui, E. J., & Sugai, G. (1993). Reconceptualizing behavior management and school-wide discipline in general education. *Education and Treatment of Children, 16,* 361-381.

Gall, M. D., Borg, W. R., & Gall, J. P. (1996). *Educational research* (6th ed.). White Plains, NY: Longman.

Kauffman, J. M. (1996). Research to practice issues. *Behavioral Disorders, 21*(1), 55-60.

Kauffman, J. M. (1997). *Characteristics of emotional and behavioral disorders of children and youth.* Columbus, OH: Merrill.

Kauffman, J. M. (1999). How we prevent the prevention of emotional and behavioral disorders. *Exceptional Children, 65,* 448-468.

Kerr, M. M., & Nelson, C. M. (1989). *Strategies for managing behavior problems in the classroom.* Columbus, OH: Merrill.

Marr, M. B., Audette, R., White, R., Ellis, E., & Algozzine, B. (in press). School-wide discipline and classroom ecology. *Special Services in the Schools.*

Stallings, J. (1975). Implementation and child effects of teaching practices in Follow Through classrooms. *Monographs of the Society for Research in Child Development, 40*(7-8, Serial No. 163).

Stallings, J. (1980). Allocated academic learning time revisited, or beyond time on task. *Educational Researcher, 8*(11), 11-16.

Sugai, G., & Horner, R. H. (1999). Discipline and behavior support: Preferred processes and practices. *Effective School Practice, 17*(4), 10-22.

Taylor-Greene, S., Brown, D., Nelson, L., Longton, J., Gassman, T., Cohen, J., Swartz, J., Horner, R. H., Sugai, G., & Hall, S. (1997). School-wide behavioral support: Starting the year off right. *Journal of Behavioral Support, 7,* 99-112.

White, R. (1996). Unified discipline. In B. Algozzine (Ed.), *Problem behavior management: An educator's resource service.* Gaithersburg, MD: Aspen Publishers.

6 Building Effective Parent-Teacher Partnerships

Pam Kay
Martha Fitzgerald
Stephanie H. McConaughy

I was so afraid if Hank went on the way he was that he would feel that he couldn't do anything. I felt that way when I was younger and it is not a good feeling. I have noticed that Hank is a lot happier and is making a lot of new friends. Hank don't lose his temper at a drop of a hat anymore. I thank this program for that also. I feel that because he is more confident in himself, he don't have to try to prove he is good enough, by fighting. I also think that because of the parents and teacher involvement that this wonderful thing happened. If we were not at it at both ends . . . this wouldn't have worked. I feel so good about what Hank has accomplished and I know he does too.

—Hank's mother

Most of the research on parent-professional collaboration around children with emotional or behavioral issues focuses on older children and teenagers whose problems have already disabled them educationally. By then, the parent-teacher relationships may resemble an uneasy truce rather than a partnership. In the early elementary years, strategies to prevent emotional and behavioral problems from disabling children must include the development of true partnerships between parents and teachers. These partnerships do not develop naturally.

The child's behavioral issues in school can lead parents to believe that teachers are blaming them, and vice versa, making the working relationship even more difficult. Social class and cultural differences between parents and teachers often widen the gap. The burden of making improvements in the parent-teacher relationship usually falls on teachers, yet very little work is done in this area of teacher education, either preservice or inservice.

Many parents of children who receive services for emotional and/or behavioral disorders (E/BD) report that their children's problems were recognized by the first grade. Wehby, Dodge, and Valente (1993) found that children identified as having been placed at "high risk" for E/BD by kindergarten teachers had significantly more difficulties in interactions with teachers, were more disruptive in class, and spent more time in solitary play at the end of first grade than did a matched sample of "low-risk" children. However, few schools make a systematic practice of identifying children who are at risk for E/BD and providing preventive services.

This chapter will describe how the Achieving Behaving Caring (ABC) Project at the University of Vermont builds working partnerships between families and schools. With the help of Parent Liaisons, parent-teacher teams for students at risk of emotional or behavioral problems create and carry out action plans. A process called Parent-Teacher Action Research (PTAR) enables parents and teachers to learn to work together as equal partners while they address the child's needs for consistency between home and school. A Parent Liaison provides parent support and facilitates regular meetings between the parent(s) and classroom teachers. Teachers identify first-grade students who are in need of these partnerships by screening their entire class, using an inexpensive, standardized, and easy-to-administer measure. Each school also selects a social skills curriculum and teaches it to all students in (at least) the first and second grades.

The University of Vermont study found that students whose parents and teachers worked together for 2 years improved in cooperation, self-control, and other adaptive behaviors. Teachers found that these students had fewer rule-breaking (delinquent) behaviors than those in the control group. Parents who were part of these teams said that they felt more capable of getting their children the services that they needed through the school.

Tools to Help Identify Children
Who Need Extra Support

Classroom teachers, with their extensive knowledge of the social, behavioral, and academic characteristics of children in their classes, are in the best position to participate fully . . . at the initial screening level. However, their expertise and considerable knowledge are rarely used in this context. (Walker & Severson, 1992, p. 2)

Selecting the children who need additional support is a sensitive task, and one that many primary level teachers do not relish when they first hear about it. Many teachers believe that they do not have the training to make such selections accurately. Others may regard the screening process as premature in the early grades, given the variable rates at which children develop. They fear that selecting a child for special attention around emotions and behavior amounts to a prejudicial "labeling" process. Some may recall harsh criticisms of teacher judgment in the past. A few teachers may fear parents' reactions to the selection of their child, especially if the teachers have not found the courage to talk to those parents about their observations of the child in the classroom. Given the right tools, time, and administrative support for screening groups of children, however, classroom teachers can find children who may be at risk for E/BD. By identifying these students and learning what works for them, teachers can change many patterns of poor adjustment before they interfere seriously with learning.

Screening involves reviewing an entire class for specific behaviors that may lead to E/BD. In any group, there will be several children with *internalizing,* or withdrawn, behaviors as well as several with more obvious *externalizing,* or "acting-out," behaviors. The children whose problem behaviors are directed inward are often forgotten in the discussion about E/BD; their needs are usually not met unless they surface suddenly and explosively in later years. The ABC project involved children both with internalizing and with externalizing behaviors.

The screening instrument used in the ABC project is the Systematic Screening for Behavior Disorders (SSBD; Walker & Severson, 1992).[1] The SSBD has been rigorously tested, and is a valid and reliable tool that uses a *gating* process. Its first gate yields a group of children to consider in greater depth. The second gate identifies whether certain critical events have occurred for each child in the course of the school year. Criteria for the number of these events reduce the group of children further. The third gate looks at the adaptive and maladaptive behaviors of children in this small group, and narrows the selection again. All three of these steps can be taken by classroom teachers after a brief training session.[2]

The Parent Perspective

The first two authors of this chapter know firsthand the issues faced by the parents of students with E/BD. We each have a child, now grown, who had emotional or behavioral problems while in public school. Despite backgrounds in education and counseling, we each experienced great frustration in working with school and agency personnel. However, the mid-1980s saw the beginnings of change in the ways in which the education, mental health, and social work professions began to work together and with parents to improve services for children. Both of us served on the Parents' Committee of the Child and Adolescent Service System Program (CASSP; see Knitzer, 1993) in Vermont, and we began to work together. Our ABC project was designed in 1995 to counteract many of the traditional problems that arise between parents and teachers, families and schools.

Duchnowski, Berg, and Kutash (1995) outlined five perceptions that parents often have:

♦ *Parents feel blamed.* Training for professionals in education and social services has not yet removed the stigma caused by "a series of unsubstantiated, psychodynamic hypotheses . . . that linked parental behaviors and characteristics with subsequent emotional disorders in their children" (p. 185). This inclination to blame parents entered our culture and has not been eradicated.

♦ *Parents are confused.* When diagnostic tests and the results of other professional assessments are presented to parents, professionals often use unfamiliar terminology. (We believe that classroom teachers are often similarly confused by psychoeducational jargon, but seldom protest its use in meetings.)

♦ *Parents feel patronized and not involved.* When parents do speak up in a meeting, their comments are often not taken seriously. They sense that they are invited to meetings only to rubber-stamp plans that professionals have drafted during premeeting sessions.

♦ *Parents feel their perceptions of their child are discounted.* Children's behavior may be quite different at home than in school. However, when parents point out these differences or speak of their child's strengths, their comments are often dismissed as unimportant, untrue, or simply uneducated.

♦ *Parents feel they are treated without cultural sensitivity.* Parents of color are well aware of the problem of disproportionate representation of their children in special education classes. They may come to the school doubting that either they or their child will receive fair treatment. Even in areas where there are few racial differences visible between families and school personnel, there are ethnic, cultural, and often class differences.

A prevention program that is based on effective parent-teacher partnerships must address the factors that cause these parent perceptions, while remembering that the classroom teachers often feel equally powerless and cannot be blamed for creating these difficult feelings.

The Classroom Teacher Perspective

As Irwin (1996) points out,

> Parents and students see teachers as dominant. Teachers do not feel dominant; they feel dominated by administrators, from whom they are thereby alienated as well. Administrators do not feel dominant either; they have to report to the school boards and the parents. Each of these groups fears the other. (p. 30)

Children with emotional or behavioral problems are among the most challenging students to teach, whether they have internalizing or externalizing behaviors. Teachers have heightened awareness of their responsibility for the safety of their students due to the tragic murders that have taken place in schools over the past few years. At the same time, many activist parent groups have increased their demands to participate in decisions about curriculum and classroom management. Few teacher preparation programs provide training in productive ways to work with parents. Is it any wonder that teachers are reluctant to reach out to the parents of their most challenging students?

Those who have, however, find that their perspective on families changes radically once they find ways to connect. In *Engaging Families* (Shockley, Michalove, & Allen, 1995), two classroom teachers describe their successful approach to parent involvement in literacy. "Respect and belief in family knowledge and caring are our core values," they said; "we based partnership decisions and actions on these values" (p. 95). Kottler (1997) urges teachers to think like anthropologists in order to understand how their own culture shapes their teaching. Others, such as Moll and Diaz (1993), Delgado-Gaitan (1990), and Harry (1994), challenge educators to involve families in all aspects of schooling.

After participating in the ABC project, many teachers commented that they wished they could do PTAR with the parents of *all* children, but that they just do not have the time. Administrators, too, are challenged by the puzzle of bringing parents and teachers together. We believe that there are elements in the ABC project that will help to meet the need.

QUALIFICATIONS FOR A PARENT LIAISON

1. Experience in raising a challenging child

2. Interest in promoting good communication and collaboration among families, schools, and community resources

3. Interest in helping parents become involved with their children's education, and ability to let go when others are ready to be independent

4. Skills and appropriate assertiveness in helping families develop their natural systems of support

5. Good communication skills, especially the skill of listening

6. An open mind and ability to suspend judgment about various forms of family structure and patterns of child rearing

7. Openness to the teacher's perspective as well as the family's perspective

8. Self-discipline, comfort with a flexible schedule, and ability to meet deadlines

9. Comfort in resolving conflicts

10. Persistence in the face of temporary resistance, and commitment to a "zero reject" policy

11. Access to transportation

The Parent Liaison Position

The ABC project established positions for *Parent Liaisons*. Parent Liaisons are paraprofessionals, preferably from the local community, who play a medial role between parents and teachers. The Parent Liaison is not an advocate, but a supportive peer, someone who is able to go easily between the worlds of the family and the education establishment. She or he is an empowering friend to other parents, modeling behavior and strategies that parents can use to become effective and collaborative advocates for their child. Often liaisons have worked through some similar issues with their own children. Ideally, the Parent Liaison does not work for the school system, although the school may contract with another community agency to

RESPONSIBILITIES OF AN
ABC PROJECT PARENT LIAISON

1. To provide information about the program to families of children who have been identified so that parents can make a fully informed decision about their participation

2. To maintain confidentiality and to understand its limits as established by law

3. To provide specific support and encouragement to parents to help them carry out their roles as full members of the child's team

4. To forge links between families and their natural systems of support in the community

5. To help organize and facilitate meetings of the Parent-Teacher Action Research (PTAR) teams, arranging the date, time, and place so that the parents, teachers, and other community resource people who are involved can meet

6. To help parents complete any surveys required by the program

7. To maintain notes and contact logs as required by the program

8. To meet regularly with supervisors and other parent liaisons

9. To participate in evaluations of the program

provide this service. When the Parent Liaisons stand outside of the school system, they can be regarded more easily as "one of us" by the parents.

Parent Liaisons are chosen for their ability to listen and talk easily with both parents and teachers. They bridge the cultures of home and school, explaining each to the other in clear, comprehensible terms. They facilitate face-to-face meetings, support both parents and teachers in taking action, and refer families to appropriate community services. A good Parent Liaison is skilled in developing the natural systems of support for families in the community. The intent of all liaisons is to remove themselves from the picture once parents feel empowered to maintain communications on their own.

The parents of students who have been identified through screening are contacted by a Parent Liaison, who explains Parent-Teacher Action Research and answers questions. Once the parents agree to participate, the Parent Liaison stays with that family throughout the process. Parent Liaisons

---

WAYS TO FIND GOOD CANDIDATES
FOR THE PARENT LIAISON POSITION

♦ Ask teachers, administrators, and early childhood educators for the names of people who have these qualifications.

♦ Call the local chapter of Parent-to-Parent, the Federation of Families for Children's Mental Health, and other advocacy groups. To locate these organizations, contact The National Information Center for Children and Youth With Disabilities at www.nichcy.org/index.html, or 1-800-695-0285.

♦ Ask at the local Parent-Child Center or Head Start office; hang a notice on their bulletin boards.

♦ Ask each of these contact people who else to call.

---

help ensure parity between parents and teachers through such means as holding meetings on neutral ground (neither home or school), having parents speak first in meetings, and helping parents and teachers address each other in a similar fashion (e.g., both using either formal or first names alike). They provide and facilitate a structured agenda that keeps the focus on mutual goals for the child. They gently persist in holding parents and teachers accountable for their parts of the action plans, and give lots of praise.

When the child makes a transition from grade to grade, moves, or changes schools for other reasons, Parent Liaisons continue to work with the family. If the new school is within a reasonable distance, they are able to help personnel in that school select the best classroom for the child. They also help the parent establish a PTAR team with the new teacher, if that teacher is willing. If the move spans too great a distance for follow-up, the Parent Liaison stays in touch with the parent(s) by telephone for a few weeks during the transition.

Although we recommend that the Parent Liaisons be employed by a Parent-Child Center or other agency that stands outside of the school system, the funding and impetus for this collaboration usually needs to come from the school. Title I funds, monies to prevent drug and alcohol abuse, and United Way support should all be considered. Such issues as supervision, payment of mileage and other expenses, and agreements on confidentiality all need to be addressed in an agreement between the school system and the cooperating agency.[3]

The Parent-Teacher Action
Research Process

Over the past 50 years, *action research* has been used in education to improve both individual teacher practices and faculty collegiality. Action research involves a continuous cycle of problem definition, observation and data collection, theory building, and action planning. Teachers use action research to make changes in their individual professional practices. When action research is applied to school improvement, teachers implement change collaboratively, building trust, adopting and adapting techniques from one another, learning to manage group process and to create ties with colleagues.

In the past decade, several school improvement initiatives have used collaborative action research to incorporate parents into the group of reformers at each school (Davies, Palanki, & Burch, 1993). After using Parent-Teacher Action Research to study the impact of school reform on collaboration between home and school, the authors of this chapter outlined ways for special educators to use PTAR in their practices (Kay & Fitzgerald, 1997). A similar approach was used by Cheney (1998) to address emotional and behavioral issues in middle school students. More recently, our research team has focused on the power of PTAR as a preventive intervention, increasing communication and consistency between home and school for individual children who are at risk of developing E/BD (McConaughy, Kay, & Fitzgerald, 1998, 1999, 2000).

The definition of action research that we use in the ABC project is *the systematic study of a practical issue by those most directly affected by it, in order to take corrective action.* As in any research, systematic study involves several steps: definition of a research question or the puzzle to be solved; collection of data according to a plan; analysis of those data; theory building; and theory testing. In action research, that cycle is often repeated numerous times as a means of continuous improvement. The child is the focus of the Parent-Teacher Action Research (PTAR) team's work. The parent and the classroom teacher are considered the heart of the team; each has both expertise and an essential perspective on the child. Both are considered co-practitioners in PTAR. Parents have critical knowledge or expertise about their children, even though they may not recognize their own wisdom. Teachers are recognized as experts in curriculum, instruction, and classroom management. Through their schools and professional contacts, they have other experts with whom to consult about specific behavioral concerns. However, those others, such as guidance counselors, special educators, school psychologists, or social workers, may not attend the PTAR meeting unless both parents and teachers have agreed to invite them.

GROUND RULES FOR PTAR MEETINGS

- ◆ Parents talk first, then teachers.

- ◆ Everyone is free to "pass" or to stop at any time.

- ◆ All ideas are to be expressed as positively as possible.

- ◆ Everything will be written down in your own words.

Meeting Time and Place. PTAR teams meet at first in a safe, neutral place, neither home nor school. This helps to reduce any perceptions of either parent or teacher having power over the other. Some parents are extremely uncomfortable going into school, especially when school was not a positive experience for them. Some teachers feel unsafe going into homes, even when accompanied by the Parent Liaison. There are places where the Parent Liaisons should not go alone; even the initial meetings with parents may take place at a local fast-food restaurant.

The ABC project schools are largely in rural areas, presenting a challenge to Parent Liaisons to locate meeting places. We meet in town libraries, branch bank conference rooms, the firehouse, and even in the corners of coffee shops when they are not busy. Sometimes there is no place except the school; then the Parent Liaisons arrange to use any private space that is not the teacher's classroom. Rarely, meetings take place at the parents' home. Over the 2 years in which the PTAR meetings take place, the Parent Liaison's goal is to have the meetings move to the classroom. When the support of the project has ended, parents need to feel confident contacting teachers at school and talking to them as equals in the classroom.

Initially the meetings take place at a time that is convenient for the parents; principals help teachers make accommodation in their scheduling. Over time, the Parent Liaison helps the teacher and parent find creative ways to adjust their schedules to one another.

MAPS and Goals. Before beginning the first meeting, the Parent Liaison establishes *ground rules* to ensure equal participation by both parent and teacher and to maintain a positive focus.

The Parent Liaison guides the parent and teacher through the MAPS (Making Action Plans; Forest & Lusthaus, 1989) process to create a strengths-based description of the child. The MAPS questions culminate in

QUESTIONS USED IN THE ABC MAPS PROCESS

Who is this child?

- ◆ What does she or he do well?

- ◆ What does he or she like? How does she or he let us know?

- ◆ What does he or she dislike? How does she or he let us know?

- ◆ Who are his or her friends or regular playmates?

What is this child's story?

- ◆ Where was he or she born?

- ◆ What places has he or she lived in?

- ◆ What is special to him or her in life? (People, places, things)

- ◆ What health issues has he or she faced?

What are your dreams for this child?

- ◆ What do you hope for in his or her life?

- ◆ What would you like to see him or her learn soon?

What are your concerns?

- ◆ What should we watch out for?

- ◆ What are the clues that something is wrong?

- ◆ What do you NOT want to see happen in his or her life?

the hopes and dreams, then fears and worries, that both parents and teacher have for the child. This is often a powerful moment in the life of the PTAR team. When the Parent Liaison has been able to create a safe space in which parent and teacher can establish trust, one or both may feel free to share important information. One parent revealed that the child's father was dying; another disclosed her own fatal disease. Several parents expressed fears that their children would be drawn into drugs or alcohol, as their older brothers had been. Others worried about sexual abuse. Sadly, many had no dreams for their children or themselves.

Teachers are pleased by the insights that these questions give them into the child's home life. Many are sobered by the parents' lack of dreams or hope. Some teachers are honest about their fears for the children, and others veer away from the question.

With all of this information spread out on chart paper, the Parent Liaison helps the team to define their mutual goals. Very few of the goals specify academic achievements (e.g., "Fran[4] will come up to her own age group in reading and math"), but all goals impact the children's lives in school as well as at home ("Hank will make transitions more quickly, quietly, and happily"; "Ellie will make one good friend this year"). Occasionally the parents and teacher are unable to agree on mutual goals; the Parent Liaison asks them to work toward each other's goals and continue to talk about areas where they might agree.

For each goal, the facilitator asks the team to name *clues,* or observable indicators that will tell them that the child has accomplished the goal. For example, Monty's father and his first-grade teacher set the goal that "Monty will be able to open up and be more sociable." If they reached that goal, Dad said, Monty would no longer hide behind him in the grocery store when a neighbor spoke to him. The teacher said that she would notice Monty talking with other children when he came into the classroom in the morning.

The Action Research Cycle. Once the parent and teacher have agreed on one or more goals for the year, they begin the Action Research Cycle pictured in Figure 6.1. The Parent Liaison moves the PTAR team through the cycle, spiraling back to previous sectors as necessary. Although it is important to move toward an action plan, the Parent Liaison needs to encourage parents and teachers to take the time to reflect on the meaning of the data. Often the very act of focusing positive attention on the child begins to solve the problem.

Data Collection. The data in action research come from the parents' and teachers' observations of the child. PTAR team members use the *ABC* approach, which in this case stands for Antecedent, Behavior, and Consequences. The question to answer in A is "What was happening before the behavior took place?" In answering B ("What was the behavior?"), parents and teachers try to *describe* the behavior, not label it or characterize it. For example, they note that "John stamped his feet and yelled," rather than "John had one of his temper tantrums." Finally, in noting C, they answer the question, "Then what happened?" Here they may speak about their own actions, those of others in charge, or those of the child's peers.

Parents and teachers choose their own methods for collecting data. Some teachers expand their anecdotal record systems to include a focus on the specific goals for that child. Other teams use a home/school journal, in

FIGURE 6.1. Parent-Teacher Action Research Cycle

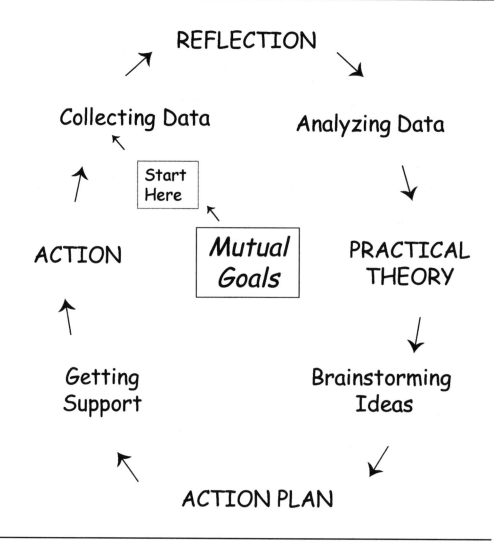

which both teacher and parents write on a regular basis. One team created a "Self-Esteem Log" in which they noted each time the child exhibited positive self-esteem, at home as well as at school.

When parents have difficulty with observations, the team may create a list of questions that the parent will ask the child 2 or 3 days a week after school. Depending on the goal, these questions might be, "Who ate lunch with you today?" "What did your teacher tell you that you did well?" or "What work was easiest for you?" When literacy is an issue, the Parent

Liaison may help parents collect data by calling them once a week and writing down their comments on what they have noticed about the child's progress.

One parent for whom reading and writing was difficult demonstrated that she understood the significance of the data collection process. She and the teacher had drafted a short list of questions for her to ask her son about his day in school, and created worksheets on which she could write the answers. "When I sit down to ask Kim the questions," she commented, "his older brother wants me to ask him, too. I do, but I don't have a place to write down his answers. Writing them down makes them more important."

Data Analysis: Time for Reflection. When the parent and teacher come together as a PTAR team, they share their data with one another. In the conversation, each has an opportunity to reflect on what she has observed. Part of this reflection process involves asking, "How does what I do as a parent or a teacher contribute to this behavior?" This is a very important step, and requires a high level of trust between parents and teachers. Facilitators need to be comfortable with long silences during this part of the meeting, and careful not to jump in with their own thoughts and observations. It may take several meetings before parent or teacher will talk aloud about changing their practices. The decision to make a change is more powerful and likely to happen when it arises from self-reflection.

Developing Practical Theory. When both the parent and the teacher have shared their data aloud, the Parent Liaison asks, "Why do you think the child behaves this way?" Those who are familiar with Functional Analysis will recognize this question as, "What function does this behavior perform for the child?" The practical theory is the best guess that the parent-teacher team can make at that point in time. Again, the Parent Liaison needs to be careful not to get to this step too soon. Often more data are needed, or the data need to come from other observations. For example, asking the child a series of questions on a regular basis can open up a good dialogue about the issues that are troubling him or her, and produce new insights into the behavior. Students in the second grade occasionally attend PTAR meetings, and their self-knowledge amazes their parents and teachers.

This is the point in the cycle at which outside expertise is most often needed. Research-based publications, Web sites, and materials provided by the National Association of School Psychologists have been very helpful.[5] When counselors, special educators, or other family members are invited to come to the PTAR meeting, the Parent Liaison keeps the focus on the child, and the decisions in the hands of the parent and teacher.

RULES FOR BRAINSTORMING

♦ All ideas are good ideas when they are first expressed.

♦ The facilitator will write down each idea in exactly the words used.

♦ "Piggybacking" on someone else's idea is allowed . . . even encouraged!

♦ No one may "put down" anyone else's idea.

♦ Set a short time limit and stick to it.

Brainstorming Ideas for Action. Once the team has agreed on its practical theory, they need to think through its implications for action. Again, the Parent Liaison encourages them to take their time, not settling on the first idea expressed.

The Action Plan. The action plans are as simple as possible. The Parent Liaison writes down what the action will be, who will be responsible, and when it will occur. Part of the plan is an agreement on the kind of data that both parent and teacher will continue to collect as the plan is implemented.

Getting Support and/or Permission. Some action plans are easier to follow than others. The Parent Liaison notices the demands that the plan places on the parents. Sometimes they need extra support from the Parent Liaison in order to carry out their responsibilities. Sometimes it is only a reminder, or a friendly phone call that asks, "How are you doing with the new plan?" that is needed.

Occasionally a plan will require the permission of someone who is not on the team, such as the principal. Part of the plan includes getting that permission. Would it be better for the teacher to get it, the parent, or both together, which can be very persuasive to an administrator. The Parent Liaison may also play a role here; each situation is different.

Taking Action and Returning to Data Collection. As the plan is carried out, both parent and teacher continue collecting data on the child. They use this information to assess the child's progress, and to determine whether their plan is working. They give the plan enough time for a fair trial, but are ready to make a change if their new data indicate a strong negative reaction from the child.

PTAR Team Meetings. Teams meet for approximately one hour on an average of once a month during the school year; one or two have held meetings over the summer as well. The goals and the action research cycle drive the agenda for each meeting. The facilitators begin each meeting with a review of the previous meeting's notes. Following the ground rules, they ask parents to speak first, then teachers, sharing their data with one another.

Teachers are often the first to notice how their observations shape their view of the child's behavior. Barbara went out on the playground to observe Chip on a day when she did not have playground duty. She was somewhat abashed as she reported, "I discovered that other boys are setting him up to get into trouble!" As another teacher said, "When you tune in to a child like this, you realize what you are *not* seeing about children in your class." A parent noted that her daughter was her third child to go through their local school, and that she had not been paying as much attention to her daughter's needs as she had to her older children, when the process was relatively new for her. Collecting data helped her to see her daughter as an individual with specific needs around school.

After carrying out their plans, parents and teachers begin the action research cycle again, observing the child, noting the context and consequences of his or her behaviors, and collecting data to bring to their next meeting. As one teacher noted, "The most important reason for the success experienced in this program was the structure of the meetings: the review of prior meetings, the sharing of current observations, and the identification of next steps." Her Parent Liaison was equally pleased at the success of her teams. "It is amazing that something so simple results in such achievement!"

Results of the Achieving Behaving Caring Project

The effectiveness of the ABC project was demonstrated by decreases in problem behavior and increases in adaptive behavior during the 2-year period. Specifically, we compared behavioral ratings from the fall of Grade 1 (start of intervention) and the spring of Grade 2 (end of intervention). Behavioral ratings were obtained from three perspectives: teachers, parents, and independent observers. For more information on the specific measures used, please see Chapter 10.

On the Teacher Report Form (TRF; Achenbach, 1991b), teachers reported significant reductions in both internalizing behavior and rule-breaking (delinquent) behavior over time for the group of students whose parents and teachers participated in PTAR, compared with a matching group of students who received only the social skills lessons in their classrooms. Teachers also reported a significant overall reduction in withdrawn behavior and significant gains in competent behaviors over the 2-year period across both groups. Using the Social Skills Rating System—Teacher Version (SSRS; Gresham & Elliott, 1990), teachers reported increases in total social skills, cooperation, assertiveness, and self-control across both groups.

The parents who participated in PTAR for their children reported significant reductions in total problems and rule-breaking (delinquent) behavior, using the Child Behavior Checklist (CBCL; Achenbach, 1991a), and externalizing behaviors on the SSRS-P, compared with parents of social skills-only children. Across both groups, parents also reported significant overall reductions in CBCL internalizing, externalizing, withdrawn, thought problems and aggressive behavior, and SSRS-P total problems and hyperactive behavior over the 2-year period.

In addition, parents of the PTAR group children observed significant increases in their competent behavior over time compared with parents of social skills-only children. PTAR group parents observed greater gains in their children for cooperation and self-control on the SSRS-P, and total competence on the CBCL. Finally, the PTAR families reported a greater sense of empowerment in obtaining school-based services for their children over the 2-year period compared with control families; the measure used here was an adaptation of the Family Empowerment Scale (FES; Koren, DeChillo, & Friesen, 1992), focusing on school-based services.

Because both parents and teachers were involved in the PTAR intervention, we employed independent observers who did not know the children and were kept blind to their group assignment. These observers provided further evidence of the effectiveness of the PTAR intervention. Observers rated PTAR group children significantly lower on internalizing, nervous/obsessive, and depressed behavior over time, and rated the social skills-only children higher on all of these scales over time. In anecdotal evidence, parents and teachers have been consistent in their praise for the ABC project. Indeed, only 3 out of 43 PTAR teams failed to complete the initial 2-year cycle. We are encouraged to continue to build these partnerships by comments like the following:

Sonya, a teacher, wrote,

> For the past two years, I feel extremely fortunate to have had the opportunity to "go the extra mile" for two students in my classroom. This was done by meeting monthly as part of a team whose sole mission was that of creating a network of support for these children. The implications of meeting with a child's parent each month are astounding. Every meeting was a celebration of growth which was observed together—and a time to brainstorm objectives and plans to ensure

future growth. This positive communication which resulted has been powerful. It has also allowed for consistency in language and expectations at school and at home. One of the most important reasons for the success experienced in this program is the structure of the meetings: the review of prior meetings, the sharing of current observations and the identifications of next steps. Although at times I felt that this process was repetitious and tedious, I always walked away feeling that anything less would not have given us a clear picture.

A mother gave this very positive evaluation of the ABC project:

> The PTAR process worked well for me because we were able to set reasonable goals and to accomplish them. I recommend this to any family who is ever given the opportunity. This is one honest chance at really being involved in a healthy growth for your child in and out of school. I hope to see more programs available to the schools and also for Amanda [the Parent Liaison] to be someone I may get a chance to work with again. Amanda and the PTAR process were wonderful and I thank you wholeheartedly for them.

Work to Be Done

As reviewers for research journals have pointed out, the ABC project needs to be tested with a control group that does not receive social skills training in the general education classroom. We believe that all schools should teach a social skills curriculum as part of their universal prevention for E/BD, as Chapter 4 suggests. However, at this time, we cannot attribute the success of the ABC project to any one of its components in isolation: social skills training, the Parent Liaison, and the Parent-Teacher Action Research process.

Also, the ABC project and the PTAR process have yet to be tested in urban and multiethnic areas. The rural New England towns where it was developed have multicultural populations, but few racially or ethnically mixed areas. Nonetheless, the principles of selecting a Parent Liaison from the local community and enabling parents and teachers to work together as equals, with a focus on the child, would seem to be equally viable in multiethnic schools. As Winters writes in the conclusion of her study, *African American Mothers and Urban Schools,* "The participation of parents leaves a positive imprint, an indelible image of empowerment upon the children's impressionable minds, the school, and all of society" (1993, p. 111).

NOTES

1. Walker and Severson, the developers of the SSBD, have produced a similar screening measure for use with young children, the Early Screening Project (ESP). For more information on obtaining either of these measures, see www.sopriswest.com.

2. The SSBD provides yet another screen, which involves direct observation by a trained professional other than the classroom teacher. The ABC project does not utilize this level of screening since we want to find all of the students who are in need of secondary prevention. Students who need tertiary interventions are referred immediately to student assistance teams, if the teacher has not done so already.

3. For more information on school-agency agreements, see literature on full-service schools, school-linked services, and Systems of Care. Two Web sites of interest are www.gse.harvard.edu/~ciss/ and http://smhp.psych.ucla.edu.

4. All names used for parents, teachers, children, and schools are pseudonyms.

5. For information available through the National Association of School Psychologists, see the NASP Web site at www.naspweb.org.

REFERENCES

Achenbach, T. M. (1991a). *Manual for the Child Behavior Checklist/4-18 and 1991 Profile.* Burlington: University of Vermont, Department of Psychiatry.

Achenbach, T. M. (1991b). *Manual for the Teacher's Report Form and 1991 Profile.* Burlington: University of Vermont, Department of Psychiatry.

Cheney, D. (1998). Using action research as a collaborative process to enhance educators' and families' knowledge and skills for youth with emotional and behavioral disorders. *Preventing School Failure, 42*(2), 88-93.

Davies, D., Palanki, A., & Burch, P. (1993). *Getting started: Action research in family-school-community partnerships.* Baltimore: Johns Hopkins University, Center on Families, Communities, Schools, and Children's Learning.

Delgado-Gaitan, C. (1990). *Literacy for empowerment.* Philadelphia: Falmer.

Duchnowski, A. J., Berg, K., & Kutash, K. (1995). Parent participation in and perception of placement decisions. In J. M. Kauffman, J. W. Lloyd, D. P. Hallahan, & T. A. Astuto (Eds.), *Issues in educational placement: Students with emotional and behavioral disorders.* Hillsdale, NJ: Lawrence Erlbaum.

Forest, M., & Lusthaus, E. (1989). Promoting educational equality for all students: Circles and MAPs. In S. Stainback, W. Stainback, & M. Forest (Eds.), *Educating all students in the mainstream of regular education* (pp. 43-57). Baltimore: Brookes Publishing.

Gresham, F. M., & Elliott, S. N. (1990). *Social Skills Rating System manual.* Circle Pines, MN: American Guidance Service.

Harry, B. (1994). Behavioral disorders in the context of families. In R. L. Peterson & S. Ishii-Jordan (Eds.), *Multicultural issues in the education of students with behavioral disorders.* Cambridge, MA: Brookline Books.

Irwin, J. W. (1996). *Empowering ourselves and transforming schools: Educators making a difference.* Albany: SUNY Press.

Kay, P. J., & Fitzgerald, M. (1997). Parents + teachers + action research = real improvement. *Teaching Exceptional Children, 30,* 8-11.

Knitzer, J. (1993). Children's mental health policy: Challenging the future. *Journal of Emotional and Behavioral Disorders, 1,* 8-16.

Koren, P. E., DeChillo, N., & Friesen, B. J. (1992). Measuring empowerment in families whose children have emotional disabilities: A brief questionnaire. *Rehabilitation Psychology, 37,* 305-321.

Kottler, J. A. (1997). *What's really said in the teachers' lounge: Provocative ideas about cultures and classrooms.* Thousand Oaks, CA: Corwin Press.

McConaughy, S. H., Kay, P. J., & Fitzgerald, M. (1998). Preventing SED through parent-teacher action research and social skills instruction: First year outcomes. *Journal of Emotional and Behavioral Disorders, 6,* 81-93.

McConaughy, S., Kay, P. J., & Fitzgerald, M. F. (1999). The Achieving Behaving Caring Project for preventing ED: Two-year outcomes. *Journal of Emotional and Behavioral Disorders, 7,* 224-239.

McConaughy, S., Kay, P. J., & Fitzgerald, M. F. (2000). How long is long enough? Outcomes for a school-based prevention program. *Exceptional Children, 67*(1), 21-34.

Moll, L. C., & Diaz, S. (1993). Change as the goal of educational research. In E. Jacob & C. Jordan (Eds.), *Minority education: Anthropological perspectives.* Norwood, NJ: Ablex.

Shockley, B., Michalove, B., & Allen, J. (1995). *Engaging families: Connecting home and school literacy communities.* Portsmouth, NH: Heinemann.

Walker, H., & Severson, H. (1992). Users guide and administration manual. *Systematic Screening for Behavior Disorders (SSBD).* Longmont, CO: Sopris West.

Wehby, J. H., Dodge, K., & Valente, E. (1993). School behavior of first grade children identified as at-risk for development of conduct problems. *Behavioral Disorders, 19,* 67-78.

Winters, W. G. (1993). *African American mothers and urban schools: The power of participation.* New York: Lexington Books.

RESOURCES

Achenbach, T. M. (1986). *Direct Observation Form of the Child Behavior Checklist* (Rev. ed.). Burlington: University of Vermont, Department of Psychiatry.

Burch, P. (1993, October). *Action research in family-school-community partnerships: The experience of one rural elementary school.* Paper presented at the 85th annual meeting of the National Rural Education Association, Burlington, VT.

Calhoun, E. (1993). Action research: Three approaches. *Educational Leadership, 51,* 62-65.

Calhoun, E. (1994). *How to use action research in the self-renewing school.* Alexandria, VA: Association for Supervision and Curriculum Development.

Cheney, D., & Osher, T. (1997). Collaborate with families. *Journal of Emotional and Behavioral Disorders, 5*(1), 36-44.

Cochran-Smith, M., & Lytle, S. L. (1993). *Inside/outside: Teacher research and knowledge.* New York: Teachers College Press.

Corey, S. M. (1953). *Action research to improve school practices.* New York: Teachers College Press.

Forest, M., & Pearpoint, J. C. D. (1992). Putting all kids on the MAP. *Educational Leadership, 50,* 26-31.

Friedman, R. M., Silver, S. E., Duchnowski, A. J., Kutash, K., Eisen, M., Brandenburg, N. A., & Prange, M. (1988). *Characteristics of children with serious emotional disturbances identified by public systems as requiring services.* Tampa: University of South Florida, Florida Mental Health Institute.

Glickman, C. D. (1990). *Supervision of instruction: A developmental approach.* Boston: Allyn & Bacon.

Harvard Graduate School of Education. (1999). *Full service schools: New practices and policies for children, youth and families.* Cambridge, MA: Collaborative for Integrated School Services.

Knitzer, J., Steinberg, Z., & Fleish, B. (1990). *At the school house door.* New York: Bank Street College of Education.

Kurcinka, M. S. (1992). *Raising your spirited child: A guide for parents whose child is **more**.* New York: HarperCollins.

Lareau, A. (1989). *Home advantage.* Philadelphia: Falmer.

Noffke, S. (1997). Professional, personal, and political dimensions of action research. In M. Apple (Ed.), *Review of Research in Education, 22,* 305-343.

O'Brien, J., & Forest, M. (with Snow, J., & Hasbury, D.) (1989). *Action for inclusion.* Toronto: Frontier College Press.

Oja, S. N., & Smulyan, L. (1989). *Collaborative action research: A developmental approach.* Boston: Allyn & Bacon.

Sagor, R. (1991). What project LEARN reveals about collaborative action research. *Educational Leadership, 48*(6), 6-10.

Shartrand, A. M., Weiss, H. B., Kreider, H. M., & Lopez, M. E. (1997). *New skills for new schools: Preparing teachers in family involvement.* Cambridge, MA: Harvard Graduate School of Education, Harvard Family Research Project.

U.S. Department of Education. (1998). *Twentieth annual report to Congress on the implementation of the Individuals With Disabilities Education Act.* Washington, DC: Author.

Ysseldyke, J. E., & Christenson, S. L. (1993-1994). *TIES II: The Instructional Environment System—II. A system to identify a student's instructional needs.* Longmont, CO: Sopris West.

7 Building Linkages to Learning Through Community Partnerships

Peter E. Leone
Robert J. Evert
Karen A. Friedman

The teachers complained that my son did not pay attention to schoolwork and that he hit other children. I lived in fear they would say that he could not attend school anymore. I was seeing the Linkages to Learning counselor about other problems in my family. He helped to enroll my son in activities after school where he had fun with other children. Before this, because I have to work most of the time, he had to stay alone with a baby-sitter, and he did not have a chance to play. My child still has problems in school, but his behavior and grades are improving. I tell him, "I have big dreams for you and me. I must work and attend GED class, because these are the first steps for a better future."
—Carla, from Nicaragua

Low-income families and immigrant families face monumental challenges in raising and supporting their children in school. When non-native English-speaking families and other groups lack material and social supports, their ability to nurture their children as students is compromised. Those families, particularly the ones who have recently immigrated, often face an additional difficulty—"they do not speak the language of the school" (Harry, 1992, p. xiii). The process of relocating to a new country can have both material and psychological costs. Helping families and their children can prevent the development of emotional or behavioral problems in school and promote academic achievement. Often, fragmented service systems fail to meet the most basic needs of disadvantaged families (Schorr, 1989).

In response to the needs of immigrant and low-income families and their school-age children, Montgomery County, Maryland, developed an interagency program, Linkages to Learning (LTL), in the early 1990s. The program currently serves youth and families in seven elementary and two middle schools in the county. Through a flexible service delivery system, the program provides social services (including financial and food assistance), counseling, physical and mental health care, translation, and educational support. However, since the inception of Linkages to Learning in 1993, there has been very limited information on the efficacy of the program (Leone, Lane, Arlen, & Peter, 1996). This chapter focuses on the connections between an elementary school and its community and how the Linkages to Learning program assisted families in supporting their children. Besides describing the operation of the program, we discuss the core elements and practices that have shaped Linkages to Learning at one school site. The chapter concludes with a brief discussion and an evaluation of child and parent outcomes and an assessment of parent satisfaction.

Linkages to Learning at Broad Acres

In 1995, with support from the U.S. Department of Education, researchers at the University of Maryland collaborated with the Montgomery County Public Schools, the Montgomery County Department of Health and Human Services, and several private agencies to develop a Linkages program at Broad Acres Elementary School. The grant from the Department of Education funded direct services to low-income students and their families to prevent the development of emotional and behavioral disorders, and supported an evaluation of the program (see Fox et al., 1999).

Broad Acres Elementary School serves children in kindergarten through fifth grade. The school has on-site both Head Start and day care programs. There are two self-contained special education classrooms in the school. At the time the Linkages to Learning program began, the total student population at Broad Acres was 505 students. About 95% of the students at Broad Acres live within walking distance of the school.

Broad Acres has one of the highest mobility rates within the local public school system. Approximately 30% to 40% of students enter or leave the school in a given academic year. Broad Acres also has a culturally diverse student body, representing more than 40 nations and 10 languages. Roughly 75% of parents in the Broad Acres community are recent immigrants: The student body is 55% Hispanic, 27% African American, 18%

When Marie first learned about Linkages, she was a single mother with three school-aged children. Her daughter was in the hospital, she had no personal transportation, and one of her sons, according to her, "was tearing up the school." Marie's son received individual counseling and she attended parent support groups for 2 years.

Thao and Tran immigrated from Vietnam with their two sons. The parents had difficulty learning English, and felt trapped in low-income jobs. When the oldest son had academic and behavioral difficulties, a Vietnamese instructional assistant referred the family to Linkages. Through a translator, the mother said later, "Without the counselor, English classes, translation of letters and forms, and transportation to the doctor . . . I would be sinking."

Asian, and 1% Caucasian. During the 1998/1999 school year, 32% of students received ESOL (English for Speakers of Other Languages) services.

The Broad Acres community is culturally diverse, yet largely economically disadvantaged. During the 1998-1999 school year, 90% of students in the school were eligible for Free and Reduced Meals (FARMS), a frequently cited poverty indicator. Of 96 parents interviewed in the spring of 1996, the mean annual family income reported ranged from $12,000 to $20,000. Only 2% of parents reported an annual family income greater than $35,000. The text box provides examples of families served by the Linkages program.

Services for Children and Families

At Broad Acres, mental health, social, education, and health services are available to children and their families through Linkages to Learning. Mental health services include assessments, individual and group counseling, support groups for parents, and staff development for teachers. Social services include translation and transportation assistance, housing assistance, after-school and summer recreation programs, and assistance in connecting with other agencies. Education support has ranged from tutoring and mentoring for children, to adult education classes and groups in English and computer literacy for parents. Students have also obtained basic health care services through Linkages such as hearing and vision screening, emergency services, immunizations, referral, and case management. Beyond basic mental health, social services, education, and health services, the needs identified by the parents have driven the range of supports available each semester.

A major emphasis of the program has been preventing and reducing the social, emotional, and health problems of children that interfere with their ability to succeed in school. Part of the process of reducing risk factors for children has involved supporting their families and giving them the support and skills that enable them to help their children independently of the program (Oppenheim & Evert, 2000).

Problem Analysis, Program Development, and Core Program Elements

Several core elements shaped the Linkages program and practices at Broad Acres Elementary School. The core elements include (a) stable and consistent funding, (b) critical mass of resources, (c) cultural competence among staff, and (d) a collaborative program culture. These program features have enabled the program to build effective partnerships between the Linkages staff and the local school staff. Underlying these core elements is a belief that problem management and problem-solving activities, essential aspects of program development, need to be directed at the appropriate level of the operation: the *practice* level, the *program* level, or the *system* level (Eber, 1997). The *practice* level includes the interactions among the Linkages staff, the children and families, and the school staff. The middle, or the *program,* level refers to the policies, understandings, and the interactions among the Linkages leadership, the school administration, and the neighborhood of families. The *system* level involves the upper management of the direct service providers, the political leadership in the county, and the division heads of the social services agencies and the public schools. Program success in building community-based partnerships is contingent in part on problems being managed at the appropriate level. Time and resources are wasted when solutions are sought at too low or too high a level—when staff chase the wrong "fire engines" in attempting to solve problems. Through experience, the Linkages staff has learned how to manage problems at the appropriate level.

For example, when the program was moving from portable classrooms into a new health center facility attached to the school there was confusion, misinformation, and miscommunication about the transition to the new space. Dates for the move were changed at the system level without staff at the program level being consulted or informed by the participating agencies in a timely manner. At one point, phones were not operating for several months. Although some glitches are inevitable and highly probable when several agencies work together to coordinate a program, interagency programs like Linkages have to learn how to solve problems at the appropriate level. Linkages brought agencies and staff together—at the system level initially, and then at the program and practice levels—to hammer out exactly how the school, social service, and private partners would be working together, and how problems and conflicts should be addressed.

Another example of learning to address problems at the appropriate level involved figuring out how to meet the reporting requirements of different agencies and the school. Each system used a variety of data management tools. Reporting was a laborious process that took valuable time from direct service to clients. The school and all the participating agencies needed monthly and yearly data on the operation of the program and services to children and families. Devising a collaborative data management process at the system level at the outset, deciding on common goals and outcomes across agencies, and identifying both resources and clerical support necessary for the job might have saved headaches and lessened the burden on staff at the program and practice level.

Core Elements

The first core element that shaped program practice was *stable and consistent funding*. Because the sources of support for the Linkages program come from several different sources, achieving and sustaining this core element has not been easy. As the program began at Broad Acres, the school district's financial contribution consisted primarily of maintaining the Linkages office; the social services agency purchased the first Linkages trailer. The health center that became part of the Linkages program was completed after a tortuous 4-year saga of system-level politics and delays. Advocates at the system level who pushed this issue forward were essential. The effort of a well-connected, former Broad Acres principal helped resolve resource and responsibility issues between the school district and the social service agency.

Although some aspects of program funding were predictable, conflicts among agencies and providers challenged program stability at times. Salaries for Linkages staff at Broad Acres were paid through subcontracts from the University of Maryland grant and through a Robert Wood Johnson grant for health services. However, tension existed between the desire of the private subcontractor providing the Linkages mental health services to increase billable hours and the program staff's attempt to promote the maximum use of resources by families. The Linkages mental health team (employed by a private contractor) was unable to meet its targeted budget because it was unable to generate enough fees for services. The private contractor's income projections were based on an outpatient clinic model that did not fit a school-based center serving low-income families.

Much time was spent creating and sustaining relationships among Linkages staff, school staff, and providers to provide financial stability to the program. As the external funding through the University of Maryland grant ended, the fee-for-service funding leveled out and generated approximately $30,000 in annual revenues. At the same time, the Linkages staff asked Montgomery County to step in and supply funds previously covered by the University. The private mental health agency came within days of leaving the program because the new funding level was too low to guarantee the positive outcomes for children and families that were demonstrated by the program evaluation (discussed later in the chapter). Resolution of the funding crises eventually involved a decision by the County Executive and agency heads to fund the program at Broad Acres with new local money at the level previously supported through external grants. Although stable and consistent funding was a core element of the Linkages program at Broad Acres, achieving this and providing program stability for children, parents, and staff took 4 years to achieve.

The second core element was a *critical mass of resources*. The words "critical mass" suggest a level of resources essential for program operation. For example, we found that adding or subtracting a relatively small amount of resources had a disproportionately large effect on the program. We also discovered that a different form or arrangement of an asset was critical to effective service delivery.

Office space was an important asset. Acquiring enough office space was itself a difficult journey. Over the 4 years of the project, the Linkages mental health and social services elements of the program were moved from a trailer to two portable classrooms to a semipermanent structure. Each time the program moved, we gained more room. However, when we moved into our current offices with the health staff, for the first time we were working with the health staff in the same offices every day. This rearrangement of our working space produced a dramatic leap in collaboration among the social services, mental health, and the school health staff. Policies and procedures were clarified, communication improved, and most important, parents and children had access to a much more efficient and collaborative system of services. The final move made it easy for health staff to accompany parents to talk with a caseworker or therapist as needed. As consultations and referrals between health and mental health staff increased, the program had an opportunity to expand and strengthen the collaborative program culture (another core element of the program). Placing the health, mental health, and social service aspects of the program in contiguous office space produced a greater positive impact on the program than doubling the office space.

Nowhere does the idea of a critical mass of resources appear to be truer at the practice level than around staffing. One key asset of our staffing in the Linkage program at Broad Acres was our ability to hire part-time licensed clinical social workers and licensed psychologists. Having these mental health individuals on the staff brought experience and expertise to the program and made it possible for the program to have graduate interns in both social work and psychology. In the fourth year of operations, four interns increased the program's case management and clinical staff time by 64 hours a week. Interns also increased the ethnic diversity and language capabilities of our staff. Trainees also brought energy, enthusiasm, and creativity to the program.

Besides office space and staffing, other essential elements that represented critical mass for the program were office equipment and political capital. Obtaining and maintaining these resources was a challenge. For example, as the program moved from one temporary space to another, we gained and lost key office resources, including phones, facsimile machines, copiers, and computers. Initially the staff had to make do with donated, used computers and other equipment and borrowed phones. When the program was moved to permanent office space, the staff had saved enough money from the monthly office materials allocation to buy a TV/VCR, an overhead projector, and a new computer. At times staff members were seriously compromised in their ability to complete their work. This situation created high levels of frustration, low morale, and feelings of helplessness among staff. If agreements about resources and infrastructure necessary to run the program had been developed by the partner agencies before trying to initiate services in a new site, these problems could have been prevented.

With regard to political capital, the program, through the school principal and county politicians, was able to obtain critical funding and funding mechanisms to get the program off the ground. At the time the Linkages to Learning program was started at Broad Acres, the county was funding three other Linkages sites and would not allocate more funds for the new program. The school district resisted providing support for social services because as an education agency, it saw its primary responsibility as ensuring children were educated. When the University of Maryland received its research grant, the funding for staff was covered but there was no space for the program at Broad Acres.

Historically, a school-linked service program at Broad Acres was to begin as a health center with private funds in March 1995. When funding for the health center fell through, the principal, with approval from the school district, invited a local private nonprofit agency to send a therapist to Broad Acres after school to provide therapy for children and families on a fee-for-services basis. A few months after the plans to launch a health center failed, the school was left with partial funding for a Linkages center (through the University of Maryland grant) and a fee-for-service licensed clinical social worker who by then was working during school hours. Initial recruitment of children and families for the evaluation of the Linkages program began in September 1995, but the service delivery could not begin without space for clinicians and caseworkers. After many phone calls by the Broad Acres principal and key politicians, the Department of Health and Human Services found and parked a trailer outside the school. At many key junctures during the first 4 years of Linkages at Broad Acres, the difference between losing the program and growing the program was the critical mass of political capital at the system level and the ability of the principal to access it.

The third core element of the Linkages program is *cultural competence*. Cultural competence extends beyond having a staff that is bilingual; it includes an awareness and understanding of the differences between the dominant American culture and the *high-context* culture of many families served by the program. For example, in high-context cultures, communication involves connecting with others in ways that they recognize, understand, and value. This means developing respectful, welcoming relationships with families as a prerequisite to working with or helping them. From this perspective, a necessary step before parents will use program resources is building a trusting relationship. Developing trust requires talking with individuals informally and often at unscheduled times. Because families from higher-context cultures communicate differently, we found taking the time to build relationships with families essential. In high-context cultures, the nonverbal communication of the relationship and the setting are all-important. Cultural competence at the program level meant structuring our time to be flexible and responsive to build relationships and communicate with our families. It meant less reliance on flyers, letters, and posted announcements to inform parents about program services and more phone calls, home visits, and informal contacts outside the school.

Being culturally competent as a program meant that the Linkages office needed to stay open weeknights and weekends when parents were free to visit. However, spending the time with a parent when the opportunity presents itself wreaks havoc on scheduled appointments with school staff. By necessity most school cultures are very low context and highly scheduled. The need to structure the program to be responsive to parents from a higher-context culture can precipitate a problem for any regularly scheduled meeting between school staff and Linkages staff. The common example of this phenomenon on the practice level occurs when a teacher schedules back-to-back, half-hour parent-teacher meetings and a parent arrives half an hour late. The teacher feels that she has no flexibility to meet with the late parent (it's not fair to the next parent) and politely tells him or her to reschedule the meeting. The parent probably walks away feeling dismissed, not because of the content of the message but because of the brevity of the conversation.

The Linkages staff used the weekly 2-hour staff meetings as the opportunity for inservices and consultation with the school on acculturation and cultural competence issues. For example, Linkages staff members participated in meetings involving a parent, a teacher, and the principal. These situations provided an opportunity to discuss with the principal and school staff how the differences in culture (high vs. low context) played out in the ongoing miscommunication with some families.

Staff commitment to a *collaborative culture* represents the fourth core element of the Linkages program. A collaborative culture involves a shared vision of the anticipated outcomes for clients and a commitment to working together to reach common goals. In other words, a collaborative culture is a high-context culture. A collaborative program means that the coordinated effort is achieved through high-context communication (i.e., a network of relationships).

When all staff members within an organization share the same cultural background and work within the same organizational culture, there is less need for a collaborative culture. However, when the staff is culturally diverse and comes from different organizational cultures (school, child welfare, private provider business, etc.), a collaborative program culture is essential. When a team within an organization is multicultural, then the team must be culturally competent. Because Linkages to Learning involved staff from different organizational and professional cultures serving clients from different ethnic backgrounds, a collaborative culture was essential. The collaborative culture that evolved at Linkages included responsiveness to children and families from different ethnic backgrounds and to program and school staff from different professional and organizational cultures.

As the collaborative culture at Broad Acres developed, Linkages staff learned to understand the perspectives, needs, and stresses experienced by teachers in the school. By the same token, school staff developed realistic expectations about what Linkages therapists and case managers could and couldn't do, and an understanding of the importance of confidentiality between clients and therapists. The Linkages and school staffs worked out referral procedures, integrated educational and mental health teams, and coordinated policies for crises within a collaborative culture. This could not happen in an environment where staff failed to trust one another and felt the need to compete for resources. Over time, the Linkages therapist participated in the weekly educational support team meetings in the school, and the Linkages site coordinator became part of the school planning committee. Linkages staff members regularly participate in the meetings to coordinate parent programs in the school, and the principal has become a member of the Linkages advisory board. Both staffs have participated in each other's meetings to develop vision and mission statements.

At the end of each school year the Linkages staff and the school staff met as part of a yearly evaluation and to promote communication. At these meetings, staff members were asked to evaluate how well staff from the other program (school or Linkages) met their expectations. As each staff member presented critical and positive feedback at these meetings, other staff quietly listened without questions. After discussion, the common points were identified and both staffs chose the top three priorities on which to work during the next school year. Building a collaborative culture between the school and the Linkages staffs took a large commitment of time over several years. Without a critical mass of time allocated to create and sustain the relationships through feedback sessions, retreats, and team meetings, it would have been difficult to create a collaborative culture.

A critical aspect of the program is the collaborative culture with the parents. The Linkages staff built relationships with them by first organizing the program in a culturally competent way. In the fall of 1996 we held three open forums for parents. Parents hadn't participated in creating the program, but they could influence its growth. At all three forums parents said that they wanted the program to provide English classes and computer training. English classes were organized that year, and computer classes were developed later when the program had computers on which to train parents. Although a parent advisory board was started, confusion about the roles of the PTA and the advisory board resulted in disbanding the advisory board. However, parents were asked periodically to participate in focus groups to give us feedback about aspects of the program. In developing a collaborative culture with parents, Linkages staff sought to listen first to the parents and their needs. Among other things, the staff worked with them to learn the language of this country. We helped them learn "the language of the school." They taught us the language of their experience.

In the sections that follow, we briefly describe an extensive evaluation of the Linkages to Learning program. The information demonstrates the effectiveness of the intervention.

Evaluating the Effect of Linkages to Learning on Children and Families

In order to assess the effects of the LTL program on children and families, we compared Broad Acres with another elementary school. Midway through the project we also interviewed eight families who were representative of the families served by the program. The outcomes reported in this chapter summarize findings presented in our final report and the findings from our parent satisfaction study (see Fox et al., 1999).

The evaluation design compared children and families at Broad Acres with a comparison or control school. Over the 4 years, a total of 119 children and 69 parents were part of the evaluation. The sample consisted of families from whom data were collected just before Linkages started at Broad Acres and 3 years later. The small size of the sample, relative to the number of children and families served by Linkages, reflects the unusually high mobility rates at both the experimental and control schools. Because this project was designed as a comparison-school study, we expected that children and families at both schools would share many common characteristics. Unfortunately, major differences existed. Not only were there differences in ethnicity, income level, education, and length of time in the United States, but other schoolwide demographic differences were also found. Overall, the experimental school, Broad Acres, served a population at greater risk for difficulties than the control school. The control school was selected by public school administrators and not by the researchers for the project. Other elementary schools whose demographic profile more closely resembled Broad Acres were not selected, in part because they were receiving other special programs and compensatory services.

Many parents who declined to participate in the evaluation of Linkages were part of the program and they and their children received Linkages services. An analysis of the children and families participating in the evaluation and those not participating revealed no significant differences on any measures.

Measures of child behavior problems and academic performance from the pretest also showed children at Broad Acres having more difficulties than children at the control school. For example, we found that according to teachers, the children at Broad Acres demonstrated more acting-out behaviors, such as being disruptive in class, and more learning difficulties, such as poor concentration, than students at the control school. According to mothers, children at Broad Acres demonstrated more total problem behaviors, such as symptoms of aggression and depression, than children at the control school. And, Broad Acres students demonstrated poorer academic performance on measures of math, reading, and writing abilities.

Procedure

During the fall of the first project year, information about the Linkages to Learning evaluation project was distributed to all parents with children in Grades K-2 at the experimental and control schools. Bilingual staff distributed informational flyers and answered questions at parent meetings, PTA functions, and other school activities. All flyers and consent forms were available in English, Spanish, and Vietnamese. In addition, teachers in Grades K-2 distributed to all children in their classrooms consent forms and endorsement letters from the principals. Parents or guardians who agreed to participate in the evaluation of Linkages to Learning and their children were interviewed and assessed each year.

In addition, teachers were asked to complete two questionnaires each year and assess the behavior of each child participating in the program. A summary of the research instruments can be found in Chapter 10.

Parent Report of Emotional and Behavioral Outcomes. Parents at Broad Acres reported a significant decrease of children's negative behaviors over 3 years. Decreases were reported on both the externalizing and internalizing subscales of the Child Behavior Checklist. Children at Broad Acres exhibited more negative behaviors than children in the control school before the start of the project. By the end of the third year, children at Broad Acres had fewer negative behaviors than children at the control school. This suggests that Linkages may have had a positive, schoolwide impact on the prevalence of parent-reported behavior problems.

Differences in CBCL Scores by Services. We also evaluated differences among children in three groups. We examined children at the control school, children at Broad Acres who had received direct services through Linkages, and children at Broad Acres who had not received services. Over time, we found significant differences among the three groups on both the externalizing and internalizing subscales of the CBCL. Children who had the highest scores on the CBCL were those who were receiving Linkages services. This suggests that the children who needed services most were the ones who received them. The externalizing problem scores for children receiving services were, on average, more than two points higher than those of children not receiving services in the same school, and four points higher than scores of children in the control school.

By the end of the study, parent-reported problems for children receiving services at Broad Acres had dropped to the level of children at the control school. We found that children at Broad Acres who were not receiving services also showed a dramatic decline in parent-reported problem behaviors. In fact, the decline for this group was even greater than for those receiving services, particularly on the internalizing subscale. This finding suggests that the Linkages to Learning program may have affected the emotional climate of the school. Even parents of those children not directly receiving services were reporting significant improvements in the behaviors of their children. Perhaps these children, whose behavioral problems were less severe and entrenched than those of children receiving services, were more likely to make behavioral gains with even a minimal level of intervention (e.g., program presence in the school, program impact on teacher or parent attitudes, etc.). Evidence also suggests that several students at Broad Acres with emotional and behavioral disorders were able to remain at the school and not be placed in a specialized and segregated treatment program.

Teacher Report of Emotional and Behavioral Outcomes. Data on children's behavior in the classroom were collected from teachers using the Teacher-Child Rating Scale (T-CRS). Teachers completed checklists each year to document the behavioral strengths and weaknesses they observed among their students. The T-CRS groups items into positive and negative behaviors. Negative behaviors include things like being disruptive in class, poor motivation, and defiant behavior. Examples of positive behaviors include coping well with failure, being sensitive to other children's feelings, and tolerating frustration well. Our evaluation found differences between groups on negative behaviors but not on positive behaviors.

Overall, children at the control school demonstrated an increase in negative behaviors as they got older, while children at the experimental school did not show a similar trend, though they had more risk factors. One possible explanation is that as children get into the higher elementary grades, the classroom becomes a more structured environment. Negative, acting-out behaviors become more apparent, particularly among children at risk for academic and behavioral problems. It is also possible that as children get older, teachers' expectations for conforming behaviors get higher. When children fall behind academically, they may be more likely to respond by acting out. Such behaviors can be attempts to distract from their academic difficulties, or may be expressions of frustration, anger, or poor self-image.

Child Report of Emotional Outcomes. Children were asked about their own emotional well-being. For this measure, children reported on the extent to which they experienced anxiety, depression, distractibility, and poor self-esteem. At the beginning of the evaluation, Broad Acres and the control school were significantly different from each other, with children at the control school reporting significantly lower levels of emotional distress. Over the 3-year period, however, levels of distress among children at Broad Acres remained stable while the scores for the children in the control school increased significantly, exceeding the distress scores for children at Broad Acres.

We can only speculate about the reasons for an increase in distress symptoms among children at the control school. As children mature and develop greater self-awareness, they are more able and more likely to report on their internal experiences of sadness, anxiety, or low self-concept. Common stresses experienced by school aged-children include those related to academic success, social acceptability, and family factors such as divorce. Many children are first referred for special education services for emotional disturbance during the first few years of school when they exhibit behavior problems. While we would expect that children at both schools would be similarly vulnerable to the effects of such stresses, only those at the control school show increases in distress levels over time. This finding suggests that Linkages at Broad Acres may serve as a protective factor against increases in emotional distress.

Academic Outcomes. The performances of children within the two groups at Broad Acres were different. While the children not receiving direct services from Linkages started with higher math achievement scores, by the end of the study the children receiving services had made such gains that they were now approaching the achievement scores of their peers in the no-service group.

This positive impact of the Linkages to Learning program on math achievement was not found for either the reading subscale or the writing subscale of the achievement measure. One important consideration is the fact that a significant number of the children at Broad Acres had limited English proficiency, which could have confounded reading and writing scores. Math scores, because they are less language-dependent, may be less influenced by this factor.

Parent Outcomes. Our evaluation of parenting practices showed that parents at Broad Acres who received Linkages services made the greatest gains in consistency of parenting skills over time, while parents at the control school showed slight increases. We also examined parents' satisfaction with the program and the extent to which it met their needs. We conducted a series of interviews with parents and identified aspects of the program that they found most useful (Meisel, 1997). In general, parents were very satisfied with the program. They identified improved academic, behavioral, and social skills of children; improved communication with school staff; and improved parenting skills as the most important outcomes of the program. Parents said that individual and group counseling, academic tutoring, and after-school and summer activities were the most important services their children received. For themselves, parents reported that English language classes, access to other social service agencies, and parenting classes were most helpful.

One parent, in response to a question about her satisfaction with the program, said, "The Linkages services helped my daughter very much. She would inflict harm on herself when she was reprimanded, and would frequently fight with her siblings and classmates. She received counseling, and I did too, and now life is much smoother for us." Another commented, "I have only had a few appointments, but I feel like I see the Linkages staff all the time because I am in the school a lot . . . so I can talk to them for a few minutes without an appointment and clear up simple things that way."

Community Partnerships. Another outcome more difficult to quantify than changes in children's social behavior or academic performance involves the partnerships that developed into the Linkages to Learning program. In addition to the private mental health agency, the public schools, and the social service agency, the Linkages staff has developed and continues to develop partnerships with groups such as the Vietnamese Professional Association of America, Bikes for Tykes, MANNA Food Bank, local businesses, and several local congregations. These partnerships provide additional links and supports and opportunities for Linkages families. On the drawing board are partnerships with computer companies that are interested in training and hiring skilled technicians.

Perspective on Linking Learning and Community Partnerships

Linkages to Learning, a school-based program designed to support families and prevent the development of emotional and behavioral problems among their children, may be a promising approach to meeting the needs of low-income and immigrant families. We believe that the core elements—stable funding, critical mass of resources, cultural competence, and a collaborative culture—were essential elements in setting the stage for the positive outcomes for children and parents.

Findings from our evaluation at Broad Acres Elementary School are quite encouraging. Information from multiple sources suggests positive outcomes for children and families. In some areas, functioning of children and parents at Broad Acres improved over time, while functioning of children and families at the control school did not. This suggests that the presence of the Linkages to Learning program at Broad Acres may have been serving to prevent such behavioral and emotional problems from increasing.

The Linkages to Learning program at Broad Acres has developed new initiatives for family members of the children at Broad Acres to promote the sustainability of positive outcomes for children. Besides continuing parent education and support, the training and collaborative activities under way involve job readiness, computer training, and acculturation. With Linkages, not only are parents learning to speak the language of the school, but also the school is learning to hear the needs of the community.

REFERENCES

Eber, L. (1997). *Applying "System of care" approaches through schools?* (Presentation at the First National School-Based Mental Health Conference). College Park: University of Maryland, University College.

Fox, N., Leone, P., Rubin, K., Oppenheim, J., Miller, M., & Friedman, K. (1999). *Final report on the Linkages to Learning program and evaluation at Broad Acres Elementary School.* College Park: University of Maryland.

Harry, B. (1992). *Cultural diversity, families, and the special education system.* New York: Teachers College Press.

Leone, P. E., Lane, S. A., Arlen, N., & Peter, H. (1996). School-linked services in context: A formative evaluation of Linkages to Learning. *Special Services in the Schools, 11*(1/2), 119-133.

Meisel, S. M. (1997). *Evaluation of low-income families' satisfaction with school-linked social services.* Unpublished manuscript, University of Maryland, Department of Special Education.

Oppenheim, J. A., & Evert, R. J. (2000). *Reflections on the development and implementation of the Linkages to Learning program at Broad Acres Elementary School.* Unpublished manuscript. Available from Broad Acres Elementary School, Silver Spring, MD.

Schorr, L. (1989). *Within our reach: Breaking the cycle of disadvantage.* Garden City, NY: Doubleday.

8 Using Conflict Resolution and Peer Mediation to Support Positive Behavior

Stephen W. Smith
Ann P. Daunic

Recently, the specter of school violence has caused American citizens to reconsider their beliefs about the safety of schools. High-profile, senseless shootings have left administrators, teachers, parents, students, and communities stunned and distraught. Incidents of students killing students and other people in Colorado, Kentucky, Oregon, Michigan, and elsewhere have created demands for school safety and security that are unprecedented in our country's history. Engaging students in activities designed to find an answer or solution to a disagreement or conflict has promising potential in preventing disharmony, aggression, and violence and in promoting positive behavior in schools.

For years, professionals who work with school-aged children have been concerned about problems associated with destructively aggressive behavior. These problems are nothing new; however, school safety issues have become increasingly urgent with the recent occurrence of high-profile, violent events in schools across the country. School administrators continue to seek out procedures and programs that may reduce aggression among students and prevent serious incidents from occurring. Many traditional practices, such as detention or suspension, are often punitive and adult-directed, do not teach students positive conflict management, and do not have lasting effects. Consequently, researchers and school-based professionals have begun to advocate preventive approaches to behavior problems that combine student-centered, skill-building interventions with changes in the ecological context in which behaviors occur (see Andrews, 1995; Leone, Mayer, Malmgren, & Meisel, 2000). Conflict resolution (CR) programs that incorporate peer mediation (PM) training exemplify such an approach. They have proliferated over the past decade and provide educators with an alternative to reactive, adult-directed strategies.

Conflict resolution, as a school-based program, usually includes instruction to make conflict a constructive, rather than destructive, process. It is designed to be preventive. Conflict resolution concepts can be taught in self-contained units or infused within other academic content, and they can be taught to all students or to selected groups.

Peer mediation is an intervention, often used in conjunction with a conflict resolution curriculum, in which specially trained students follow specific procedures to help their peers negotiate a positive resolution to a conflict. While curriculum in conflict resolution is designed to teach students general concepts about positive approaches to conflict in daily life, peer mediation is a specific and formal opportunity for students to practice learned skills. Peer mediation may be taught to selected cadres of students who serve as mediators, or it can be a universal approach in which each student has an opportunity to act as a mediator on a rotating basis.

Peer mediation (Benson & Benson, 1993; Deutsch, 1994; Schrumpf, Crawford, & Usadel, 1991), as part of a conflict resolution program, is a significant move away from reactive, punitive, and seclusionary methods, and its proponents suggest that it can

- ◆ Provide students with a framework for resolving conflicts

- ◆ Give students an opportunity to assume responsibility for their own behavior

- ◆ Lower teachers' stress by reducing the number of student conflicts they have to handle

- ◆ Increase instructional time

- ◆ Help students understand how cultural diversity can affect interpersonal communication and human interactions

Teaching students to resolve their conflicts constructively can have positive effects on the school environment, particularly because students' chronic behavior problems demand considerable time and attention from teachers and administrative staff. Conflict resolution and peer mediation programs can focus not only on teaching students skills for managing conflict constructively, but also on creating environments that empower students and provide them opportunities to practice what they have learned. By developing a positive school approach to interpersonal conflict, teachers and administrators can help students develop the personal, social, and academic skills necessary for success in school and beyond.

In this chapter, we will (a) describe the components and functions of conflict resolution and peer mediation programs and their rationale within a developmental framework, (b) briefly review some of the relevant research, (c) describe our work in three middle schools and what we found, and (d) conclude with recommendations about how to implement and maintain an effective program and suggestions about the implications of helping students turn inevitable conflicts into opportunities for growth and learning.

What Is Involved in Conflict Resolution and Peer Mediation?

Johnson and Johnson (1996) argue that conflict, if managed constructively without violence, may be desirable. Conflict resolution and peer mediation are recommended procedures for addressing in positive ways the conflict that is inevitable in the schools.

Conflict Resolution

Conflict resolution programs typically include a curriculum designed to provide basic knowledge to students about individual differences, changing win-lose situations to win-win solutions and using negotiation to resolve conflicts effectively. A conflict resolution curriculum can focus on social skills such as empathy training, effective communication, and stress and anger management; attitudes about conflict; bias awareness; and/or negotiation and large-group problem solving. Teachers or other school professionals help students learn a process for handling interpersonal conflict by focusing on skill development within a general conceptual framework rather than on how to solve an immediate, specific problem. Students tend to view conflict situations as occasions in which there are winners and losers (Carlsson-Paige & Levin, 1992). Introducing them to scenarios where all parties can win offers a framework within which to view conflict as a learning opportunity to solve mutual problems and strengthen social relations. Conflict resolution curricula can introduce students to the productive aspects of conflict instead of focusing only on eliminating or preventing it. They may be especially effective when teachers use cooperative learning strategies to foster integrative, rather than competitive, approaches to learning (Stevahn, Johnson, Johnson, & Real, 1996).

Conflict resolution programs should be student- rather than adult-centered. Adults are not always available to help students negotiate solutions to their day-to-day conflicts. Programs that depend solely on adult decision making fail to teach students appropriate resolution skills to use in the absence of adult supervision. Through a variety of learning experiences, such as discussion, role plays, and simulations, and through a focus on student empowerment, conflict resolution curricula can (a) facilitate the understanding of conflict and its determinants, (b) teach students effective communication, problem solving, and negotiation, and (c) provide a foundation for education about peace and nonviolence.

Peer Mediation

Not only should adults teach students about conflict, they must also provide students with opportunities to practice what they learn in real-life conflict situations. Students are constantly exposed to violence and aggression in the media, often as win-lose situations, and they may be exposed to similar circumstances in their homes and communities. To counter the effects of such negative exposure, students need opportunities to observe appropriate, positive negotiations and to practice conflict resolution skills in unthreatening environments. Peer mediation, an explicit intervention in which students help their peers solve conflicts, offers such an opportunity. Mediation avoids an imposed adult solution and the resentment of authority that may come as a consequence of adult control. When mediators and disputants can work autonomously, school professionals are relieved of time-consuming attention to frequently occurring conflicts, and students are empowered to take responsibility for successfully resolving their disputes.

Peer mediation in the schools is conflict resolution conducted by and for students, allowing them a say in how their disputes will be resolved. It is a structured process consisting of specific steps student mediators use to help disputants define and solve a problem between them. As a significant part of an overall conflict resolution program, peer mediation can provide students with methods for resolving conflict peacefully and with skills to approach future conflict as a constructive opportunity. Peer mediation differs from other programs facilitated by peers, such as peer counselors or peer helpers, because it involves a clearly defined, formal process with distinct roles for each participant.

Schoolwide peer mediators are typically a group of students who receive specific, intensive training in mediation. There are several models of mediation, but all tend to follow the same general process in which mediators (a) provide a supportive environment in which disputants tell their versions of the problem, (b) focus disputants on mutually identified problems, (c) help disputants develop a list of possible solutions through brainstorming, and (d) guide disputants to mutually agreed upon resolutions. The negotiation skills required for mediators and disputants include self-control, effective communication, problem solving, critical thinking, and appropriate planning.

Providing students with the opportunity to develop negotiation skills should help to improve their self-esteem and contribute to a school climate that fosters peaceful solutions to interpersonal problems. After students have had positive experiences in settling their own disputes, they are better able to accept structure and guidance and are more self-motivated. The experiences gained through peer mediation can thus increase how much students benefit from traditional classroom settings. Other positive outcomes may include (a) a regard for conflict as a learning opportunity, (b) a nonpunitive method of discipline that has long-lasting benefits, (c) a reduction in violence, vandalism, and absenteeism, and (d) a better understanding of individual differences (see Goldstein & Glick, 1987, and Schrumpf et al., 1991, for more information on long-term effects of teaching negotiation and mediation skills).

How Does Conflict Resolution Fit in Middle Schools?

We can view the prevention of chronic behavior problems through conflict resolution strategies within a developmental frame of reference. Although younger children can learn to use conflict resolution strategies, we think these techniques are particularly relevant during the middle school years. In middle school, children are becoming increasingly independent of adults and more influenced by their peers. Programs that are appealing and instructive help students effectively meet the challenges encountered during this critical transition from childhood to adolescence.

Students who develop positive coping strategies for the environmental demands they encounter have an improved chance of growing into emotionally healthy adults. Such development requires that students learn new ways of conceptualizing and dealing with situations when their prior responses no longer work. Developmental psychologists call this process of creating new cognitive structures *accommodation* (Berger, 1994). Accommodation takes place when a person's former developmental level is no longer adequate to meet new environmental demands, and it occurs most readily under conditions that provide optimal levels of both *challenge* and *support* (Ivey, 1991). Sufficient challenge is required to create a need to develop new ways of solving problems. Sufficient support is needed to create a climate in which the individual feels safe enough to risk trying new coping strategies. Successful development occurs when a challenge is balanced with available support.

A significant source of challenge for middle school students is conflict with their peers. Peer conflicts are troublesome for students who experience them and can significantly affect the entire school, the families involved, and the community. Peer mediation can offer a support system for some of the social challenges students experience and contribute to a developmentally appropriate environment within the school setting. The primary developmental tasks of adolescents are (a) achieving emotional independence from parents and other adults, (b) desiring and achieving socially responsible behavior, and (c) acquiring a set of values and an ethical system to guide behavior (Havighurst, 1972). Conflict resolution principles practiced through peer mediation can contribute to students' successful social adjustment and self-enhancement.

The work of Lawrence Kohlberg (1963, 1984) provides additional insight about how conflict resolution might enhance the development of middle school students' ethical and moral decision making. Two of Kohlberg's levels of moral development are relevant: Level I, preconventional, and Level II, conventional. During the preconventional stage, young children are motivated by a need to obey rules and avoid punishment. As children grow older and enter the conventional stage of development, motivating factors increasingly involve social rules and group expectations. Learning the principles of conflict resolution and how to use mediation effectively to resolve conflicts (in lieu of a more traditional trip to the principal's office) is consistent with movement from a preconventional, punishment-obedience orientation to a conventional, social orientation. Development of a conventional orientation is an important step toward becoming self-directed.

A Conflict Resolution and Peer Mediation Program

Over a 4-year period, we collaborated with school personnel in three middle schools in the Southeast to establish and evaluate a conflict resolution program that included peer mediation. The school populations ranged from 780 to 1,135 students and were ethnically and socioeconomically diverse. From 32% to 61% of the students received a free or reduced-price lunch, and from 12% to 16% were designated as having a disability. Our goals included introducing students and staff to the basic tenets of conflict resolution, establishing positive attitudes about conflict within the school community, and reducing student office referrals for interpersonal conflict.

Conflict Resolution Curriculum

The task in teaching effective conflict resolution is to help students realize that their approach to conflict, rather than the existence of conflict itself, determines their successful social development. Our main objective was to show students how to make dealing with conflict a productive exercise. We developed a curriculum to foster a problem-solving approach to conflict and to encourage students to seek mutually agreeable solutions. We designed twelve 40- to 50-minute lessons within four topic areas: understanding conflict, effective communication, understanding anger, and handling anger. An additional lesson provided an introduction to the process of peer mediation. Lessons included student activities and role plays for practicing newly learned skills. We provided teachers with all materials, including instructional directions and sample scripts, overhead transparencies, and student worksheets. For example, students learned about the "Relax-Breathe-Think" model to practice thinking through difficult situations, rather than reacting impulsively, in a lesson on handling anger. Teachers then presented students with several scenarios and instructed them to answer the question, "Who's the boss, me or the problem?" in each case.

Administrative personnel in each school determined how the CR lessons would be integrated into their overall programs. In one case, a newly instituted course in critical thinking for students at all three grade levels provided an appropriate vehicle. In another school, a homeroom period at the beginning of the day was long enough to allow teachers to deliver the curriculum schoolwide. We encouraged teachers to highlight the lessons throughout the school year, providing opportunities for students to recognize and handle their anger, think through cooperative solutions to conflict, and practice effective listening and communication skills.

Peer Mediation Program

Along with teaching students about effective conflict resolution skills, we also helped school personnel establish a peer mediation program. We provided training, program parameters, and implementation strategies, but each school developed its own method for selecting mediators and establishing mediation protocols. In each case, however, 25 to 30 students representing all three middle school grade levels served to mediate disputes throughout the year.

The peer mediation (PM) training included concepts similar to those covered by the schoolwide curriculum, such as understanding the nature of conflict and effective communication. It also focused on issues such as cultural influences, confidentiality, skills related to effective communication, and the specific procedures of the mediation process. Training included role plays and mediation simulations. Those who successfully completed the training were able to execute the mediation process with minimal supervision or intervention by adults.

A systematic referral process provided schoolwide student access to peer mediation. Referral forms were available to students and staff (e.g., in classrooms or guidance office), providing a record of the referring party, conflict location, brief description of the problem, and disputant names. Most important, participation in the peer mediation process was always voluntary. At the conclusion of each mediation, mediators and disputants signed an agreement form that included the date, type of conflict, and agreed-upon resolution. Although a teacher or counselor was available during mediation in case adult intervention became necessary, the supervision they provided was minimal. According to the teachers with whom we worked, students' feelings of independence in handling their own disputes positively influenced their attitude toward the program and their willingness to take their responsibilities seriously.

The more challenging aspects of a schoolwide program are assuring that mediations occur as soon as possible after a referral is made and providing ample opportunities for all trained mediators to mediate disputes. An additional challenge is matching mediators appropriately with disputants (e.g., age, gender). School personnel paired mediators to provide mutual support, more frequent mediation opportunities, and to facilitate discussion during debriefings. We found the availability of a class period during which program facilitators could schedule mediations and meet regularly with mediators to debrief (e.g., a homeroom period) to be a help, if not a necessity. It may be possible to devise a schedule for varying the periods during which mediations occur, but it is not always easy to find suitable locations and provide supervision. Academic considerations also were given appropriate priority to prevent mediators from missing a test or important class presentation, if possible.

To summarize, setting up the peer mediation programs required significant planning and school resources. Those in charge of its implementation had to address the following questions as they considered the logistics of referrals and the mediation process:

- How and by whom would students be referred?

- What kinds of conflicts are suitable for mediation?

- Where would mediation take place?

- Who would supervise the mediations?

- How would the mediators be made available?

- How often would mediators miss class?

- Could teachers refuse to release a mediator (or disputant) from class to attend a mediation?

How Conflict Resolution Worked
in Three Middle Schools

As we assisted in the implementation of the conflict resolution and peer mediation program in three middle schools and collected mediation data, we examined the patterns of office referrals, conflict issues, and mediation resolutions. Our findings are specific to the populations in the three schools, yet they generally correspond to those of other researchers. They also provide insight into how students use peer mediation and whether they consider it a viable alternative to less constructive conflict resolution strategies.

Who Are the Disputants?

Younger middle-school students appear to be more open than their older peers to using mediation to settle disputes. Sixth-grade students were involved in the majority of referrals to mediation. Of course, more disputes that can be handled appropriately through mediation, such as conflicts over relationship issues or feelings, may occur among sixth graders than among seventh or eighth graders. A higher frequency of these issues among younger students would result in a disproportionate number of sixth-grade mediations. From a developmental standpoint, however, there is reason to believe that as students progress through middle school, their need for independence grows. This may include a need for independence from any kind of help in settling conflicts, including the help of peers. One mediator told us that some students would feel embarrassed if they went to mediation, because their friends would ask them where they went. These students thought they risked their reputation if their friends found out they requested help.

We also found that more girls than boys participated in mediation. Some of the peer mediators suggested that mediation may be inherently less appealing to boys because they may perceive its use as a sign of weakness (Robinson, Smith, & Daunic, 2000). For example, one student interviewed stated that his male peers might not use mediation because they wanted to put up a "tough" front with their friends and thereby "boost their reputation." Some boys might avoid *any* process that implied a need for assistance or a reluctance to solve interpersonal conflicts through force. To have a positive effect on school climate, peer mediation has to be socially acceptable to as many students as possible and particularly to those inclined to use aggression.

What Are the Conflict Issues?

Verbal harassment such as name-calling, threatening, or insulting a family member was the reason for most of the mediations. Spreading a

rumor or talking behind someone's back (i.e., gossiping) were other frequently named issues. We found mild forms of physical aggression, such as
pushing or hitting, to be less prevalent. Boys were more likely to be
involved in some form of physical aggression, and girls were more likely to
be concerned with relationship issues, such as broken friendships or gossip.

The high occurrence of verbal harassment issues in mediation has
important implications for the prevention of serious conflict. Aggression
theorists (e.g., Bandura) assert that verbal taunting, name-calling, or
threats can escalate into physical aggression. This is especially the case for
students who are deficient in the verbal skills necessary to de-escalate
potentially violent situations. For these students, peer mediation is an
opportunity to resolve negative verbal incidents by practicing effective verbal strategies in a structured environment and avoid an escalating chain of
destructive events. If mediation can diffuse the effects of minor verbal
threats or incidents before they become serious, it will serve an important
preventive function.

An interesting question is whether the tendency for girls to be less
involved in physical incidents and more involved in verbal ones is related to
their greater tendency to refer themselves to mediation. Perhaps a prefer-
ence for verbal strategies in negotiating social relationships in general
makes girls respond more positively to a process that depends upon the use
of verbal skills. If so, it underscores the need for program coordinators to
address the social acceptability of peer mediation for male students. Some
researchers (Lochman, Dunn, & Klimes-Dougan, 1993) have suggested
that there is a relationship between level of verbal skill and use of physical
aggression among preadolescents. The more verbally skilled a child is, the
less likely he or she may be to use physical force in resolving conflicts. If so,
it is important (a) to teach students to negotiate verbally and (b) to give
them opportunities to practice the required skills. Properly implemented
peer mediation programs provide a vehicle for enhancing verbal skills during a critical developmental period.

What Are the Typical Student Resolutions?

First, we observed over several years that more than 95% of mediations resulted in a resolution acceptable to both disputing parties. This
finding supports the notion that middle school students can, at the very
least, successfully follow a structured procedure and help disputants reach
some mutually agreeable conflict solution. The quality of the solutions they
reached is also of interest. In our study, students most frequently resolved
to avoid each other, stop the offending behavior, or "agree to get along."
These data support findings from other studies of peer mediation at the elementary or middle school level in which researchers looked at the type of

resolution reached (see Johnson & Johnson, 1996, for a thorough review of the effects of conflict resolution).

The quality of an agreement reached by students through peer mediation may result from a variety of factors. First, we found that the older the *peer mediators,* the more likely resolutions involved an agreement to "get along" rather than simply to avoid each other or stop the offending behavior. This implies a developmental progression in ability to facilitate productive communication and/or to stick with the negotiation process until disputants reach a more socially constructive solution. Early into our work in conflict resolution, we did not consider avoiding each other or simply terminating verbal or physical aggression to be desirable resolutions that would serve to strengthen the relationship between the disputing parties. As we continued our study, we realized that the willingness and ability of 11- and 12-year-old mediators and disputants to follow a process of negotiation through to any acceptable solution is a significant achievement and may provide a foundation for lifelong negotiation skills.

What Are the Overall Program Effects?

We intended to measure the effect of a comprehensive conflict resolution/peer mediation program on the rate of referrals for disciplinary incidents, and on the attitudes of various members of the school community. We accomplished that by examining school discipline records and by administering teacher and student attitude surveys about school conflict and school climate. With one exception in more than 20 student or teacher subscales, including those in surveys given to peer mediators, we did not find any significant changes in survey responses following program implementation. We believe that competing school priorities, which resulted in a curriculum of only five lessons per academic year, diminished the program's overall effect on student attitudes and school culture. We did, however, find a promising downward trend in disciplinary incidents, particularly at the school where staff were most involved. At that school, the peer mediation program was started early in the fall semester each year, the responsibility for training and student support was clearly assigned, and a homeroom period for mediations was available every day. This classroom period also provided a time for mediators to debrief with teachers and discuss their experiences. We consider each of these factors important for effective program implementation, and they may have resulted from a strong commitment and ownership of the program on the part of school administration and faculty. Our findings suggest that these accommodations affected the program's impact on school discipline. Concurrently, the factors themselves may also have contributed to the level of program acceptance by making the required activities more feasible to carry out.

Despite little evidence of schoolwide attitude change, mediators and disputants expressed high levels of satisfaction with the mediation process and its capacity for solving conflicts. Peer mediators and their parents reported that mediation skills learned during training were used frequently when conflicts arose at school outside of formal mediation or at home. Disputants, who were surveyed at least a week following mediation, reported continued adherence to their mediation agreement and high satisfaction with the process.

The only consistent attitudinal change we found was in how mediators rated their teachers' communication. Following training in mediation, students' ratings of teacher communication were significantly lower than before training, when compared to the ratings of a control group who had not received training in mediation. More specifically, after students learned about the importance of (a) effective listening and speaking, (b) being open to others' ideas even when they are opposed to one's own, and (c) giving others a chance to express their ideas, students apparently raised the standards they used to judge their teachers in these areas.

The change in student perceptions of teacher communication following student training is an important finding. Since a significant portion of the peer mediation training was about the development of effective communication, students trained in mediation skills evaluated their teachers more harshly than their untrained peers did. This finding underscores the importance of establishing a school culture that supports the principles of positive conflict resolution and mediation. If teachers do not model effective communication and negotiation skills, the long-term impact of a program that incorporates peer mediation to influence patterns of student communication and conflict management is likely to be compromised.

Building Sustainability

Each school building has its own community and culture, and the success of a new program will necessarily be a function of the larger environment in which it is based. Moreover, there are certain general conditions that facilitate or impede the effective implementation of any schoolwide program, such as the school schedule, competing curricular demands, available space and resources, and the priority assigned to the program. Given these parameters, and with insight gained from our experience and that of other researchers, we suggest that program developers consider several factors as key to successfully implementing and sustaining a school peer mediation program. They are committed leadership, consistency of promoting and monitoring the program, and the peer mediator selection process.

Committed Leadership

The following characteristics are typically addressed in discussions of effective schools and the programs within them:

◆ A clear and focused mission on learning for all

◆ Instructional leadership

◆ High expectations of all stakeholders

◆ Opportunity to learn and student time on task

◆ Frequent monitoring of student progress

◆ Safe and orderly environment for learning

◆ Positive home/school/community relations

The importance of administrators, teachers, and other school personnel in realizing these characteristics has bearing on achieving and sustaining effective conflict resolution and peer mediation programs.

Administrators. Schools are under increasing pressure from parents and community members to provide safe environments for the children they serve. Many administrators, particularly those immediately responsible for schoolwide discipline, are compelled to develop responsive antiviolence and safe-school programs. Coupled with escalating demands for academic improvement in schools with increasingly diverse student populations, the urgency to demonstrate antiviolence measures often makes it tempting to initiate new programs without fully exploring the resources and effort necessary to make them effective. To ensure a program's long-term success—in this case, a peer mediation program—one or more school administrators must commit to providing essential resources and responsible follow-through. For example, a committed administrator would (a) assign to an individual (or team) the primary responsibility for program implementation, (b) make sure that person (or team) has time to perform the required duties effectively, and (c) solicit feedback periodically about the program status and needs. This administrative commitment is probably the single most important factor in sustaining a viable program.

Faculty and Other School Personnel. Along with commitment of top-level administrators, we suggest that establishing a "school mediation team," including teachers from each grade level and administrators or guidance counselors who would be directly involved in program supervision, enhances program success. The "buy-in" of this core group is also critical.

If team members view peer mediation as potentially beneficial to both staff and students, they naturally encourage the involvement of the remaining faculty. Conversely, if a school administrator assigns responsibility for the program to a teacher or group of teachers without their input, incentives, or a commitment to follow through, the interest those teachers have in the program's success is seriously diminished (Matloff & Smith, 1999). Teachers with the most information and direct experience with the program are most likely to feel comfortable using it.

Even willing faculty who enthusiastically support a conflict resolution program can be cautious about using it if they lack program experience. Only after teachers or other school professionals have become knowledgeable and directly involved are they likely to be fully committed. Further, the school mediation team must make a variety of decisions regarding curriculum delivery, program logistics, and peer mediator selection. They must make these decisions according to the needs of each school and cannot rely on "packaged" prescriptions. Team members need incentives for these efforts, along with sufficient planning time and resources. When time and resources are lacking, the team cannot be expected to invest the effort required to initiate and sustain a comprehensive schoolwide program.

Finally, if educators truly wish to affect school culture as a whole and help students develop lasting constructive and cooperative conflict resolution strategies, they need to examine how conflict is addressed, among faculty as well as students. Through exposure to conflict resolution concepts infused in curriculum, students can learn to respond appropriately to simulated and real conflict situations. They will also be heavily influenced, however, by the larger school culture in which they are immersed. For instance, a principal with whom we worked voiced concern that teachers at the school needed instruction in appropriate conflict resolution as much as students did. Adults are not likely to be effective role models if students see that they are not constructive conflict managers themselves. School personnel need to foster an environment conducive to the peaceful and constructive resolution of conflicts, whether between students or adults.

Consistency of Promotion and Follow-Up

Students who have experienced traditional, adult-dependent school discipline may not think automatically about using peer mediation to help settle interpersonal conflicts. Students at the middle school level may continue to call on readily available adults unless they are actively and consistently encouraged to use an alternative, even when the alternative appeals to their developing need for independence. School professionals should address how they will publicize the availability of peer mediation as a disciplinary option on an ongoing basis. For example, the teachers in our study often mentioned how positively students viewed peer mediation and were surprised by the decline in number of mediations as the school year progressed. In retrospect, they believed that waning program publicity contributed to this decline. Some suggestions for publicizing peer mediation to students and faculty on an ongoing basis are as follows:

- ◆ Frequent announcements to remind students and teachers of mediation as an alternative to discipline referrals

- ◆ Posters advertising the program

- ◆ Flyers distributed to homeroom teachers

- ◆ T-shirts worn by peer mediators

- ◆ School- and districtwide recognition of the contributions of peer mediators

In summary, school mediation team members should continually assess how well the word is getting out to students and staff that mediation is a viable option, particularly if it represents a change in the school's disciplinary practices.

Also important to the integrity and sustainability of a peer mediation program is an ongoing check on how the disputants view the process. Having them complete a brief survey a few days following mediation is one way to assess their satisfaction. For example, a member of the school mediation team can administer questionnaires to disputants to solicit their perspectives about (a) the value of the mediation process, (b) whether required steps were followed by the mediators, (c) how helpful the mediation was in settling their dispute, and (d) how well they adhered to the signed agreement. This kind of follow-up is important in assessing the fidelity of the mediation process and its acceptability to students.

Equally important are frequent opportunities for mediators and teachers to discuss their mediation experiences. The mediation process requires sophisticated and sometimes subtle skills that are difficult for even adults to master. We cannot expect students to become overnight experts or to maintain the skills they learned during training without regular meetings to review concepts about mediation and effective communication and discuss their experiences. Therefore, effective program implementation requires a built-in time for mediators to debrief with school mediation team members who can monitor how well the students are following specified procedures. Students can use this opportunity to learn from each other's experiences and discuss how to enhance the desirability of mediation for fellow students, as well.

Selection of Peer Mediators

A key to the schoolwide acceptability of a peer mediation program may be in the way educators select student mediators. The selection process can be based on student applications, student nominations, teacher nominations, or a combination of these processes. In our experience, mediators most often were "successful" or "leader-type" students rather than truly representative of the student body, even though they were diverse demographically. To illustrate, the peer mediators in our study differed from a control group matched on demographic variables, *prior* to their training in mediation, in their attitudes toward conflict, school, communication, and openness. In each case, the mediators' scores were more positive than those of their non-trained peers (matched on school, grade level, gender, race, SES, and placement in special program). Scores indicate that mediators were more positive about school and probably were more effective communicators—that is, they were perhaps the more "successful" students in general.

School staff must understandably consider how serious, conscientious, and competent students would be in the role of peer mediators, but a dilemma arises when only the "best" students are chosen for the job. When this happens, students in need of mediation may view the mediators as a select group who are less apt to understand their problems. They may also see the whole program as "belonging to the establishment" and not something they should consider. The social acceptability of mediation as an alternative response to conflict depends, in part, on its appeal to a broad range of students, particularly those most likely to engage in disruptive or aggressive behavior. Moreover, peer mediation training includes problem-solving steps that are part of several well-researched interventions aimed at reducing aggressive student behavior (Lochman et al., 1993). Program coordinators miss an opportunity to engage students who may become socially isolated if they fail to include them in mediation training. Although not specific to peer mediation, there is recent evidence that students with pronounced behavioral problems can become positive influences when training their peers in social interaction skills using a formal social skills curriculum (Blake, Wang, Cartledge, & Gardner, 2000). In this study, both peer trainers and student trainees showed an increase in positive peer interactions. Thus students with high levels of interpersonal conflict at school could become effective peer mediators and may enhance the program's acceptability to students who might otherwise feel reluctant to share problems.

Perspective on Conflict Resolution Programs in Schools

Students benefit from conflict resolution and peer mediation programs. They learn about effective communication, critical thinking, and problem solving in mediating disputes and how to make conflict a constructive opportunity. They can learn formal mediation procedures and help their peers negotiate positive solutions to conflicts. We found that peer mediators consider mediation a satisfactory way to resolve disputes and an effective alternative to traditional discipline. In the vast majority of conflicts referred to mediation in our study, disputants reached a mutually agreeable solution and were highly satisfied with the process.

Teachers report spending valuable instructional time managing conflicts about spreading rumors and verbal harassment. Even though these issues may seem relatively harmless and typical for middle school students, they can escalate to more serious conflicts or contribute to feelings of alienation. Teaching students how to resolve disputes so that they control the outcome and develop life-long social skills counters violence and alienation and increases time for teaching and learning.

More often than not, middle school students using peer mediation choose unsophisticated resolutions to their conflicts. If we judge these resolutions (e.g., avoiding each other, stopping an offensive behavior) by the degree to which they strengthen relationships, they are not highly productive, yet they still provide an alternative to the destructive escalation of conflict. When combined with a conflict resolution curriculum, practice in mediation can increase students' negotiation skills and possibly lead to more constructive agreements over time. Further research is needed to study the long-term effects of conflict resolution programs and how much curriculum exposure and mediation training are necessary to increase constructive approaches to conflict.

At the outset of our work, we were focused on traditional outcome measures to validate how a conflict resolution and peer mediation program influenced students' views and management of conflict. We intended to investigate the program's effectiveness by looking at changes in school climate, suspension rates, and number of office referrals. As our study progressed, however, we became equally interested in student use of the mediation process as a desirable end in itself. We found that mediators and disputants could learn to use mediation, and they perceived it to be useful and effective. Mediators' parents were satisfied with the effects of the program and reported that their children used mediation when conflict occurred at home.

Our experience as researchers taught us that we can learn from attending to how well students engaged in the process as well as to traditional outcome measures. Peer mediation allowed students to negotiate a variety of disputes independently and constructively, modeling the concepts and skills taught during training. Reduction in office referrals and suspensions are important traditional indicants of long-term program effectiveness. At the same time, offering students a socially acceptable process as an alternative to violence is also an important consideration.

Finally, there are two distinct approaches that CR/PM program developers might consider. In the first approach, students who have requisite skills for mediation (i.e., students with leadership qualities, high social status, effective communication skills) would constitute the mediator cohort. The program focus would be on the quickest way to reduce office referrals and teacher time spent on student conflicts. This approach has obvious merits and is probably adopted most often by school administrators. The odds of quickly establishing a smoothly running program increase when student leaders are involved. The primary target for change would be the attitudes and behavior of students referred to mediation rather than those of the student mediators. Broader goals would involve improving school climate through a schoolwide conflict resolution curriculum and reducing suspension rates.

A different approach would be to implement a program whose primary goal is to develop or remediate students' social behaviors through training in conflict resolution and peer mediation. Students who lack skills in leadership and communication and those across the social status spectrum could work with student leaders to learn and to practice the skills required in formal mediations. Students with learning, behavioral, or social problems that place them at risk for school failure could learn to deal more effectively with conflict by serving as peer mediators. Although this approach might not be as efficient initially, its value would be in changing outcomes for the students who serve as mediators, as well as for disputants and the school as a whole.

The work conducted in the field of school conflict resolution and peer mediation programs shows promise. We need to further our understanding through longitudinal studies of well-implemented programs that track mediator learning, disputant attitudes, the nature of student resolutions over time, and the programs' effects on aggressive behavior. To effect schoolwide change, school professionals need to make constructive conflict resolution an accepted and meaningful part of their culture. As we continue to study the effects of conflict resolution and peer mediation programs over the long term, we will learn more about how our schools can benefit from a positive, student-based approach to resolving the inevitable conflicts that are part of everyday school life.

REFERENCES

Andrews, D. W. (1995). The adolescent transitions program for high-risk teens and their parents: Toward a school-based intervention. *Education and Treatment of Children, 18*(4), 478-498.

Benson, A. J., & Benson, J. M. (1993). Peer mediation: Conflict resolution in schools. *Journal of School Psychology, 31,* 427-430

Berger, K. S. (1994). *The developing person through the life span* (3rd ed.). New York: Worth.

Blake, C., Wang, W., Cartledge, G., & Gardner, R. (2000). Middle school students with serious emotional disturbances serve as social skills trainers and reinforcers for peers with SED. *Behavioral Disorders, 25*(4), 280-298.

Carlsson-Paige, N., & Levin, D. E. (1992). Making peace in violent times: A constructivist approach to conflict resolution. *Young Children, 48*(1), 4-13.

Deutsch, M. (1994). Constructive conflict resolution: Principles, training, and research. *Journal of Social Issues, 50*(1), 13-32.

Goldstein, A. P., & Glick, B. (1987). *Aggression replacement training: A comprehensive intervention for aggressive youth.* Champaign, IL: Research Press.

Havighurst, R. J. (1972). *Developmental tasks and education* (3rd ed.). New York: McKay.

Ivey, A. E. (1991). *Development strategies for helpers.* Pacific Grove, CA: Brooks/Cole.

Johnson, D. W., & Johnson, R. T. (1996). Conflict resolution and peer mediation programs in elementary and secondary schools: A review of the research. *Review of Educational Research, 66*(4), 459-506.

Kohlberg, L. (1963). The development of children's orientation toward a moral order. *Vita Humana, 6,* 11-33.

Kohlberg, L. (1984). *The psychology of moral development: The nature and validity of moral stages.* San Francisco: Harper & Row.

Leone, P. E., Mayer, M. J., Malmgren, K., & Meisel, S. M. (2000). School violence and disruption: Rhetoric, reality, and reasonable balance. *Focus on Exceptional Children, 33*(1), 1-20.

Lochman, J. E., Dunn, S. E., & Klimes-Dougan, B. (1993). An intervention and consultation model from a social cognitive perspective: A description of the Anger Coping Program. *School Psychology Review, 22*(3), 458-471.

Matloff, G., & Smith, S. W. (1999). Responding to a schoolwide conflict resolution-peer mediation program: Case study of middle school faculty. *Mediation Quarterly, 17,* 125-141.

Robinson, T. R., Smith, S. W., & Daunic, A. P. (2000). Middle school students' views on the social validity of peer mediation. *Middle School Journal, 31*(5), 23-29.

Schrumpf, F., Crawford, D., & Usadel, H. C. (1991). *Peer mediation: Conflict resolution in the schools.* Champaign, IL: Research Press.

Stevahn, L., Johnson, D. W., Johnson, R. T., & Real, D. (1996). The impact of a cooperative or individualistic context on the effect of conflict resolution training. *American Educational Research Journal, 33,* 801-823.

9 Making Connections That Keep Students Coming to School

Mary F. Sinclair
Christine M. Hurley
David L. Evelo
Sandra L. Christenson
Martha L. Thurlow

It has been known for many years that young people who don't complete school face many more problems in later life than do people who graduate. But, while national leaders have demanded that schools, communities, and families make a major effort to retain students, the dropout rate remains high. Keeping students in school is a national priority.

Regular attendance, involvement in classroom activities, and sharing common values with classmates and teachers are all indicators of a student's connection with school. These indicators of connection, also referred to as school engagement, are powerful predictors of successful school completion. Educators and parents of youth with a history of course failures, suspensions, and dropping out know that some students have a tenuous connection with school. *Alienation* is a word that more accurately characterizes this group. Many recommended school practices and policies, such as schoolwide discipline, Total Quality Education, and a welcoming climate, have been shown to promote students' connection with school. When supportive school policies are not used systematically, outreach to alienated students and their families is often compromised. If families are highly mobile, the most powerful school-based support services will have a limited impact on those who move on within a year.

The *Check & Connect* model, described in this chapter, can be used to build connections with disenfranchised youth and families. Key components featured here include the role of the person responsible for facilitating students' connection with school (the monitor) and the procedures used to encourage school engagement (checking and connecting). In brief, a caring adult works with disengaged students and families over an extended period of time. This adult systematically checks student levels of engagement with school and provides timely individualized intervention to build and maintain connections to school and learning. Check & Connect is data based and grounded in research on resiliency and home-school collaboration. The chapter is concluded with a discussion of implementation issues including staffing and program costs.

Why Focus on Building Connections?

Research on resiliency in children and adults has sought to explain survival and success in the face of adversity. Life outcomes are typically described in terms of interactions among risk and protective factors. Protective factors, such as a caring adult in a child's life, are most important for those who experience greater risk. Using a resiliency framework, it is not difficult to understand how the connection with a determined parent, teacher, or community mentor can have a profound impact on the educational life of a student with an emotional or behavioral disability placed at high risk for school failure.

Common characteristics of youth with an emotional or behavioral disability include limited personal and financial resources (e.g., learning and mental health challenges by definition of the disability, poverty, siblings and parents who have had negative school experiences) compounded often by mobility associated with either residential movement or administrative transfers. Those students in transition from elementary school to middle or junior high school confront an even greater challenge. The typical decrease in responsiveness of secondary schools can intensify problems for students and families who had become accustomed to the accommodating nature of the elementary system.

Furthermore, we know students do not learn and develop in a vacuum. For decades, scholars have argued that children's development is influenced by more than maturation, calling attention to the impact of culture and socialization on a child's ability to learn and cultivating the notion that child and adolescent behavior is best interpreted in context. The context of student alienation has been studied extensively by Bronfenbrenner (1979, 1986), who documented that students experience greatest risk when problems stem from multiple spheres of influence including home, school, and community. Bronfenbrenner would anticipate that school-related behavior and performance of high-risk youth would be adversely affected by stressful circumstances in adults' personal lives (parents and teachers), poor coordination within systems and services, and inconsistent and incongruent messages about learning which are apparent to youth: "The forces that produce youthful alienation are growing . . . and the best way to counteract alienation is through the creation of connections or links throughout our culture. The schools can build such links" (Bronfenbrenner, 1986, p. 430).

Effective schools help students achieve their educational goals by attending to the needs of the whole child. Coleman (1987) accentuated the importance of a child-centered focus in his discussion of the erosion of social capital. In both dual-income families and families nurtured by one adult, youth are less likely to experience routine, frequent interaction with their parent(s) about academic work and personal matters. Furthermore, many families feel alienated from their communities and have a limited social network on which to rely. Some families also may have limited cultural capital, which refers to less knowledge about or experience with the school culture. As a result, both students and families can be at a loss for knowing how to create the optimal environmental conditions that promote student success in school. Failure to support these students and families has led to an ongoing cycle of alienation.

Building Connections Using Check & Connect

When Anthony (a pseudonym) was first referred to Check & Connect, he was in seventh grade. He was supposed to be in eighth grade, but was held back for excessive absences the year prior. Anthony lived with his mother and never had much contact with his father. He was particularly upset the week he started with Check & Connect, because he found out his family had to move again. His older sibling got them kicked out of their apartment for having too many parties. Anthony's school records indicated that he had been suspended from school several times the first few months of the school year for verbally abusing school staff. His counselor reported that some of Anthony's teachers were fearful his aggressive language would turn physical.

Check & Connect is a model designed to assist students like Anthony. The goal is to promote engagement with school through the connection with a persistent and caring adult who is focused specifically on the student's educational success. The model was developed in the context of two urban middle schools in the Midwest, as part of a middle school study to reduce dropout rates among youth with disabilities, and was funded by the Office of Special Education Programs. Intervention began with the seventh graders receiving special education services for a learning or emotional/behavioral disability. One group of youth participated in Check & Connect through eighth grade and a second group participated through ninth grade (through the transition to high school).

Check & Connect was developed in participation with a community advisory committee. The committee met regularly over a year and a half and included students with disabilities, their parents, regular and special education teacher, youth advocates, and community outreach workers. The participation of advisors from the "front line" was purposefully solicited to increase the likelihood the model we developed would be practical and to promote buy-in from those who would be asked to field-test it.

As a team of researchers and practitioners, we brought to the advisory committee a set of theoretically grounded assumptions upon which to build the model. First, solving the dropout problem would require a comprehensive and multicomponent effort of home, school, community, and youth. Students drop out of school for a variety of reasons for which there is no single solution, nor a simple solution. Second, leaving school prior to graduation is not an instantaneous event. Solutions would require a long-term response focused on those predictors that educators and families are able to change. Third, students must be empowered through knowledge and skill acquisition to take control of their own school completion and behavior. And fourth, schools must take leadership in reaching out to parents and families, in partnership with community members, to strengthen the support network for students struggling with school.

The advisory members agreed with these assumptions and advocated a response to the dropout problem that would address family-school trust building, use of out-of-school time, problem solving, alternative instructional strategies, tutoring and mentoring support, and transitions from one school to another. The Check & Connect model evolved with ongoing input from members of the community advisory committee over an additional 3½ years after its initial development. To explain how Check & Connect works, we have described the *role* of the person responsible for promoting students' engagement in school and the primary procedural aspects of the model that guide intervention—*checking and connecting* (see Table 9.1).

The Role of the Monitor

The person responsible for facilitating a student's connection with school and learning is referred to as the *monitor*. The role of the monitor is modeled after one of the commonly identified protective factors in resiliency

TABLE 9.1 What Is Checking and Connecting?

Check . . .   involved regularly monitoring student's participation in school and academic progress using existing school records.

> Q. Was the student engaged in school?
>
> . . . tardy to school, skipped classes, absent, suspended from school, disciplinary infractions for other behaviors (e.g., referral to the office, in-school suspension, bus incident), failed classes, or unsatisfactory marks in reading or math?

> Q. How did the student's level of engagement compare to the days, weeks, months, and years before today?
>
> . . . has percentage of time engaged in school improved, declined or stayed the same?

Connect . . .   involved providing timely support to students and families to increase or maintain student participation in school.

> Q. What were the connect interventions?
>
> Middle school interventions generally fell into one of three broad categories: conflict resolution and coping via problem solving, academic support, or recreation and community service exploration.

> Q. How was the specific intervention determined?
>
> The specific intervention was based upon a combination of factors: individual needs of the student; past efforts of the student, parent, and school to engage the youth in school and learning; and availability of supplemental resources in the home, school, and community.

> Q. Was there an intervention that all Check & Connect students received, regardless of their particular level of engagement with school?
>
> Yes, this is referred to as *basic intervention.* Each student was engaged in a conversation on a monthly basis. The conversation covered the student's progress in school, the relationship between school completion and the "check" indicators of engagement, the importance of staying in school, and review of problem-solving steps to resolve conflict and cope with life's challenges.

> Q. How much intervention did a student receive?
>
> Student levels of engagement were used as a guideline to determine the level of intervention support. Those who were engaged in school received *basic intervention* only. Students who were disengaged received *intensive interventions,* which include *basic* plus individualized interventions.

FIGURE 9.1.   The Monitor's Message

A CARING ADULT BELIEVES SCHOOL IS IMPORTANT,
YOU CAN SUCCEED, YOU CAN DO THE WORK,
ATTEND CLASS, BE ON TIME,
EXPRESS FRUSTRATION CONSTRUCTIVELY,
AND STAY IN SCHOOL—
EDUCATION IS IMPORTANT FOR YOUR FUTURE.

literature—the presence of an adult in the child's life to fuel the motivation and foster the development of life skills needed to overcome obstacles. The monitor's primary goal is to promote regular school participation and to keep education a salient issue for students, parents, and teachers. The role of the monitor can be characterized as a cross between a mentor, an advocate, and a service coordinator. One of the students who participated in the middle school study described the role of the monitor as "the person who stay[ed] on my back about coming to school." Monitors' interactions with students, parents, educators, and others are guided by the check and connect components of the model (see Table 9.1).

Principles underlying the monitors' approach to building relationships—whether with a student, parent, or teacher—include persistence, continuity, and consistency. *Persistence* means there is someone who is not going to give up on the student's educational attainment or allow the student to be distracted from the importance of school. *Continuity* means there is someone who knows the student's educational history, is familiar with the student's family background, and is available throughout the school year, the summer, and into the next year. *Consistency* means each monitor reinforces the same message (see Figure 9.1).

Trust and familiarity are developed over time through persistent efforts. Efforts include regularly checking on student attendance and academic performance, providing ongoing feedback about student progress, modeling the use of problem-solving skills, frequently communicating with families about both good and bad news, and being available to the youth to listen to personal concerns. We found that students and families were more willing to extend their trust to monitors because the monitors were independent of the schools and social services system—institutions in which these families typically had little confidence.

The size of a monitor's caseload is based on the number of hours hired to work per week multiplied by 1.25 students. Thus a monitor working 30 hours per week carries a maximum caseload of 37 students. During our middle school study, the length of time the same monitor worked with his or her caseload of students ranged from 1 to 3 years. Ideally, the continuity of staff should continue across several years (at least 2 years). This continuity allows the monitor to be a historical resource for teachers and a familiar face to parents. When it is not possible to maintain the same monitor over time, the *message* to the student from a caring adult stays the same (see Figure 9.1).

The position is year-round, as interventions are continued through the summer. Essential qualifications for the position include the following skills and attitudes: persistence; belief that all children have abilities; willingness to work closely with families, using a non-blaming approach; advocacy skills, including the ability to negotiate, compromise, and confront conflict; good organizational skills and accurate documentation of intervention efforts; and the ability to work well independently in a variety of settings. Monitors worked as employees of the University for the middle school study. The individuals who staffed these positions typically held bachelor's degrees in human services-related fields and had at least 1 to 2 years' experience (paid and volunteer) working with youth and/or families. Graduate students in licensure programs for school psychology and special education also staffed the positions.

A special education coordinator with the school district, who was affiliated with the project, provided weekly case consultation and ongoing supervision to the monitors. This supervisor provided the essential link to the schools, hooking monitors up to critical school and community resources, providing vital expertise regarding appropriate intervention and procedures, and lending legitimacy to the program among school staff.

Checking

The check component is designed to facilitate the continuous assessment of student levels of engagement with school and to guide intervention response. Levels of engagement are measured according to several indicators that are alterable, or within the power of educators and parents to change. The alterable indicators include attendance (skipping classes, absenteeism), social/behavior performance (out-of-school suspension, other disciplinary consequences such as behavior referrals, detention, in-school suspension), and academic performance (course failures). Levels of engagement are systematically monitored and documented (daily to at least weekly) using a monitoring sheet. A section of Anthony's sheet from eighth grade showed that he was at risk for absences and out-of-school suspensions (see Figure 9.2).

FIGURE 9.2. Monitoring Sheet

Check & Connect Monitoring Sheet

Student: __Anthony__ ID: __123456__

School Year: 1992-93 Start Date: __11-2-1992__

Monitor: __David__ Grade: 7 DOB: __10-2-1978__

SCHOOL	Sept	Oct	Nov	Dec	Jan	Feb	March
Name	*Jefferson*	*Jefferson*	*Jefferson*	*Jefferson*	*Jefferson*	*Jefferson*	*Jefferson*
Setting	*traditional*	*traditional*	*traditional*	*traditional*	*halftime spec ed*	*halftime spec ed*	*halftime spec ed*

CHECK	Sept	Oct	Nov	Dec	Jan	Feb	March
Tardy	0	0	0	0	0	0	0
Skip	0	4	0	0	1	0	0
Absent	2	5	6	2	1	1	2
Suspension	1	2	3	0	0	1	0
Other Beh	*no*	*yes*	*no*	*no*	*no*	*no*	*no*
Fs/ Total # Classes				1st period 2 / 6		2nd period 1 / 6	
Credits (total number to date)				*not applicable*		*not applicable*	

CONNECT	Sept	Oct	Nov	Dec	Jan	Feb	March
Student	1 2 3 4 / 5 6 7 8 9 10 11 / 12 13 14 15 16 17 18 / 19 20 21 22 23 24 25 / 26 27 28 29 30	31 / 1 2 / 3 4 5 6 7 8 9 / 10 11 12 13 14 15 16 / 17 18 19 20 21 22 23 / 24 25 26 27 28 29 30	1 2 3 4 5 6 / 7 8 9 10 11 12 13 / 14 15 16 17 18 19 20 / 21 22 23 24 25 26 27 / 28 29 30	1 2 3 4 / 5 6 7 8 9 10 11 / 12 13 14 15 16 17 18 / 19 20 21 22 23 24 25 / 26 27 28 29 30 31	30 31 / 1 / 2 3 4 5 6 7 8 / 9 10 11 12 13 14 15 / 16 17 18 19 20 21 22 / 23 24 25 26 27 28 29	1 2 3 4 5 / 6 7 8 9 10 11 12 / 13 14 15 16 17 18 19 / 20 21 22 23 24 25 26 / 27 28 29	1 2 3 4 / 5 6 7 8 9 10 11 / 12 13 14 15 16 17 18 / 19 20 21 22 23 24 25 / 26 27 28 29 30 31
Family	1 2 3 4 / 5 6 7 8 9 10 11 / 12 13 14 15 16 17 18 / 19 20 21 22 23 24 25 / 26 27 28 29 30	31 / 1 2 / 3 4 5 6 7 8 9 / 10 11 12 13 14 15 16 / 17 18 19 20 21 22 23 / 24 25 26 27 28 29 30	1 2 3 4 5 6 / 7 8 9 10 11 12 13 / 14 15 16 17 18 19 20 / 21 22 23 24 25 26 27 / 28 29 30	1 2 3 4 5 6 / 5 6 7 8 9 10 11 / 12 13 14 15 16 17 18 / 19 20 21 22 23 24 25 / 26 27 28 29 30 31	30 31 / 1 / 2 3 4 5 6 7 8 / 9 10 11 12 13 14 15 / 16 17 18 19 20 21 22 / 23 24 25 26 27 28 29	1 2 3 4 5 / 6 7 8 9 10 11 12 / 13 14 15 16 17 18 19 / 20 21 22 23 24 25 26 / 27 28 29	1 2 3 4 / 5 6 7 8 9 10 11 / 12 13 14 15 16 17 18 / 19 20 21 22 23 24 25 / 26 27 28 29 30 31
School Staff	1 2 3 4 / 5 6 7 8 9 10 11 / 12 13 14 15 16 17 18 / 19 20 21 22 23 24 25 / 26 27 28 29 30	31 / 1 2 / 3 4 5 6 7 8 9 / 10 11 12 13 14 15 16 / 17 18 19 20 21 22 23 / 24 25 26 27 28 29 30	1 2 3 4 5 6 / 7 8 9 10 11 12 13 / 14 15 16 17 18 19 20 / 21 22 23 24 25 26 27 / 28 29 30	1 2 3 4 / 5 6 7 8 9 10 11 / 12 13 14 15 16 17 18 / 19 20 21 22 23 24 25 / 26 27 28 29 30 31	30 31 / 1 / 2 3 4 5 6 7 8 / 9 10 11 12 13 14 15 / 16 17 18 19 20 21 22 / 23 24 25 26 27 28 29	1 2 3 4 5 / 6 7 8 9 10 11 12 / 13 14 15 16 17 18 19 / 20 21 22 23 24 25 26 / 27 28 29	1 2 3 4 / 5 6 7 8 9 10 11 / 12 13 14 15 16 17 18 / 19 20 21 22 23 24 25 / 26 27 28 29 30 31
Social Worker	1 2 3 4 / 5 6 7 8 9 10 11 / 12 13 14 15 16 17 18 / 19 20 21 22 23 24 25 / 26 27 28 29 30	31 / 1 2 / 3 4 5 6 7 8 9 / 10 11 12 13 14 15 16 / 17 18 19 20 21 22 23 / 24 25 26 27 28 29 30	1 2 3 4 5 6 / 7 8 9 10 11 12 13 / 14 15 16 17 18 19 20 / 21 22 23 24 25 26 27 / 28 29 30	1 2 3 4 / 5 6 7 8 9 10 11 / 12 13 14 15 16 17 18 / 19 20 21 22 23 24 25 / 26 27 28 29 30 31	30 31 / 1 / 2 3 4 5 6 7 8 / 9 10 11 12 13 14 15 / 16 17 18 19 20 21 22 / 23 24 25 26 27 28 29	1 2 3 4 5 / 6 7 8 9 10 11 12 / 13 14 15 16 17 18 19 / 20 21 22 23 24 25 26 / 27 28 29	1 2 3 4 / 5 6 7 8 9 10 11 / 12 13 14 15 16 17 18 / 19 20 21 22 23 24 25 / 26 27 28 29 30 31
Probation Officer	1 2 3 4 / 5 6 7 8 9 10 11 / 12 13 14 15 16 17 18 / 19 20 21 22 23 24 25 / 26 27 28 29 30	31 / 1 2 / 3 4 5 6 7 8 9 / 10 11 12 13 14 15 16 / 17 18 19 20 21 22 23 / 24 25 26 27 28 29 30	1 2 3 4 5 6 / 7 8 9 10 11 12 13 / 14 15 16 17 18 19 20 / 21 22 23 24 25 26 27 / 28 29 30	1 2 3 4 / 5 6 7 8 9 10 11 / 12 13 14 15 16 17 18 / 19 20 21 22 23 24 25 / 26 27 28 29 30 31	30 31 / 1 / 2 3 4 5 6 7 8 / 9 10 11 12 13 14 15 / 16 17 18 19 20 21 22 / 23 24 25 26 27 28 29	1 2 3 4 5 / 6 7 8 9 10 11 12 / 13 14 15 16 17 18 19 / 20 21 22 23 24 25 26 / 27 28 29	1 2 3 4 / 5 6 7 8 9 10 11 / 12 13 14 15 16 17 18 / 19 20 21 22 23 24 25 / 26 27 28 29 30 31
Other	1 2 3 4 / 5 6 7 8 9 10 11 / 12 13 14 15 16 17 18 / 19 20 21 22 23 24 25 / 26 27 28 29 30	31 / 1 2 / 3 4 5 6 7 8 9 / 10 11 12 13 14 15 16 / 17 18 19 20 21 22 23 / 24 25 26 27 28 29 30	1 2 3 4 5 6 / 7 8 9 10 11 12 13 / 14 15 16 17 18 19 20 / 21 22 23 24 25 26 27 / 28 29 30	1 2 3 4 / 5 6 7 8 9 10 11 / 12 13 14 15 16 17 18 / 19 20 21 22 23 24 25 / 26 27 28 29 30 31	30 31 / 1 / 2 3 4 5 6 7 8 / 9 10 11 12 13 14 15 / 16 17 18 19 20 21 22 / 23 24 25 26 27 28 29	1 2 3 4 5 / 6 7 8 9 10 11 12 / 13 14 15 16 17 18 19 / 20 21 22 23 24 25 26 / 27 28 29	1 2 3 4 / 5 6 7 8 9 10 11 / 12 13 14 15 16 17 18 / 19 20 21 22 23 24 25 / 26 27 28 29 30 31
Basic	*na*	*na*	X	X	X	X	X
Intensive	*na*	*na*	X	X	X	X	X

The monitors obtained the attendance information and the other indicators of participation primarily from school records (an online district database). Information not available online was obtained from several sources, including attendance clerks, teachers, and assistant principals. These individuals were also consulted to verify contradictory information, as was the student or parent(s).

Connecting

Connecting involved providing timely support to students and families to increase or maintain participation in school. Procedures were used for students and parents.

Student-Connect Procedures. Two levels of student-focused interventions were developed to maximize the use of finite resources: *basic intervention,* which was the same for all students and delivered at least one time per month, and *intensive interventions,* which were more frequent and individualized. All students received basic interventions (even if receiving intensive interventions), whereas indicators of school engagement were used to guide who received the delivery of more intensive interventions. Individual needs of the student and family dictate what specific intervention strategy was used. The two levels of intervention help the monitors to manage their time and resources more efficiently and responsively.

As a sustained preventive measure, basic intervention is administered to all targeted students. Basic intervention uses minimal resources in an effort to keep education a salient issue, especially after a working relationship has been established among the monitor, student, parents, and school staff. It begins with introductions and sharing general information about the monitor's role and the Check & Connect model with the student and his or her family. The substance of basic intervention is a monthly conversation with each student. The conversation covers the student's progress in school, the relationship between school completion and the "check" indicators of engagement, the importance of staying in school, and review of problem-solving steps used to resolve conflict and cope with life's challenges. For problem solving, students are guided through real and/or hypothetical problems using a five-step cognitive-behavioral problem-solving strategy: (a) "Stop. Think about the problem." (b) "What are the choices?" (c) "Choose one." (d) "Do it." and (e) "How did it work?" Monthly conversations were a systematic opportunity for monitors to share information and reinforce skills that students needed to promote their own connection with school actively.

> Anthony's monitor found it most effective to connect with him over lunch or during study hall. They spent a good deal of conversation and time on the first step of the problem-solving strategy. Stopping, before acting, was a difficult skill for Anthony to master.

Intensive interventions are administered for students showing high risk in relation to any of the early warning signs of withdrawal. At least three quarters of the students received intensive intervention at any given time during the study. These interventions are tailored to the individual needs of the student and family, but can be characterized as falling into one of three broad types: problem solving, academic support, and recreation and community service exploration. Existing support services were used as much as possible to promote the student's community participation and to minimize service duplication.

Problem solving is based on a five-step cognitive-behavioral approach used to teach students how to resolve conflicts constructively and to cope with the daily challenges of life. Such interventions in the middle school project included immediate problem-solving sessions with students exhibiting high-risk behaviors. Thus the five-step plan was used for a real-life situation. Individualized behavioral contracts were used, in which rewards varied from simple praise, to school supplies, to gift certificates at local fast food restaurants, to shared time together out of school. The monitors and special education case managers worked closely with assistant principals so that due process rights of students with emotional and behavioral disabilities were considered as part of the disciplinary consequences. Commercially available social skills curriculum materials (e.g., *Tough Kids, Skill-streaming*) were also used to supplement skill acquisition (see Chapter 4 for details on these and other social skills curricula).

> While checking in on Anthony, his monitor heard that he had been suspended from school for 10 days on a weapons violation. Upon further investigation, the monitor learned that Anthony had been shooting paper clips with a rubber band in history class. The teacher argued that the items were being used like a slingshot and could have seriously injured someone's eyes. The monitor consulted the teacher and talked with the assistant principal to shorten the length of the suspension. He argued that Anthony already missed too much school, that a weapons violation was probably not the most accurate categorization of the offense, and that the incident could be related to his disability. The monitor offered to facilitate a conversation between the student, history teacher, special education case manager, and parent.

Academic support included individualized academic contracts, similar to behavioral contracts. Some students were connected with a tutor or mentor to help with assignments, to provide additional math or reading practice, to provide academic motivational support, and/or to reinforce the importance of staying in school. Extra steps were taken to increase the likelihood that the student actually connected with the tutor or mentor, which included helping the student or parent fill out program registration forms, personally introducing the tutor to the student, or accompanying the student to the first few sessions.

Recreation and community service exploration involved hooking students up with school-based activities and programs, as well as relevant community-based programs, throughout the school year or over the summer. Project resources were focused on helping students access existing programs, rather than developing new activities or duplicating services. Monitors made home visits to get students' permission forms signed, helped students fill out forms to waive participation fees, explained program options and brought students to the first meeting, invited program coordinators of recreational and life skills programs in the community to attend project parent meetings to share information with parents, co-staffed some of the after-school activities, and helped coordinate transportation.

Parent-Connect Procedures. While this procedure is described separately, in practice it is intertwined with student outreach efforts. Family members are brought into the process as resources and partners. A non-blaming approach is used to redirect the tendency to find blame and to push efforts toward generating a new action plan and moving forward. Family members are contacted either by phone or home visit, as monitors seek to share and exchange information about their child's educational progress. Parent support for learning is promoted individually, as part of intensive interventions, as well as through opportunities offered to all targeted parents regardless of their child's level of engagement with school.

Individual interventions focus on minimizing education-related barriers identified by the family (e.g., communication between caregivers and school staff) or on facilitating access to resources that directly or indirectly promote the student's connection with school (e.g., helping the parent enroll younger children in Head Start so the middle school youth was not kept home to baby-sit). Another common intensive intervention during the middle school project focused on helping caregivers, typically mothers, exchange ideas about alternative discipline strategies and how to set boundaries for their adolescents.

In addition to individualized outreach, two additional opportunities were offered to all of the participating middle school parents at the suggestion of our consumer advisory committee. One opportunity was paid part-time positions at the middle schools, referred to as "parent workers." These positions offered minimum wage and were considered a precursor to the paraprofessional position with the district. The goal of the parent worker was to help students—those in the program as well as others—stay engaged and on task with classroom instruction. A parent worker might rouse a sleepy student and spend several minutes by the youth, while the teacher was allowed to continue on with the lesson. The specific job description varied as a function of the needs of the teacher(s) with whom the parent worker partnered. Students often called the parent worker "Mom." Of the 40 parent workers employed over a 3-year period, most were dependent on welfare and few had previously maintained steady employment. The program coordinator spent a good deal of time helping parents learn job skills or completing forms to prevent loss of their welfare eligibility.

Another feature of Check & Connect outreach to families is regular parent meetings. During the middle school project, these meetings were held monthly, in the evenings, in neutral community settings. Students and their teachers and resource staff were invited. The agenda was developed with the participating families, and always linked as directly as possible to students' educational progress. The topics of the meetings often focused on issues of adolescent development and strategies for promoting the use of constructive problem-solving skills for both the parents and the students. Parents were offered assistance with transportation and day care, meals were served, and a nominal stipend was offered to parents and teachers for their consultation and participation.

> Anthony's mom attended most meetings, missing a few during periods when they were moving from one residence to another. She was at a loss as to how she could prevent him from staying out past curfew. Physical intimidation was no longer effective, now that Anthony outsized her by one foot and 50 pounds.

What Do We Know About the Effectiveness of Check & Connect?

The effectiveness of Check & Connect for the middle school study was evaluated using a rigorous experimental design. The evaluation focused on critical outcomes for urban students with learning and emotional/behavioral disabilities who were placed at high risk for dropping out of school. All seventh graders receiving special education services for a learning or emotional and behavioral disability from three middle schools were targeted for the study. Students were assigned to one of three groups: a contrast group that received no Check & Connect services, a treatment group that received Check & Connect services in Grades 7 and 8, or another treatment group that received Check & Connect through Grade 9. Thus the study included the evaluation of benefits derived from receiving an additional year of Check & Connect—the year during which the student moved from a middle school environment to a high school environment.

The sampling procedure was designed to account for potential differences across several key variables including ethnicity, sex, socioeconomic status, disability, age, and initial school of attendance. At the end of eighth grade, an additional variable was examined to control for potential differences across the two treatment groups in terms of student levels of engagement with school, referred to as a *profile rating*. The profile rating measures engagement using a 4-point composite score based on absenteeism, behavior incidents, and course failures. Low-profile students had two or fewer absences per month, no significant behavior problems, and were passing all courses, whereas high-profile students had more than four absences per month, repeated suspensions or behavior referrals, and more than three Ds or Fs for grades.

Strong evidence of effectiveness was obtained for the middle school study, which demonstrated that students with emotional and behavioral disorders and learning disabilities could be engaged in school. However, to increase relevancy of the results previously published, data from the middle school study were reanalyzed for this chapter excluding 44 students receiving special education services for a severe learning disability with no identified emotional or behavioral needs. The final samples for this chapter include 39 students who received Check & Connect through Grade 8, another 36 students who received Check & Connect through Grade 9 (the transition to high school), and 56 students in the control group. The data specifically related to the construct of *participation in school* were reanalyzed. Paricipation in school was one of six critical constructs examined in the middle school study. The Check & Connect monitoring sheet was a primary source of participation information and included outcome data on three participation indicators.

Evidence of program effectiveness was found for all three indicators of participation, beginning with *enrollment status* at the end of ninth grade. Enrolled in school refers to a student enrolled in a formal education program such as a traditional school or alternative program. Students were considered dropouts if they were no longer attending school at the end of the year (absent 15 or more consecutive days, without an excuse). The youth who received Check & Connect from Grades 7 through 9 were more likely to be enrolled at the end of the ninth grade (92%) compared to similar students in Check & Connect through eighth grade as well as similar youth in the contrast group (about three quarters for both).

The second indicator of participation is the rate of *persistence*. This second approach was investigated because the standard dropout rate formulas do not differentiate between students who consistently stay in school and those who drop in and out of school. Specifically, "persisters" were students who did not drop out during ninth grade (i.e., absent for 15 or more consecutive days without an excuse). "Interrupters" were the youth who dropped out at least once during ninth grade, regardless of their enrollment status at the end of the year. Persistence rates similarly indicated the effectiveness of Check & Connect. The youth who received the Check & Connect intervention from Grades 7 through 9 were more likely to persist in school (83%) compared to similar students in Check & Connect through eighth grade (67%), as well as similar youth in the contrast group (61%).

The third indicator of participation is the rate of *reentry*. This measure reflects the extent to which youth who stop going to school are willing to give formal schooling another try. The reentry rate includes all the students involved in the middle school study who interrupted their schooling at least once during a 3-year period beginning in Grade 7. About 67% of the youth in the treatment groups returned to and remained in school within the same year compared to 45% of similar students in the contrast group who received no Check & Connect services.

> In the fall following ninth grade, Anthony was living with his sister in their grandmother's hometown about 4 hours outside of the city. Anthony's mom stayed in touch with him, although she was living in a homeless shelter at the time. His monitor continued to call him every couple of months. Anthony reported that he was doing well, going to school, and earning credits toward graduation.

The Check & Connect model is presently being replicated in urban and suburban settings, from kindergarten through twelfth grade, and targeting students with and without disabilities. Preliminary effectiveness data are promising, yielding impact similar to the original study.

What Does Check & Connect Cost?

The costs of allowing youth with emotional and behavioral challenges to drop out of school far exceed the resources required to keep these youth engaged in school and on track to graduate with the skills and confidence needed to become contributing members of society. The primary expense category for the Check & Connect middle school study was personnel. The monitor, who delivered intervention and collected program evaluation data, earned a salary and benefits similar to a paraprofessional's. Recall that a monitor working 40 hours per week served between 40 and 50 students.

A program coordinator was also required, at a minimum of 2 days per week. This person has typically been a special education coordinator or school psychologist. Operational costs were the next significant line item, expenses associated mostly with mileage reimbursement for the monitors and program coordinator (making home visits, attending community meetings, travel between schools) and communication support (voicemail, pager). Another operational cost was associated with program evaluation, including data entry, analysis, and production of technical reports. The final budget category included staff development materials, student and parent outreach rewards of about $20 per student annually, photocopies, and consumable office supplies. The estimated program costs for a current replication study targeting elementary students with and without disabilities, followed through middle/junior high school, is about $1,100 per student annually.

The costs to the individual are as devastating as the costs to society. Youth who do not complete high school are more likely to experience unemployment, underemployment, incarceration, and long-term dependency on social services. Eight out of every 10 workers in the labor force have completed high school, compared to fewer than 5 out of 10 just 40 years ago. Students with serious emotional disturbance who drop out of school are three to five times more likely than graduates to be arrested just a few years after leaving school. Of the youth who are employed, average annual earnings for high school graduates a few years out is approximately $6,415 more per year than for high school dropouts.

Costs to society of students who drop out of school are increasing. Four out of five federal prisoners have not completed high school, at an annual cost of approximately $51,000 per person for incarceration (U. S. Select Committee, 1992). The annual cost of providing for dropouts and their families was estimated at $76 billion a year more than 10 years ago; presently more than $800 annually per taxpayer (Joint Economic Committee, 1991). In the context of our middle school study, the estimated loss of per pupil revenues (PPR) for students in the contrast group was $63,000 annually (25% dropped out, where $n = 14$ students $\times$ $4,500 PPR). In comparison, loss of per pupil revenues for students who participated in Check & Connect through ninth grade was about $13,500 (8% dropped out, where $n = 3$ students $\times$ $4,500 PPR). Thus the program could potentially have retained $49,500 annually in per-pupil revenues for the district. While high school completion does not guarantee a positive and productive niche in life, remaining in school through graduation does reduce the likelihood that a youth will engage in destructive activities commonly associated with negative life outcomes.

Implementation Issues and Considerations for Adopting the Practice

During the past 10 years, the Check & Connect model has been refined and field-tested in a dozen school districts, with students in elementary, middle, and high school. Target students have included youth with and without disabilities. With each effort to replicate the model, several implementation factors have remained constant. It has been our experience that adhering to these factors has helped to preserve the integrity of the model and to maximize the potential impact of the program.

First, Check & Connect is intended to be a *long-term intervention.* Youth targeted for the program are referred for their history of negative school experiences, a history that is not likely to be resolved in a few weeks. The model is based on the assumption that a minimum of a 2-year commitment will be made to the students and families, as well as to the school staff.

Second, the willingness of district and building leaders to *address systemic issues* as they impact individual learners with emotional and behavioral disabilities is critical, as is their support of specific program needs. Particular policies and practices that influence student levels of engagement with school include schoolwide discipline practices (especially out-of-school suspensions and administrative transfers), social promotion/grade retention policies, and opportunities for students with disabilities to access engaging instruction through the general education curriculum. Supportive assistant principals, for example, have considered alternatives to out-of-school suspension or at least reduced the number of days students are suspended and subsequently excluded from instruction. Supportive principals have provided space to Check & Connect staff, allocated time for program updates at staff meetings, and given recognition to the attendance clerks or other school staff for their contributions to the program.

Third, monitors are coached to earn the *trust* of school staff, with emphasis on reliability, follow-through, and timely communication. They begin by introducing the program and themselves through informal conversations with school staff, informational memos, and brief presentations at various staff meetings. Monitors and the program supervisor typically meet individually with each of the attendance clerks and other building staff responsible for maintaining the student data to provide an explanation of the program as well as its importance. Teachers and resource staff are consulted on past efforts to increase students' engagement as well as future attempts to connect students with school.

Fourth, Check & Connect monitors are expected to *follow their caseload* of students and families from school to school, program to program. While student referrals from a specific building or cluster of schools are assigned to a designated monitor, the monitor does not discontinue services if the youth moves to another school in the service area. Less than 10% of cases are transferred between monitors in order to reduce the number of buildings to which a monitor must travel. Flexibility is also built into the defined workday, because home visits and evening and weekend hours are needed to reach out effectively to many youth and families. Furthermore, new staff members are asked to honor a minimum commitment of 2 years to the program. Relationship building and trust are essential tools for the monitor and both take time to develop.

Fifth, professional development is another critical factor that can help to ensure the model is being implemented as intended. The learning curve for the monitoring position is steep. Timely technical assistance from the program supervisor is essential, as is routine professional development. The program supervisor facilitates weekly to semimonthly staff meetings. The meetings are used to review appropriate procedures and practices, exchange information about useful resources, provide case consultation, and clarify roles in relation to other professionals and develop strategies for communicating this information back to other professionals and families. Time is made available for monitors to attend community and district workshops on topics ranging from home-school collaboration, to mandated reporting, to problem-solving and conflict resolution.

Sixth, the primary referral criterion is attendance (absenteeism, tardiness to school, or skipping classes) at a rate of 15% or more of the school year. In a sense, the model is tailored for students whose sporadic physical presence in school and in the classroom is a concern. However, academic, social, and behavioral performances are considered at referral for each student as well as any sibling or parent history of school problems. Final referrals are decided together by the school staff and Check & Connect personnel.

Seventh, the orientation to parent outreach has mirrored dimensions that are the foundation of family-centered practice. Monitors have a family-centered orientation, directing education-related services to the family, not just the child. Interactions are characterized by positiveness (belief in parents' abilities) and a sensitivity to anticipate how parents might feel given a variety of circumstances. Monitors must be responsive, listening and paying attention to parents' needs in relation to their child's educational progress. Relationships are reciprocal in nature and monitors maintain a level of friendliness conveying support, encouragement, and genuine care for the youth. Finally, monitors act as a resource for families, facilitating access to information and services.

Parents are first introduced to the program through personal contact, by telephone or a home visit. The monitor or a school staff member whose relationship with the family will increase the likelihood of their participation makes the visit. Written information about Check & Connect is also forwarded. Permission is most effectively obtained using a multi-method, multi-attempt approach including home visits, phone calls, and a mailing with a self-addressed, stamped envelope. When no one is home or the legal guardian is not available, handwritten notes are left behind to stress the personal nature of the invitation. Voice mail messages are also left for the same purpose. This strategy has resulted in a refusal rate of less than 10% among parents of urban middle school students with emotional and behavioral challenges. These efforts to obtain parent permission and/or participation are viewed as the first steps of Check & Connect intervention.

Some parents talk about participation in the program with their child before signing permission. Sometimes, the youth are present when the monitor explains the program to the parent. For others, the students' first introduction to the program comes from the monitor at school. For those students who are not found in school, monitors seek out the youth either at home or out-and-about in the youth's neighborhood. The student introduction begins with a face-to-face conversation, during which the monitor describes his or her role and the purpose of the program.

The final implementation issue for consideration is evaluation. The model is uniquely designed to be a data-based practice. The information routinely collected to guide intervention can also be used for program evaluation. It is no coincidence that the predictors of school completion are the same variables the monitors gather from school records and personnel. Program staff members need time to collect and maintain up-to-date records. When resources for a comparison group are not available, program impact has been measured as a function of change over baseline—performance during the last 4 months in the program compared to performance the year and/or months prior to referral. Absences and the other indicators of engagement are reported as a percentage of time; for example, number of days absent divided by number of days enrolled. Substantial changes in levels of engagement are not anticipated until students have participated in the program for at least 2 years (see Chapter 10 for more information on program evaluation).

Perspective on Keeping
Students Coming to School

This model, designed to promote students' connection with school, has been described by its three primary components: the monitor, the check procedures, and the connect procedures. The components draw upon research in resiliency and the protective influence of a caring adult (the monitor) to assist youth placed at high risk for school failure. Furthermore, the components of the model focus on the predictors of school completion that educators and family members have an ability to change (school engagement and the check procedures). The members of the community advisory committee continually raised the issue of balancing feasibility with comprehensiveness, which evolved into an efficient and timely link between student's engagement and intervention (the connect procedures).

We hypothesize that the most unique feature of the Check & Connect model is that outreach is provided by someone who is familiar to the student and family and who is trusted to act on behalf of the youth. The specific interventions used by the monitor may be the same strategies tried by others in the past. However, monitors are more likely to achieve follow-through because of their established relationship with all the key constituents and long-term commitment to the effort. When students were asked how they knew they could trust their monitor, one student replied, "because he showed up at my doorstep over the summer." Another student commented, "I knew I could really trust this person when I started classes at my new school, and there she was." The ongoing relationship allows the monitor continually to demonstrate and model a persistent commitment to formal education to both the student and the parents.

The check component of the model is intended to keep intervention efforts focused on those predictors of school completion over which educators and families have some control (participation in school, identification with school, academic progress). Because a large percentage of students with emotional and behavioral disabilities also experience a number of non-school-related stress factors, educators can easily become overwhelmed by the challenges intertwined with helping a student succeed. Nonschool factors also strongly associated with dropping out—such as poverty, substance abuse by the student or family members, frequent crises, or physical and mental health challenges—are addressed by the monitor to the extent they impede a student's engagement with school. For example, a student may struggle to get to school on time because his parent is abusing substances, staying up all night and sleeping in until midday. A monitor's role is first to listen to and acknowledge students' personal concerns. In addition to following mandated reporting requirements, a monitor might first provide the student with a personal alarm clock, call in the mornings, and talk with the parent about the importance of getting the youth to bed on time.

The two levels of connect intervention, basic and intensive, were developed to maximize the use of finite resources. Furthermore, we found that student levels of engagement changed from month to month, sometimes requiring only a few moments of the monitor's time and at other periods requiring several days of concentrated attention. Using data to create a strong assessment-intervention link, a minimum set of responses to be provided to all students was defined and tested. This all gave monitors the ability to provide timely, individualized support to students demonstrating low levels of engagement with school.

REFERENCES

Bronfenbrenner, U. (1979). *The ecology of human development: Experiments by nature and design.* Cambridge, MA: Harvard University Press.

Bronfenbrenner, U. (1986, February). Alienation and the four worlds of childhood. *Phi Delta Kappan,* pp. 430-436.

Coleman, J. (1987, August-September). Family ties and schools. *Educational Researcher,* pp. 32-38.

Joint Economic Committee. (1991, August). *Doing drugs and dropping out: A report prepared for the use of the subcommittee on economic growth, trade, and taxes of the joint economic committee.* Washington, DC: Government Printing Office.

U.S. Select Committee. (1992, March). *On the edge of the American dream: A social and economic profile in 1992.* Select Committee on Narcotics Abuse and Control. Washington, DC: Government Printing Office.

RESOURCES

Check & Connect Web [online]. Available: http://ici.umn.edu/checkandconnect.

Christenson, S. L., & Conoley, J. C. (Eds). (1992). *Home-school collaboration: Enhancing children's academic and social competence.* Silver Spring, MD: National Association of School Psychologists.

Coley, R. J. (1995). *Dreams deferred: High school dropout rates in the United States.* Princeton, NJ: Policy Information Center, Educational Testing Service.

Delgado-Gaitan, C. (1991). Involving parents in the schools: A process of empowerment. *American Journal of Education, 100*(1), 20-46.

Finn, J. D. (1989). Withdrawing from school. *Review of Educational Research, 59*(2), 117-124.

Finn, J. D. (1993). *School engagement and students at risk* (U.S. Department of Education, National Center for Educational Statistics). Buffalo, NY: State University.

Masten, A. S., Best, K. M., & Garmezy, N. (1990). Resilience and development: Contributions from the study of children who overcome adversity. *Development & Psychopathology, 2*(4), 425-444.

McWilliam, R. A., Tocci, L., & Harbin, G. L. (1998). Family centered services: Service providers' discourse and behavior. *Topics in Early Childhood Special Education, 18,* 206-221.

Sinclair, M. F., Christenson, S. L., Hurley, C., & Evelo, D. (1998). Dropout prevention for high-risk youth with disabilities: Efficacy of a sustained school engagement procedure. *Exceptional Children, 65*(1), 7-21.

Sinclair, M. F., Thurlow, M. L., Christenson, S. L., & Evelo, D. (1995). Check & Connect partnership for school success: Dropout prevention and intervention project targeting middle school youth with learning disabilities and emotional/behavioral disorders at risk for dropping out of school. In H. Thornton (Ed.), *Staying in school: A technical report of three dropout prevention projects for middle school students with learning and emotional disabilities.* Minneapolis: University of Minnesota, College of Education and Human Development, Institute on Community Integration.

Statistical Abstracts of the United States. (1986). Washington, DC: U.S. Bureau of the Census.

Vygotsky, L. S. (1962). *Thought and language.* Cambridge: MIT Press.

Wagner, M. (1991, September). *Dropouts with disabilities: What do we know? What can we do?* A report from the national longitudinal transition study of special education students. Washington, DC: U.S. Department of Education, Office of Special Education Programs.

Measuring the Success of Prevention Programs 10

Stephanie H. McConaughy
Peter E. Leone

*In contrast to formal published missions, the actual
missions in most public schools are based on what is
most publicly measured and most widely recognized.
It is the actual mission that determines teachers' priorities
and the processes of learning and teaching associated
with their classrooms. There seems to be little doubt that
in the traditional American public school, curriculum
coverage and high scores on tests constitute the actual
mission of public education.*
> —Audette and colleagues,
> Chapter 3 in this volume

Prevention programs operate on the premise that early responses to learning, behavioral, and emotional problems can reduce children's risk for developing more severe problems that require intensive interventions like special education. Because they are major arenas for social interactions among children, schools provide ideal settings for programs to prevent social and emotional problems. Schools have the advantages of access to large numbers of children simultaneously and possibilities for meshing prevention strategies with daily routines and educational curricula. In school settings, universal prevention programs (also termed "primary prevention") involve all children in a particular setting, such as a classroom or the entire school building. Focused prevention efforts (termed "secondary prevention") are targeted at particular individuals considered to be at risk for more serious future problems. Focused prevention programs might also be targeted at particular schools considered to be at risk, rather than individual students. However, until prevention programs are "publicly measured" and "widely recognized," they will not become part of the *actual* mission of any schools.

In this chapter, we discuss procedures for measuring the success of prevention programs, including universal and focused efforts. To provide concrete illustrations and practical recommendations for administrators and evaluators, we draw from the various projects described in other chapters for examples of instruments and evaluation procedures. The first section focuses on assessment procedures for identifying at-risk status, including school demographic factors, student demographic factors, and student problem behaviors. Next, we discuss procedures for measuring outcomes of prevention programs. In doing so, we have included detailed lists of descriptive measures and published instruments that administrators and evaluators can consider for use in their own programs. In the third section, we describe different types of evaluation designs, including single-case and group designs. We also address key measurement issues and alert administrators and evaluators to common hazards to avoid in program evaluations. In the final section, we discuss how program evaluators might disseminate their results most effectively to key stakeholders in order to ensure sustainability of prevention programs.

Identifying Participants
for Prevention Programs

The first step in designing school-based prevention strategies is to determine which students will be the participants in the program. As indicated earlier, universal prevention efforts are targeted on all students in a particular setting, such as a school or classroom. For example, a universal prevention program, such as social skills instruction, might be introduced as a standard part of the curriculum for all elementary students in a school or district. Or the social skills program might be implemented for all students in particular classrooms or particular schools considered to be at risk because of the demographics of the student population. Focused prevention efforts, in contrast, are targeted at individual students considered to be at risk for future problems. In focused prevention programs, only the students considered at risk in a classroom or school would participate in the program. To select participants for prevention programs, administrators can rely on descriptive procedures or published screening procedures.

Descriptive Identification Procedures

Descriptive identification procedures can focus on student or family demographic factors or specific types of student behavior that may lead to referral for services. Table 10.1 lists examples of the many descriptive factors that were considered in identifying recipients of the prevention projects described in preceding chapters. The first column lists specific factors or problems that were examined, while the second column lists measurement procedures. The third and fourth columns identify the projects that used the various identification procedures and the chapter where the projects are discussed in detail.

Administrators for projects described in this book considered demographic factors when deciding whether to implement a universal or focused prevention program in their schools. For example, schools participating in the Unified Discipline project had high rates of special education placement in conjunction with low rates of school achievement. Some schools were also located in high-crime neighborhoods. The Linkages to Learning and Check & Connect projects were implemented in schools with high rates of student mobility or absenteeism. The Juniper Gardens Children's Project was implemented in schools where large percentages of students were behind academically. The ABC project was implemented in rural or semirural schools where access to special services was limited.

Sophisticated measurement procedures are usually not necessary for identifying schoolwide demographic factors. Instead, measurement can simply involve visual inspection of office or district records, standardized test scores and grades, or publicly available information, such as high rates of neighborhood violence or crime reported by police or local newspapers. Student or family demographic factors might also be considered. For example, several projects were implemented in districts or schools with large numbers of low-income families, as indicated by free or reduced price school lunch. Administrators may also choose to adopt prevention programs for students of families living in violent or high-crime neighborhoods or students with high rates of absenteeism or tardiness as done in the Unified Discipline and Check & Connect projects.

Descriptive measures of student problem behaviors provide another data source for deciding where to implement universal prevention programs. The last part of Table 10.1 lists descriptions of student problem behaviors that were reasons for office referrals from teachers in the Unified Discipline project. Classroom teachers completed a project-designed referral form, the Teacher's Assistance Request Form, which listed the academic and social problems shown in the first column of Table 10.1. Teachers rated each student in their class on each problem item, using a 4-point scale: 1 = infrequently (less than once a week), 2 = occasionally (once a week),

(text continues on page 188)

TABLE 10.1 Descriptive Procedures for Identifying Participants for Prevention Programs

What Is Measured	Measurement Procedure	Example Project	Chapter
Schoolwide Demographic Factors			
High rates of special education placement	School office/district records	Unified Discipline	5
Low school achievement	Standardized scores/grades	Unified Discipline	5
		Juniper Gardens	2, 4
Violent/high-crime neighborhood	Police/newspaper reports	Unified Discipline	5
High rates of student mobility/changing schools	School attendance records	Linkages to Learning	7
		Check & Connect	9
Low school engagement (on track toward graduation credits)	School office/district records	Check & Connect	9
Rural or semirural environment	Population/geography	ABC Project	6
Student/Family Demographic Factors			
Low income/poverty (e.g., <$25,000)	Free/reduced school lunch	Juniper Gardens	2, 4
		Unified Discipline	5
		Linkages to Learning	7
		Check & Connect	9
Violent/high-crime neighborhood	Police/newspaper reports	Unified Discipline	5
High absenteeism	School records	Unified Discipline	5
High absenteeism, tardiness, skipping classes, etc.	Monitor's Check Sheet (daily or weekly)	Check & Connect	9

Student Problem Behavior

Academic Referral Problems	Teacher Assistance Request Form	Unified Discipline	5
• Not attending school • Not asking for help • Poor self-esteem • Not completing school work on time • Not completing school work • Not cooperating with other learners	Computerized tracking system		
Social Referral Problems	Teacher Assistance Request Form	Unified Discipline	5
• Misbehaving out of classroom • Interrupting instruction • Voice volume • Tattling • Talking out • Pouting, crying, frequent whining	Computerized tracking system		

3 = frequently (more than once a week), and 4 = constantly (every day). Computer tracking of these data then formed the basis for choosing particular classrooms in which to train teachers in the project interventions. In this project, teachers used the same management procedures for all students in their classrooms and all school personnel supported the same discipline model.

Similar descriptive procedures can be used for focused prevention strategies that do not involve all students in a given setting. Focused prevention requires identification of individual students who are likely to be at risk for academic and/or behavioral or emotional problems. For example, administrators might select individual students with low academic achievement or high rates of academic or social problems. To do this, administrators can develop their own versions of teacher rating forms like the one used in the Unified Discipline program. The rating form could provide a standard procedure for referring individual students to a focused prevention program. "Local norms" could also be established by having teachers complete the rating form on all students in their classroom. The data could be averaged across an entire classroom or school to provide a standard for comparing an individual student to what is typical for the classroom or school. Individual students with higher problem scores than the class or school average could then be invited to participate in a focused prevention program. Computerized tracking programs can help record descriptive data on individual students' problems for identification purposes as well as measuring outcomes, as discussed later.

Published Screening Procedures

The Systematic Screening for Behavior Disorders (SSBD) is a good example of a published screening procedure for identifying at-risk students (Walker & Severson, 1990). The SSBD consists of the three stages outlined in Table 10.2. In Stage 1, a classroom teacher selects two groups of 10 students each whose behavioral characteristics most closely resemble "externalizing" or "internalizing" behaviors. Externalizing includes disruptive or aggressive behavior considered inappropriate by school personnel. Internalizing includes affective or emotional problems, such as withdrawal or fearfulness. The SSBD provides examples and non-examples for each type of behavior. After selecting the 10 students, teachers rank order them according to the severity of their problems. The top three Externalizers and top three Internalizers then move to Stage 2.

In Stage 2, classroom teachers complete three rating scales for each of the three top-ranked Externalizers and Internalizers. The Critical Events Index (CEI) lists 33 problem items (e.g., stealing, tantrums, sad affect) that are rated as present or absent. The Combined Frequency Index (CFI) includes

TABLE 10.2 The Systematic Screening for Behavior Disorders

What Is Measured	Measurement Procedure	Example Projects	Chapter
Stage 1			
Internalizing students	Teacher nominations and rank ordering	ABC Project Juniper Gardens	6 2, 4
Externalizing students	Teacher nominations and rank ordering		
Stage 2			
Critical Events Index	33 items; present/absent; cutoff scores	ABC Project Juniper Gardens	6 2, 4
Combined Frequency Index			
Adaptive behaviors	12 items; 5-point scale		
Maladaptive behaviors	11 items; 5-point scale; cutoff scores		
Stage 3			
Direct Observations		Juniper Gardens	2, 4
Academic engaged time	Two 15-minute classroom observations		
Social engagement	Two 15-minute recess observations		

NOTE: The SSBD (Walker & Severson, 1990) is available from Sopris West, Inc., P.O. Box 1809, Longmont, CO 80502-1809. Phone: (303) 651-2829.

12 adaptive behaviors and 11 maladaptive behaviors that are rated on a 5-point scale. The SSBD provides standard scores and percentiles, as well as average scores, for the CEI and CFI based on large samples of normal students. Students who exceed specific CEI and CFI cutoff scores for the SSBD normative samples then move to Stage 3 for observations in the classroom and at recess. Trained observers conduct two 15-minute observations of the student in each setting. The SSBD manual provides definitions of behaviors to be observed and coding procedures. Scores are obtained from the observations for academic engaged time and social engagement. Students who exceed SSBD age and gender normative criteria on the observation coding system are then considered at risk for school failure due to behavioral or emotional problems.

The SSBD was originally designed to screen students for pre-referral interventions or further assessment for special education or other services. The SSBD has also been used as a screening measure for identifying at-risk students in several focused prevention projects, including the ABC project and Juniper Gardens Children's Project described in other chapters. A particular advantage of the SSBD is its focus on both externalizing and internalizing problems. Students with externalizing problems are frequently referred for evaluation or services, whereas those with internalizing problems run the risk of being under-referred because they are less disruptive in classrooms.

Administrators may choose to modify SSBD procedures or to utilize normative criteria differently, depending on school demographics or the goals of a particular program. For example, the ABC project was carried out in rural or semirural schools with small class sizes. As a result, it was not feasible for teachers to select 10 Externalizers and 10 Internalizers in each class. Therefore, Stage 1 procedures were modified to screen for only five Externalizers and five Internalizers. It was also not feasible to rely on Stage 2 cutoffs on the CEI and CFI due to small class sizes. Still, the SSBD provided a useful first screen, which was later combined with other student information, to select participants and matched controls for evaluating outcomes. In another study, Gresham, MacMillan, and Bocian (1996) also adapted SSBD-CEI cutoffs to fit their purposes. They concluded that even one critical event reported on the CEI provided a good initial screen for identifying students at risk for behavioral and academic problems.

Standardized measures with cut points based on normative samples can provide an empirical or "objective" basis for defining at-risk status for focused prevention programs. The SSBD is a good example of a standardized screening measure with cut points for problems based on normative samples. Several other standardized instruments might also serve as screening measures. Examples are the Teacher's Report Form (TRF) and Child Behavior Checklist (CBCL), described later, in the section on outcome measures. Both the TRF and CBCL provide cut points and percentiles for defining "normal" versus "clinical" ranges for scores on problem scales. For example, scores above the 90th percentile on the TRF or CBCL Total Problems scale are considered to be in the "clinical range," based on scores obtained by large nationally representative samples of children who have not been referred for mental health or special education services.

Defining at-risk status according to cut points on standardized instruments requires deciding whether to maximize "sensitivity" or "specificity" in identification procedures. *Sensitivity* refers to the proportion of "true positives," who, in the case of prevention efforts, are students most likely to develop later problems. Selecting low cut points for problems on screening measures will maximize sensitivity. This reduces chances of missing children most likely to benefit from a prevention program. *Specificity* refers to the proportion of "true negatives," that is, students who most likely will not develop later problems. Selecting high cut points for problems on screening measures will maximize specificity. This reduces chances of including children who do not need the prevention program. When selecting cut points on screening measures like the SSBD, or instruments like the TRF or CBCL, administrators must think carefully about how wide a net they wish to cast in their initial selection process.

Single Versus Multiple Identification Sources

Assessing risk status for focused prevention programs can be done using a single information source or multiple sources. Relying on a single information source has the advantage of simplifying identification procedures. However, using a single source runs the risk of missing some students who might be considered at risk from a different perspective or in a different environment. Conversely, some students considered at risk by one source, such as a classroom teacher, might not be considered at risk by another source, such as a special educator or the student's parents.

School records can easily be used to identify at-risk status according to several of the family or student demographic factors listed in Table 10.1. Teacher referrals or teacher nominations can provide additional information. Using "multiple gating" screening procedures is another way to utilize multiple information sources. For example, the SSBD relies on classroom teachers' nominations and ratings of students in Stages 1 and 2, and direct observations by others in Stage 3 to identify students at risk. For students who pass SSBD risk criteria in Stage 3, teachers and parents can also complete standardized rating scales, such as the TRF or CBCL, to narrow further the pool of potential participants. Students scoring above borderline or clinical cut points on relevant TRF and/or CBCL problem scales can then be recruited as participants in a particular program. For example, students scoring high on the TRF and/or CBCL Externalizing scales can be invited to participate in programs that focus on reducing aggressive and antisocial behavior. Students scoring high on the TRF and/or CBCL Internalizing scales can be invited to participate in programs that focus on reducing emotional problems. Another option is to review school records and/or interview teachers and parents to determine whether SSBD-identified students are suitable for a particular program.

Multisource identification procedures usually require more time and effort than single source identification. However, they have the advantage of narrowing identification to only those students considered at risk by several different informants. Since students' behavior often varies across situations, multisource identification is preferable to single source identification whenever feasible. In either case, administrators must think carefully about identification procedures in order to select the most appropriate program participants.

Several of the initial screening procedures can also be used to gather baseline data for measuring problems and competences before implementation of a program. For example, initial teacher ratings of problems for an individual student or averages of problem behaviors for a particular classroom can be used as baseline, or "pretest" data. These data can then be compared to outcome data on the same measures to evaluate the effectiveness of a program, as discussed next. In a later section, we discuss evaluation designs for comparing baseline and outcome data.

Measuring Outcomes of Prevention Programs

Effective prevention programs are those that produce desired changes in student behavior and other areas targeted by the program. For students at risk for behavioral and emotional problems, changes can occur in two directions: (a) reduction of student problem behaviors targeted by the program, and (b) improvement in student competences or positive behaviors enhanced by the program. Administrators and evaluators are encouraged to select outcome measures that assess potential changes in both aspects of student behavior. Prevention programs may also produce changes in the behavior and attitudes of parents, teachers, and other school staff, as well as changes in broader aspects of the school environment, such as instructional programs and support services. Additional outcome measures can focus on these areas of change, depending on the specific goals of the prevention program. In order to interpret outcomes appropriately, it is also important to assess whether program staff actually carried out the program as intended. For example, did teachers actually provide all of the instruction required in a social skills curriculum? Or did teachers actually follow the required steps for disciplining students? Answering these types of questions requires evaluating what is termed "program fidelity." As with identification and screening, measures of outcomes and program fidelity can utilize descriptive procedures, as well as published or commercially available instruments.

Descriptive Outcome Measures

Table 10.3 lists a variety of descriptive procedures used to measure outcomes in the prevention projects described in other chapters. These include procedures to assess student problem behaviors, student positive

behaviors, and teacher behaviors. One commonly used descriptive procedure is a standard form or checklist of items to be rated on a daily, weekly,
or monthly basis. Each item can be rated present or absent or rated on
multi-point scales for frequency of occurrence (e.g., 1 = infrequently, 2 =
occasionally or sometimes, 3 = frequently, 4 = consistently; it is not a good
idea to use "never" as a zero anchor point because people tend not to
choose this option). Items may also be rated for intensity of problems (e.g.,
0 = not true, 1 = somewhat true, 2 = very true). Examples of rating scale
forms listed in Table 10.3 are the Standardized Office Referral Form (Unified
Discipline Project), the Teacher Behavior Report Form (Juniper Gardens
Children's Project), and the Monitor's Check Sheet (Check & Connect).
Table 10.3 lists examples of student problem behaviors from each form. The
specific projects are described in the chapters noted in the fourth column of
Table 10.3.

Means and standard deviations for items averaged over specific time
periods or percentages of students for whom items were scored present can
provide outcome data. Total scores can be obtained for variables that can
be easily tallied, such as number of office referrals, absenteeism, or course
failures for students who are in the program during the same time period.
Total scores can also be obtained by summing scores for individual problem items on rating scales or checklists. However, raw score tallies of variables, such as days absent or office referrals, are poor indicators of change
when the school has a high mobility rate, when students are entering or
exiting schools or programs at different times, or when baseline periods are
different.

Direct observation is another common descriptive procedure for measuring student problem behaviors. For example, in the Unified Discipline
Project, three 1-hour observations were conducted to measure 14 different
off-task behaviors. Table 10.3 lists the four off-task behaviors, plus total
off-task, that showed significant differences in outcomes for students in the
project classrooms versus those in comparison classrooms. In the Juniper
Gardens Children's Project, four student problem behaviors listed in Table
10.3 were observed in 2.5- to 3-hour sessions in the classroom or at recess.

A lower section of Table 10.3 lists student positive behaviors that
were the focus of direct observations or teacher reports. In the Unified Discipline Project, the four on-task behaviors listed in Table 10.3 showed significant differences between students in the project versus comparison
classrooms. In the Juniper Gardens Children's Project, four student positive
behaviors were observed in the classroom or at recess, and five student positive behaviors were reported weekly by teachers. After one year, observations showed that students receiving the Juniper Gardens prevention program improved more than controls in academic engagement, positive peer
interactions at recess, and appropriate requests for attention.

(text continues on page 197)

TABLE 10.3 Descriptive Outcome Measures

What Is Measured	Measurement Procedure	Example Project	Chapter
Student Problem Behavior			
Daily office referrals • Unacceptable physical contact • Classroom disruption • Fighting • Not following classroom instructions • Classroom rule violation • Profane language • Threatening another student	Standard Office Referral Form 25 items Computerized tracking system	Unified Discipline	5
Classroom rule violations • Not following directions promptly • Off-task • Talking out of turn • Not keeping to self • Not respecting others' rights/property	Individual Student Behavior Card 5 items	Unified Discipline	5
Classroom behavior problems • Out of seat/assigned area • Physically aggressive with another student • Not following directions • Annoying or disrupting others • Arguing/talking back to teacher • Arguing with other students • Destroying own/others' property	Teacher Behavior Report Form 7 items Estimated frequency/week	Juniper Gardens	2, 4

School engagement • Tardiness • Skipping Classes • Absenteeism • Residential/school mobility • Behavioral referral • Detention • Suspension • Course failures • Accrual of credits	Monitor's Check Sheet 13 items Recorded monthly	Check & Connect	9
Classroom off-task behavior • Disrupting class • Looking around • Talking inappropriately • Doing inappropriate task	Direct observations (1 hour/session) 14 items	Unified Discipline	5
Classroom/recess problem behavior • Physical aggression • Negative verbal remarks • Out of seat/area • Negative peer interactions at recess	Direct observations (2.5-3 hours/session) 4 items	Juniper Gardens	2, 4
Student Positive Behavior Classroom on-task behavior • Answering questions • Paying attention • Raising hand • Total on-task	Direct observations (1 hour/session) 10 items	Unified Discipline	5

(continued)

TABLE 10.3 Continued

What Is Measured	Measurement Procedure	Example Project	Chapter
Classroom/recess positive behavior • Academic engagement/on-task • Compliance with academic requests • Compliance with behavioral requests • Positive peer interactions at recess	Direct observations (2.5-3 hours/session) 4 items	Juniper Gardens	2, 4
• Requesting attention appropriately • Engaging in cooperative social interaction • Expressing anger appropriately • Producing quality work • Participating in class	Teacher Behavior Report Form 5 items; 5-point scale	Juniper Gardens	2, 4
Teacher Behavior			
Praise Reprimands	Direct observations (2.5-3 hours/session)	Juniper Gardens	2, 4
Monitors student behavior Uses appropriate voice tone Uses expected correction procedure • States behavior • States rule violated • States unified consequence • Offers encouragement	Direct observations with rating scale 4 items	Unified Discipline	5
Office discipline referrals	Standard Office Referral Form Computerized tracking system	Unified Discipline	5
	Office Referral Form	Conflict Resolution/ Peer Mediation	8

Direct observation can also assess changes in teacher behavior. For example, in the Juniper Gardens Children's Project, observers recorded the number of times teachers praised or reprimanded students. In the Unified Discipline project, observers used a specific coding system to periodically rate the teacher behaviors listed in the bottom of Table 10.3. These behaviors represented program strategies for disciplining students. Means and standard deviations computed for the fall and spring of each year demonstrated that teachers were actually using the strategies as directed, which served as a measure of program fidelity. (Reductions in office discipline referrals provided additional evidence of changes in teacher behavior in the Unified Discipline Project, as well as in the Conflict Resolution/Peer Mediation Project.)

Research projects often have the luxury of employing staff members who can serve as independent observers. When prevention strategies are incorporated into a school or district program, administrators must hire or select their own observers. Observers can be nonschool staff hired specifically for this purpose. More likely, due to budget constraints, administrators will recruit individuals already employed by the school district. In either case, it is important that observers have proper training in observation methods and that they are people who are not directly involved in the prevention program. When observations are obtained for program versus comparison groups, observers should not have knowledge of an individual student's group assignment. Keeping observers "blind" to group assignment will provide an independent measure of program outcomes. "Operational definitions" should also describe each behavior to be observed in easy-to-measure terms. In the ABC and the Juniper Gardens Children's Projects, independent observers provided important evidence of program effectiveness that corroborated teacher reports.

Published Outcome Measures

Psychological and educational publishing companies market many different instruments that can be used as outcome measures for prevention programs. Additional instruments are also available from researchers in prevention and psychological and behavioral assessment. Standardized instruments, in particular, have several advantages for outcome assessment:

♦ Large pools of items enable comprehensive assessment of potential problems and strengths.

♦ Sets of individual items are usually grouped together into scales and total scores for easier interpretation.

♦ The same instruments can be administered at several different time points to measure changes from baseline to completion of a project.

♦ Scores obtained for an individual or group can be compared to comparable scores from normative samples to determine whether they show unusually high levels of problems or low levels of competences and strengths.

♦ The instruments have been tested for reliability and validity.

When choosing among available instruments, administrators and teachers should review manuals to determine whether the instruments have adequate normative samples and adequate reliability and validity. The best instruments are those that provide standard scores and percentiles for males and females at different ages derived from large representative (normative) samples of the population. Users should also scrutinize scales and item pools to determine whether an instrument measures behaviors that are likely to be affected by a particular program. It is beyond the scope of this chapter to review all relevant published instruments. However, Table 10.4 lists features of the published outcome measures used in the projects described in other chapters. The outcome measures are grouped according to the type of informant who completes them: teachers, direct observers, students themselves, and parents. Within each informant category, instruments are listed for measuring student problem behaviors, student positive behaviors, and perceptions of school or family climate. (We are using *climate* as a broad term to include teachers' attitudes; students' perceptions of conflict and peer relations; and parents' perceptions of empowerment, family environment, and their own psychological functioning.) Programs using the various instruments are described in the chapters listed in the fourth column of Table 10.4. School personnel are encouraged to consult the technical manuals for instruments of interest to them. References for each instrument are listed at the end of this chapter.

In addition to outcome measures used in specific prevention programs, Table 10.4 lists two recommended standardized rating scales. The Youth Self-Report (YSR) is recommended for evaluating adolescents' perceptions of their own problems and competences (Achenbach, 1991c). The YSR is appropriate for students aged 11 to 18. It dovetails with the CBCL and TRF by containing similar items and scale scores. The YSR can be used for middle and high school students, while other self-report scales, like the Self-Perception Profile for Children, can be used with elementary students. Parental permission should be obtained before administering any of the student self-report forms. These forms should also be scored and interpreted by professionals with appropriate training.

The Behavioral and Emotional Rating Scale (BERS) is recommended for evaluating students' emotional and behavioral strengths (Epstein & Sharma, 1998). The BERS can be completed by teachers or other school

(text continues on page 206)

TABLE 10.4 Published Outcome Measures

What Is Measured	Measurement Procedure	Example Project	Chapter
Teacher Reports of Student Problem Behaviors			
Teacher's Report Form/5-18 (TRF; Achenbach, 1991b)	Standardized rating scale 118 items; 3-point scale	ABC Project Juniper Gardens	6 2, 4
Scales: Internalizing, Externalizing, Total Problems, Withdrawn, Somatic Complaints, Anxious/ Depressed, Social Problems, Thought Problems, Attention Problems, Delinquent Behavior, Aggressive Behavior	Raw scores, T scores, and percentiles		
Teacher-Child Rating Scale (T-CRS; Hightower et al., 1986)	Standardized rating scale 18 items; 5-point scale	Linkages to Learning	7
Scales: Acting Out, Shy/Anxious, Learning Difficulties	Raw scores, percentiles		
Social Skills Rating System (SSRS; Gresham & Elliot, 1990)	Standardized rating scale 18 items; 3-point scale	ABC Project Check & Connect	6 9
Scales: Internalizing, Externalizing, Hyperactive, Total Problems	Standard scores and percentiles		
Teacher Reports of Student Positive Behaviors			
Teacher's Report Form/5-18 (TRF; Achenbach, 1991b)	Standardized rating scale Academic subjects; 5-point scale	ABC Project	6
Scales: Academic Performance, Adaptive Func- tioning	Adaptive functioning 4 items; 7-point scale		

(continued)

TABLE 10.4 Continued

What Is Measured	Measurement Procedure	Example Project	Chapter
Teacher-Child Rating Scale (T-CRS; Hightower et al., 1986) Scales: Frustration Tolerance, Assertive Social Skills, Task Orientation	Standardized rating scale 18 items; 5-point scale Raw scores and percentiles	Linkages to Learning	7
Social Skills Rating System (SSRS; Gresham & Elliot, 1990) Scales: Cooperation, Assertion, Self-Control, Total Problems	Standardized rating scale 30 items; 3-point scale Standard scores and percentiles	ABC Project	6
Behavioral and Emotional Rating Scale (BERS; Epstein & Sharma, 1998) Scales: Interpersonal Strengths , Family Involvement, Intrapersonal Strengths, School Functioning, Affective Strengths	Standardized rating scale 52 items; 3-point scale Raw scores, standard scores, and percentiles	[Recommended]	
Teacher Perceptions of School Climate			
Maslach Burnout Inventory Scale (Maslach & Jackson, 1981) Scales: Emotional Exhaustion, Client Depersonalization, Lack in Personal Accomplishment	Rating scale 22 items; 7-point scale	Linkages to Learning	7
School Climate Survey (Smith, Miller, & Daunic, 1996) Scales: Collective Identity, Student Cohesiveness, Mutual Respect, Order and Discipline, Community Support, Teacher Efficacy, Racial Harmony, Homework, Conflict	Project-designed rating scale 85 items; 5-point scale Raw scores, means, and standard deviations	Conflict Resolution/ Peer Mediation	8

Direct Observations of Student Problem Behavior

Direct Observation Form (DOF; Achenbach, 1986) Scales: Internalizing, Externalizing, Total Problems, Withdrawn/Inattentive, Nervous/Obsessive, Depressed, Hyperactive, Attention Demanding, Aggressive	Standardized rating scale 10 minutes/session 96 items; 4-point scale Raw scores, T scores, and percentiles	ABC Project	6

Direct Observations of Student Positive Behavior

Direct Observation Form (DOF; Achenbach, 1986) Scale: On-task	Standardized rating scale 10 one-minute intervals/session Raw total scores	ABC Project	6
Systematic Screening for Behavior Disorders (SSBD; Walker & Severson, 1990) Scales: Academic Engaged Time; Social Engagement	Standard procedures for time sampling	Juniper Gardens	2, 4

Student Self-Reports of Problem Behaviors

Youth Self-Report/11-18 (YSR; Achenbach, 1991c) Scales: Internalizing, Externalizing, Total Problems, Withdrawn, Somatic Complaints, Anxious/Depressed, Social Problems, Thought Problems, Attention Problems, Delinquent Behavior, Aggressive Behavior	Standardized rating scale 102 items; 3-point scale Raw scores, T scores, and percentiles	[Recommended]	

(continued)

TABLE 10.4 Continued

What Is Measured	Measurement Procedure	Example Project	Chapter
Student Self-Reports of Positive Behaviors			
Youth Self-Report/11-18 (Achenbach, 1991c) Scales: Activities, Social, Total Competence	Standardized rating scale 12 items; 3-point scale Raw scores, T scores, and percentiles	[Recommended]	
Self-Perception Profile for Children (Harter, 1985) Scales: Scholastic Competence, Social Acceptance, Athletic Competence, Physical Appearance, Behavioral Conduct, Global Self-Worth	Standardized rating scale 36 items; 4-point scale Raw scores and percentiles	Linkages to Learning	7
Pictorial Scale of Perceived Competence and Social Acceptance for Young Children (Harter & Pike, 1984) Scales: Scholastic Competence, Physical/Athletic Competence, Social Acceptance, Maternal Acceptance	Standardized rating scale 24 items; 4-point scale Raw scores and percentiles	Linkages to Learning	7
Peer Mediator Questionnaire (Smith, Miller, & Daunic, 1996) Scales: Satisfaction, Generalization	Project-designed rating scale 17 items; 3- to 5-point scale Raw scores, means, and standard deviations	Conflict Resolution/ Peer Mediation	8

Student Perceptions of School Climate

Conflict Resolution Scale (Smith, Miller, & Daunic, 1996)	Project-designed rating scale	Conflict Resolution/	8
Scales: Individual Conflict/Aggression, Disciplinary Interventions, Conflict Resolution Styles, Outside Influences, Need for Help, Communication Effects, Group Aggression	25 items; 5-point scale Raw scores, means, and standard deviations	Peer Mediation	
Student Attitudinal Survey (Smith, Miller, & Daunic, 1996)	Project-designed rating scale	Conflict Resolution/	8
Scales: Communication, Openness to Differences, School Enthusiasm, Sense of Control	42 items; 5-point scale Raw scores, means, and standard deviations	Peer Mediation	
Disputant Questionnaire (Smith, Miller, & Daunic, 1996)	Project-designed rating scale	Conflict Resolution/	8
Scales: Satisfaction, Efficacy, Fidelity Procedural Check	31 items; 5-point scale; yes-no Raw scores, means, and standard deviations	Peer Mediation	

Parent Reports of Student Problem Behaviors

Child Behavior Checklist/4-18 (CBCL; Achenbach, 1991a)	Standardized rating scale	ABC Project	6
		Linkages to Learning	7
Scales: Internalizing, Externalizing, Total Problems, Withdrawn, Somatic Complaints, Anxious/Depressed, Social Problems, Thought Problems, Attention Problems, Delinquent Behavior, Aggressive Behavior	118 items; 3-point scale Raw scores, T scores, and percentiles		

(continued)

TABLE 10.4 Continued

What Is Measured	Measurement Procedure	Example Project	Chapter
Social Skills Rating System (SSRS; Gresham & Elliot, 1990) Scales: Internalizing, Externalizing, Hyperactive, Total Problems	Standardized rating scale 17 items; 3-point scale Standard scores and percentiles	ABC Project	6
Parent Reports of Student Positive Behaviors			
Child Behavior Checklist/4-18 (CBCL; Achenbach, 1991a) Scales: Activities, Social, School, Total Competence	Standardized rating scale 20 items; 3-point scale Academic subjects; 4-point scale Raw scores, T scores, and percentiles	ABC Project Linkages to Learning	6 7
Social Skills Rating System (SSRS; Gresham & Elliot, 1990) Scales: Cooperation, Assertion, Self-Control, Responsibility, Total Social Skills	Standardized rating scale 38 items; 3-point scale Standard scores and percentiles	ABC Project	6
Peer Mediator Parent Questionnaire (Smith, Miller, & Daunic, 1996) Scales: Satisfaction, Generalization	Project-designed rating scale 16 items; 3- to 5-point scale Raw scores, means, standard deviations	Conflict Resolution/ Peer Mediation	8

Measure	Format	Scoring	Source	
Behavioral Emotional Rating Scale (BERS; Epstein & Sharma, 1998) Scales: Interpersonal Strengths, Family Involvement, Intrapersonal Strengths, School Functioning, Affective Strengths	Standardized rating scale 52 items; 3-point scale	Raw score, standard scores, and percentiles	[Recommended]	
Parent Perceptions of Empowerment/Family Climate				
Family Empowerment Scale—School Version (Koren, DeChillo, & Friesen, 1992; McConaughy, Kay, & Fitzgerald, 1999) Scales: Systems Advocacy, Knowledge, Competence, Total Score	Adapted rating scale 34 items; 5-point scale	Raw scores, means, and standard deviations	ABC Project	6
Parenting Stress Index (Abidin, 1990) Scales: Child Domain, Parent Domain	Rating scale 101 items; 5-point scale	Raw scores	Linkages to Learning	7

staff for students aged 5 to 18. The BERS manual provides standard scores and percentiles based on teacher, counselor, and clinician ratings of 2,100 children without disabilities. Parents can also complete the BERS. However, until a normative sample for parent ratings is available, only BERS raw scores should be used to assess outcomes from parent reports. Several of the other rating scales listed in Table 10.4 (CBCL, TRF, and YSR) also assess competences along with behavioral and emotional problems. The Social Skills Rating System (SSRS) is another instrument that assesses social skills as well as problems. The BERS differs from these measures in focusing exclusively on strengths in several areas. Adding the BERS to a battery of other measures thus expands the focus of outcome evaluation to include changes in positive behaviors as well as changes in problems.

Importance of Multiple-Outcome Measures

Children's behavior often varies from one situation to the next, such as school versus home, or one classroom versus another. As a result, agreement between informants in different situations (e.g., teachers vs. parents) is likely to be low to moderate at best (Achenbach, McConaughy, & Howell, 1987). The relatively low level of agreement does not mean one informant is right and the other wrong. Instead, it underscores the importance of obtaining multiple perspectives of children's functioning. This can be especially challenging for evaluating outcomes of school-based prevention programs. Depending on the focus of a particular program, teachers may report changes in students' functioning in certain areas, but not other areas. At the same time, other informants, such as parents or observers, may report changes similar to those reported by teachers, little or no change, or changes in other areas not observed by teachers. A particular program may also produce changes in teachers' behavior and/or family functioning, as well as changes in students' behavior.

The ABC Project provides a good example of variations in outcomes reported by different informants (see articles by McConaughy, Kay, & Fitzgerald, 1998, 1999, and 2000, for more details). The ABC Project used several different published measures listed in Table 10.4 to evaluate outcomes for first- and second-grade students assigned to Parent-Teacher Action Research (PTAR) teams versus controls without PTAR teams in the same classrooms. Teachers completed the TRF and SSRS. Independent observers used the Direct Observation Form (DOF) to rate students' problems and on-task behavior in the classroom. Parents completed the CBCL, SSRS, and the Family Empowerment Scale—School Version (FES-S). The TRF, SSRS, DOF, and CBCL are each multi-item rating scales that provide total scores and scale scores for measuring students' problems and competences. The ABC researchers evaluated outcomes by comparing scores on each measure before and after implementing prevention strategies. At the end of 2 years of the ABC Project, both teachers and parents reported reductions in students' rule-breaking behavior and improvements in students' social skills. At the same time, teachers and observers reported greater reductions in PTAR students' internalizing problems compared to controls, whereas parents reported greater reductions in PTAR students' externalizing problems compared to controls. The differences in outcomes for PTAR students versus matched controls demonstrated the effectiveness of the PTAR teams. However, the nature of the changes in student behavior differed depending on the informant. PTAR parents also reported improvements in their feelings of empowerment in seeking school services for their children. By comparing 1- versus 2-year outcomes, the ABC researchers demonstrated further that a longer period of prevention (2 years) was much more effective than a shorter period (1 year).

The Linkages to Learning Project is another example of multi-informant outcome assessment, using published measures listed in Table 10.4. To evaluate outcomes in this project, teachers completed the Teacher-Child Rating Scale (T-CRS), TRF, and Maslach Burnout Inventory Revised. Students completed several measures to assess their own perceptions of their competence and peer acceptance, including the Self-Perception Profile for Children and Pictorial Scale of Perceived Competence and Social Acceptance for Young Children. Students were also administered a standardized achievement test. Parents completed the CBCL and several other measures of their own psychological adjustment, including the Parenting Stress Index (PSI). After one year of the Linkages to Learning Project, the parent and teacher rating scales showed decreases in problems for participating students in contrast to increases in problems for nonparticipating students. Linkages to Learning students also showed improvements in academic achievement and their parents reported decreases in family conflict at home.

In the Juniper Gardens Children's Project, teachers completed the SSBD, listed in Table 10.2, to select students at risk for behavioral and emotional problems. Outcomes for these students, plus additional students identified as having emotional and behavioral disorders (E/BD), were compared to those for students who did not participate in the prevention program. To assess outcomes, teachers provided weekly reports of student problem behavior and positive behavior, using the Teacher Behavior Report Form, listed in Table 10.3. Independent observers recorded direct observations of student problem behaviors, student positive behaviors, teacher behaviors, and aspects of the school environment (e.g., academic content and instructional groupings of students). After one year of the Juniper Gardens Children's Project, observational data indicated higher rates of academic engagement and positive interactions at recess and lower rates of aggression for program participants versus controls. Teacher reports showed more appropriate requests for attention and fewer problems following directions and disrupting class routine for program participants versus controls. Observations and teacher reports both showed less out-of-seat behavior for program participants than for controls.

All three projects described above illustrate the variability that can occur in students' behavior across settings and corresponding similarities and differences in informant reports. These findings demonstrate the importance of evaluation procedures that assess a variety of potential program outcomes. To assess multiple outcomes, administrators can select from published instruments listed in Table 10.4 and many other commercially available instruments. As illustrated in Table 10.3, administrators and researchers can also develop their own descriptive measures for use in conjunction with published instruments. Administrators are encouraged to select outcome measures that cover multiple perspectives. At the same time, administrators must remain sensitive to the time and effort required to complete several different measures and select only those that are best suited to the specific focus of the program being evaluated.

Designing Program Evaluations

Selecting participants for intervention and identifying measures that are sensitive to the effects of prevention programs are important aspects of program evaluation (see Shadish, Cook, & Leviton, 1991, for detailed discussion of evaluation designs). Another important step in program evaluation involves selecting an evaluation design that can provide evidence of the effect (or absence of effect) of the prevention program. Measuring changes in students' behavior is not difficult. The challenge for evaluators is to use an evaluation design that clearly and unequivocally enables them to link changes in behavior to the implementation of the program. A good program design will enable administrators to rule out other factors besides the program itself as potential explanations for improved behavior or performance among program participants. Examples of such other factors are developmental maturation of participants, changes in school personnel, or changes or additions in other school programs or curricula. The first step in choosing an evaluation design is to decide whether the focus will be on single cases or groups of participants.

Single-Case Designs

Single-case or single-subject designs are most suitable for measuring program effects when the intervention has targeted a limited number of participants or sites and when a control or comparison group is either unfeasible or unavailable. Single-case designs have the advantage of showing changes over time for specific individuals. In single-case evaluation designs, individual students, teachers, classrooms, or schools can represent a single case that is compared to itself or to another comparable single case. A distinguishing feature of single-case designs is multiple or continuous measurement of key behaviors or other indicators of program effects.

In single-case designs, evaluators must carefully define what is measured, when it is measured, and how it is measured. Often this involves direct observations of clearly defined discrete behaviors. It may also involve ratings of behaviors by teachers or other persons or tallies of specific types of problems or desired positive behaviors. For example, in a single-case design targeted at individual students, an evaluator might count the number of classroom rule violations and the number of classroom or recess behavior problems reported by a student's teacher. Or an evaluator might record direct observations of on-task or off-task behavior over a discrete time period. In a single-case design where a classroom or a school serves as the case, an evaluator might count the number of office discipline referrals or the number of students participating in after-school recreational activities. These data could be collected on a daily or weekly basis. Many of the descriptive outcome measures listed in Table 10.3 are appropriate for single-case evaluation designs. Functional behavior assessment (see Chapter 2) is another form of single-case assessment in which an evaluator examines antecedents and consequences of particular behavior. For evaluating the effects of prevention programs, two types of single-case designs, multiple-baseline and changing criterion designs, are most appropriate, as discussed below.

Multiple-Baseline Designs. A multiple-baseline design begins with data collection during a baseline period before implementation of a program. The strength of the program, or intervention, is measured by comparing performance after intervention with performance during baseline. In the multiple-baseline design, the baseline period is a different length of time for each case, and program effects are anticipated as each case moves from baseline to intervention. The intervention is systematically introduced to each case or subject independently at different points in time. Program effects are demonstrated when targeted behaviors or indicators change in the expected direction after the intervention is introduced. Changes in behavior for each of the cases (students, schools, or classrooms) at different points in time are generally considered convincing evidence of program effects.

Figure 10.1 displays a multiple-baseline design for disciplinary referrals for three different classrooms. The intervention, technical assistance and behavioral intervention training, was implemented for teachers in each of the three classrooms. Consistent changes in the number of referrals after the intervention at different points in time provided evidence that the technical assistance and training had its desired effects.

Changing Criterion Designs. The changing criterion design also begins with a baseline condition followed by the introduction of an intervention. In contrast to the multiple-baseline design, the changing criterion design demonstrates the effectiveness of the intervention by improved behavior at increasingly higher criteria for successful performance. That is, as participants reach a predetermined criterion of performance in the program, expectations and reinforcing conditions are changed to a higher level. For example, if a peer mediation program was designed to decrease "name-calling," "bullying," and "fighting" during recess, a changing criterion design might initially aim for a 30%, then 60%, then 90% reduction in the target behaviors over time. Figure 10.2 displays a changing criterion design that was used to evaluate the effects of such a peer mediation program.

Analysis of single-case evaluation data is usually visual. That is, inspection of graphed data points over time for the various cases reveals whether or not the prevention program is having its anticipated effect. Statistical analysis of single-case data is also possible, but often is not feasible for most school-based program evaluations, because transformations must be made in the data before using inferential statistics.

Group Designs

Group designs can use descriptive outcome measures and/or standardized instruments to measure participants' behavior or performance before and after the implementation of a prevention program. In contrast to single-case designs, group designs require gathering data from many participants and computing averages for the performance of participants at two or more points in time.

Experimental Group Designs. Experimental group designs compare the performance of a group participating in a program to a comparable group (a control group) that does not participate in the program. When the group receiving the program shows greater changes in behavior than a comparable control group, evaluators can conclude that the changes were due to the program and not other factors that might affect both groups equally, such as developmental maturation. For example, in the ABC project, beneficial effects of PTAR teams were demonstrated by greater changes in behavior of students with PTAR teams than for matched controls without PTAR teams in the same classrooms. Whenever possible, experimental group designs are preferable to group designs without control groups.

FIGURE 10.1. Multiple Baseline Across Classrooms: Disciplinary Referrals

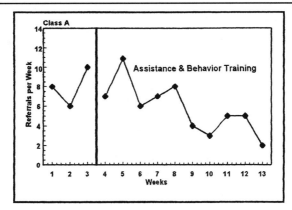

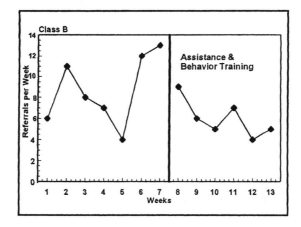

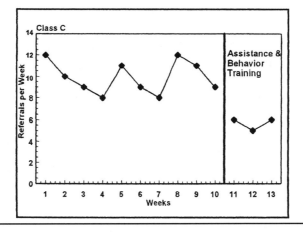

FIGURE 10.2. Changing Criterion Design: Evaluating the Success of a Peer Mediation Program

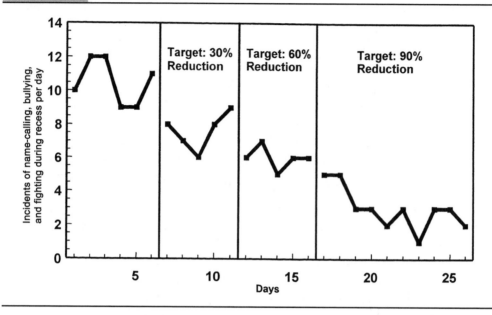

Designs Without Control Groups. When control groups are not feasible, a group evaluation design can compare the performance of a group after the implementation of a program to the same group's performance before the program began. This is sometimes referred to as pre- and posttreatment comparisons. Scores on standardized instruments for program participants can also be compared to the similar scores of the normative sample that was used to develop the standardized assessment instrument. For example, if outcome data include teacher ratings on a standardized instrument, like the TRF or BERS, then group averages on various TRF or BERS scales for the program participants can be compared to average scores on the same scales for the normative sample, assuming this information is available in the instrument's technical manual.

Evaluators need to be cautious in interpreting results of group designs without control groups. Control groups "control" for other possible explanations of changes in scores when they share the same characteristics of the group receiving a program or "treatment." Without comparisons between the treatment group and control group, there is no way to test whether changes in performance might have been due to some other factors besides the program being tested. For example, in the ABC project, it was not possible to test whether improvements in students' social skills were actually the result of classroomwide social skills instruction, because there was no control group that did not receive social skills instruction. Although the students did demonstrate better social skills after instruction, the improvements might have been due to maturation or some other factor instead of the specific instruction they received from their teachers.

Statistical Analyses. In contrast to single-case evaluation designs, group designs typically rely on statistical analyses of outcome data. Analyses of group performance can be based on descriptive or inferential statistics. Descriptive analyses might involve examining the percentage of students in a prevention program who exhibit specific problem behaviors before and after implementation of the program. In experimental group designs, evaluators can compare differences in the percentages of students exhibiting the problem behaviors in the group with the program versus a control group without the program. Descriptive statistics, like chi-square, test differences in the proportion of students in each group who show the problems versus the proportion in each group who do not show the problems.

Inferential statistics, such as the *t* test, analysis of variance, and multivariate analyses, test differences in averages, or mean scores, relative to the variance in scores for each group or sample. Inferential statistics are more powerful than descriptive statistics for showing changes in scores as evidence of program effects. Inferential statistics enable evaluators to judge whether changes or differences between groups are random or chance effects (unexplained variance) or program effects (explained variance). Inferential statistics can also be used to determine whether characteristics of specific subgroups of participants are associated with certain types of program outcomes.

Whether evaluators use descriptive or inferential statistics to examine program outcomes, it is essential that they have the necessary statistical expertise or that they confer with measurement and evaluation specialists to ensure that they are using statistical techniques appropriately. The choice between descriptive or inferential statistics with group evaluation designs may also be influenced in part by the stakeholders for whom the evaluation is being conducted. For example, prevention programs implemented within a single classroom or single school may be subjected to less intense levels of scrutiny than are programs that involve a number of classrooms, schools, or school districts. For evaluations of single-class or single-school interventions with relatively few participants, single-case deigns or group designs using descriptive statistics may be all that is necessary to demonstrate program effectiveness. However, even in these instances, evaluators need to think carefully about outcome measures and the type of evaluation design most appropriate for their particular program.

Measurement Issues

Regardless of whether evaluators choose single-case or group designs to measure program effects, it is essential that the measurement procedures have well-demonstrated reliability and validity. Reliable measurement procedures are ones that are stable and consistent over repeated applications. An instrument or procedure has good test-retest reliability when it provides the same or very similar results when administered at two different times without any intervening changes in a given situation. An instrument or procedure has good inter-rater reliability when it provides the same or very similar results when administered by two different individuals at about the same point in time. The best instruments are ones that show both high test-retest and high inter-rater reliability.

Valid measurement procedures are those that measure what they purport to measure. Validity can be tested in several ways, for example, by comparing subjects' scores on a particular instrument to scores on a similar measure (construct validity), or by testing the predictive power of the measurement procedure (criterion-related validity). Evaluators should examine the technical manuals for published instruments for studies on validity.

It is also important to examine the items and scores of an instrument to determine whether they measure the specific types of behavior or outcomes that might be reasonably expected from a given prevention program. For example, if a prevention program was designed to reduce the occurrence of aggressive behavior among primary grade students, then a valid outcome measure might involve direct observations of the children's aggressive behavior or ratings of children's aggressive behavior by appropriate informants. While the academic performance of the students might also be of interest, data on academic performance would not be a valid measure of program effectiveness, unless the program specifically targeted academic performance as well as aggressive behavior.

When designing program evaluation procedures, administrators need to consider both reliability and validity of the outcome measures they select. Table 10.4 lists published outcome measures with acceptable standards of reliability and validity that were used in the various projects described in other chapters, plus two recommended published measures. When using descriptive measures, like those listed in Table 10.3, or project-designed measures, evaluators must provide their own evidence of their reliability and validity.

Common Hazards in Program Evaluation

Several potential hazards exist in evaluating prevention programs. Anticipating hazards in advance can help reduce or eliminate their negative impact on evaluation results. One potential hazard is the use of nonequivalent treatment and comparison groups. To avoid this problem, it is essential that students in any comparison group, whether selected at the classroom or school level, share common characteristics with students participating in the prevention program. For example, if students are selected for a prevention program based on a high number of risk factors or severity of their behavior problems, a comparison group without the program should also have similarly high risk factors or similarly severe behavior problems. If the two groups differ on these selection factors, it will be extremely difficult to show that the program produced beneficial effects for the targeted group. For example, the lack of a nonequivalent comparison group was a problem encountered by the Linkages to Learning Project, where the participating school had more high-risk students than did the comparison school. This inequality occurred because the schools were selected by school district administrators and not by the program evaluators. As a result, outcomes for students at the two schools had to be interpreted with caution because of differences between schools that existed before the program began.

Another hazard not dissimilar to nonequivalent treatment and comparison groups is a statistical phenomenon termed "regression to the mean." This is a commonly observed statistical artifact, where scores at the extreme ends of a distribution of scores tend to move closer to the average, or mean, on a second assessment. Regression to the mean can occur when the participants in a prevention program are selected on the basis of extreme scores on a pretest or preprogram measure and the same measure is used later to assess outcomes of the program. Participants who obtained extreme scores on the pretest measure are more likely to score closer to the mean the next time they are assessed, regardless of whether they received the program or not. Regression to the mean thus undermines interpretations of changes as due solely to the program itself. The problem of regression to the mean can be avoided by selecting program participants based on eligibility criteria that do not include pretest scores on one of the outcome measures. For example, participants in the ABC Project were selected initially according to teacher ratings on the SSBD, and then matched to controls according to their preprogram Total Problem scores on their kindergarten teachers' TRFs. Differential changes in TRF scores from Time 1 to Time 2 for the treatment and control groups could then be interpreted appropriately as measures of the effects of the prevention program, because any regression to the mean would have affected both groups equally.

A third hazard for evaluators is maturation of participants during the course of the program. Educators and mental health professionals are often interested in promoting the social, emotional, and academic maturation of the children with whom they work. However, unless adequately accounted for in an evaluation design, the maturation of program participants might explain changes in behavior over time better than the effects of the prevention program itself. An evaluation design that uses a comparison group that is about the same age and/or grade level as the group participating in the program is less likely to mistake maturation for program effects. Because of the frequent measurement associated with single-case designs, maturation effects are less of a potential problem than they are with group designs.

A fourth hazard concerns the influence of history on program effects. Evaluators and measurement specialists use the term *history* to refer to unique experiences of participants or aspects of programs that might affect outcomes. For example, if baseline or pretreatment data were collected on student behavior just prior to a major holiday, the level of inappropriate behavior might be higher than normal. Comparisons to this unusually high level of troublesome behavior after the introduction of a prevention program would artificially inflate program effects shown by reductions in problems. The effect of history can also occur when new staff members are hired after the start of the prevention program, when schedules or location of the program changes, and when other changes to the students' routine occur after the program is introduced. Good communication between program evaluators and program staff can help to identify history that might influence outcomes.

Most evaluation hazards can be avoided when individuals evaluating programs are aware of the larger contexts within which the program operates, have a good understanding of how the program is implemented, and have the opportunity to observe the program in operation. Evaluators need to be involved in preliminary discussions with staff about evaluation design, program implementation, data collection, and data analyses. When evaluation is not considered during the planning of the prevention program, it can be very difficult to extract meaningful program effects from existing data. Thus the threats to the validity of an evaluation implemented after a program has been implemented or has been completed are considerable.

Disseminating Evaluation Information

A primary reason for program evaluation is to learn whether or not a particular program produced the desired effects. Demonstrated efficacy should be the first consideration in decisions about whether to continue a prevention program in the future. A well-conducted, clearly presented evaluation report that shows the success of a program can bolster arguments for sustaining the program, especially when budget constraints threaten its continuation. Conversely, programs that may appear promising will be more vulnerable to budget cuts when administrators are unable to provide convincing evidence of their positive impact on participants.

An evaluation report should disseminate findings to key stakeholders in an objective and unambiguous manner. To do this effectively, report writers need a clear sense of the intended audience. For example, professional audiences or journal editors usually expect a report to include a literature review and details about statistical analyses, as well as discussion of methods, results, and conclusions. Other audiences, such as school administrators, school boards, or legislators, are usually most interested in descriptions of what a program does, whom it serves, and how it was evaluated. Reports for these audiences should present clear and concise descriptions of the major features of the program, evaluation methods, key findings regarding efficacy, limitations, and conclusions. Additional information concerning evaluation instruments, statistical analyses, and background literature can be placed in footnotes or appendices for further examination by interested parties.

The major focus of this chapter has been on outcome or *product* evaluations of prevention programs. An equally important aspect of measuring the success of prevention programs involves *process* evaluations. A process evaluation is an analysis of how the program was implemented and whether persons delivering the program did what they were supposed to do. This is also called assessing "program or treatment fidelity." Key questions for process evaluations are: "Does the program reach and serve its intended participants?" and "Is the program being implemented in the ways in which it was intended?" As an example, evaluators of the Unified Discipline Project not only measured student outcomes, but also observed teachers' behaviors to determine if they were using the discipline procedures as instructed. The observed teacher behaviors are listed in the bottom part of Table 10.3.

Perspective on Measuring Success of Prevention Programs

This chapter focused on procedures for measuring the success of prevention programs. Drawing on other chapters describing specific projects, we outlined measurement procedures for identifying individual students considered to be at risk for emotional and behavioral problems and other factors for identifying at-risk schools. We also discussed measurement procedures and designs for evaluating the outcomes of prevention programs. Each school year, administrators and school boards face decisions on how to allocate their resources to best meet the needs of all children. Often these decisions involve sorting through competing demands for funding, staffing, and building space. Political pressures can also influence decisions regarding school resources and programs. In the face of such challenges, careful program evaluation is essential to preserve and sustain effective prevention programs. Without sound evidence of their success, prevention advocates will be hard-pressed to convince decision makers to continue such efforts, regardless of their positive outcomes for children.

REFERENCES

Abidin, R. R. (1990c). *Parenting Stress Index*. Odessa, FL: Psychological Assessment Resources.

Achenbach, T. M. (1986). *Direct Observation Form of the Child Behavior Checklist (Rev. ed.)*. Burlington: University of Vermont, Department of Psychiatry.

Achenbach, T. M. (1991a). *Manual for the Child Behavior Checklist/4-18 and 1991 profile*. Burlington: University of Vermont, Department of Psychiatry.

Achenbach, T. M. (1991b). *Manual for the Teacher's Report Form and 1991 profile*. Burlington: University of Vermont, Department of Psychiatry.

Achenbach, T. M. (1991c). *Manual for the Youth Self-Report Form and 1991 profile*. Burlington: University of Vermont, Department of Psychiatry.

Achenbach, T. M., McConaughy, S. H., & Howell, C. T. (1987). Child/ adolescent behavioral and emotional problems: Implications of cross-informant correlations for situational specificity. *Psychological Bulletin, 101*, 213-232.

Epstein, M. H., & Sharma, J. M. (1998). *Behavioral and Emotional Rating Scale*. Austin, TX: PRO-ED.

Gresham, F. M., & Elliott, S. N. (1990). *Social Skills Rating System*. Circle Pines, MN: American Guidance System.

Gresham, F. M., MacMillan, D. L., & Bocian, K. (1996). "Behavioral earthquakes": Low frequency behavioral events that differentiate students at-risk for behavioral disorders. *Behavioral Disorders, 21*, 277-292.

Harter, S. (1985). *Manual for the Self-Perception Profile for Children*. Denver, CO: University of Denver.

Harter, S., & Pike, R. (1984). The Pictorial Scale of Perceived Competence and Social Acceptance for Young Children. *Child Development, 55*, 1969-1982.

Hightower, A. D., Work, W. C., Cowen, E. L., Lotyczewski, B. S., Spinell, A. P., Guare, J. C., & Rohrbeck, C. A. (1986). The Teacher-Child Rating Scale: A brief objective measure of elementary children's school problem behaviors and competencies. *School Psychology Review, 3*, 393-409.

Koren, P. E., DeChillo, N., & Friesen, B. J. (1992). Measuring empowerment in families whose children have emotional disabilities: A brief questionnaire. *Rehabilitation Psychology, 37*, 305-321.

Maslach, C., & Jackson, S. E. (1981). *Maslach Burnout Inventory.* Palo Alto, CA: Consulting Psychologists Press.

McConaughy, S. H., Kay, P., & Fitzgerald, M. (1998). Preventing SED through Parent-Teacher Action Research and social skills instruction: First year outcomes. *Journal of Emotional and Behavioral Disorders, 6,* 81-93.

McConaughy, S. H., Kay, P., & Fitzgerald, M. (1999). The Achieving Behaving Caring Project for preventing ED: Two-year outcomes. *Journal of Emotional and Behavioral Disorders, 7,* 224-239.

McConaughy, S. H., Kay, P., & Fitzgerald, M. (2000). How long is long enough? Outcomes for a school-based prevention project. *Exceptional Children, 67,* 1-14.

Shadish, W. R., Cook, T. D., & Leviton, L. C. (1991). *Foundations of program evaluation: Theories of practice.* Newbury Park, CA: Sage.

Smith, S. W., Miller, M. D., & Daunic, A. P. (1996). *Conflict resolution/peer mediation project.* Available: Department of Special Education, P.O. Box 117050, University of Florida, Gainesville, FL 32611.

Walker, H. M., & Severson, H. (1990). *Systematic screening for behavior disorders.* Longmont, CO: Sopris West.

11

Building Effective Prevention Practices

Bob Algozzine

Congress finds that juveniles between the ages of 10 years and 14 years are committing increasing number of murders and other serious crimes . . . the tragedy in Jonesboro, Arkansas, is, unfortunately, an all too common occurrence in the United States.
—The Violent and Repeat Juvenile
Offender Accountability and
Rehabilitation Act of 1999

There are many misconceptions about the prevalence of youth violence in our society and it is important to peel back the veneer of hot-tempered discourse that often surrounds the issue. . . . While it is important to carefully review the circumstances surrounding these horrifying incidents so that we may learn from them, we must also be cautious about inappropriately creating a cloud of fear over every student in every classroom across the country. In the case of youth violence, it is important to note that, statistically speaking, schools are among the safest places for children to be.
—Final Report, Bipartisan Working
Group on Youth Violence

Educational researchers, administrators, teachers, and other school personnel know very well that concern for behavior in school is not new (cf. Algozzine, Audette, Ellis, Marr, & White, 2000; Brooks, Schiraldi, & Ziedenberg, 2000; Gable, 1996; Gunter & Denny, 1996; Kauffman, 1996; Lloyd & Heubusch, 1996; Mathur & Rutherford, 1996; Nelson, Crabtree, Marchand-Martella, & Martella, 1998; Sugai, Sprague, Horner, & Walker, 2000; Wehby & Symons, 1996; Whelan & Simpson,

1996). Parents, too, voice concern when sharing opinions about America's schools. Poll after poll lists behavior problems, discipline, and safety as the "biggest problems facing the public schools" (cf. Langdon & Vesper, 2000; Rose & Gallup, 1999). Concerns about discipline and safety at school are not limited to middle and high school; increasingly, elementary school students are involved in violent acts, and efforts to prevent problems in later grades must begin in elementary school (Kamps & Tankersley, 1996; Kauffman, 1999; Taylor-Greene et al., 1997).

Preventing School Violence

Administrators, teachers, and other school personnel face a variety of advice on how to make schools safe. On June 13, 1998, President Clinton directed the Departments of Education and of Justice to develop an early warning guide to help adults keep children in schools out of harm's way. *Early Warning, Timely Response: A Guide to Safe Schools* (Dwyer, Osher, & Warger, 1998) presents a brief summary of the research on violence prevention, intervention, and crisis response in schools. It describes characteristics of safe schools, provides direction on early warning signs that relate to violence and problem behavior, and delimits interventions that school personnel can take "to prevent violence and other troubling behavior, to intervene and get help for troubled children, and to respond to violence when it occurs" (U.S. Department of Education, 1998, pp. 1-2). Using information available in a public domain publication (www.ed.gov/offices/ OSERS/OSEP/earlywrn.html) and presented by Dwyer, Osher, and Hoffman (2000), we summarize the guidelines here because they support, reinforce, and promote the research-based practices that are the focus of our book.

Characteristics of Safe, Responsive Schools

In large part, schools are safe when appropriate, expected academic and social behaviors are prominent in the lives of students who attend them. Well-functioning schools encourage teaching, learning, safety, and socially appropriate behaviors. They have strong academic and behavioral goals and support students in achieving them (see Chapters 2, 3, 4, 5, 6, and 9), foster positive relationships between school staff and students (see Chapters 5, 8, and 9), and promote meaningful parental and community involvement (see Chapters 6 and 7). Most prevention programs in effective schools address multiple factors and recognize that safety and order are related to the social, emotional, and academic development of students. According to Dwyer and colleagues (1998, pp. 3-5), strategies to make this happen operate in schools that do the following:

◆ **Focus on academic achievement.** Effective schools convey the attitude that all children can achieve academically and behave appropriately, while appreciating individual differences. Expectations are communicated clearly, with the understanding that meeting them is a responsibility of the student, the home, and the school. Adequate resources and programs help ensure that expectations are met. Students who receive the support they need are more likely to behave in socially desirable ways.

◆ **Involve families in meaningful ways.** Students whose families are involved in their growth in and outside school are more likely to experience school success and less likely to become involved in antisocial activities. School communities must make parents feel welcome in school, address barriers to their participation, and keep families positively engaged in their children's education. Effective schools also support families in expressing concerns about their children—and support families in getting the help they need to address behaviors that cause concern.

◆ **Develop links to the community.** Everyone must be committed to improving schools. Schools that have close ties to families, support services, community police, the faith-based community, and the community at large can benefit from many valuable resources. When these links are weak, schools heighten the risk of violence and decrease their opportunities to serve children who are at risk for violence or whom it may affect.

◆ **Emphasize positive relationships among students and staff.** Research shows that a positive relationship with an adult who is available to provide support when needed is one of the most critical factors in preventing student violence. Students often look to adults in the school community for guidance, support, and direction. Some children need help overcoming feelings of isolation and support in developing connections to others. Effective schools make sure that opportunities exist for adults to spend quality, personal time with children. Effective schools also foster positive interpersonal relations among students—they encourage students to help each other and to feel comfortable assisting others in getting help when needed.

◆ **Discuss safety issues openly.** Children come to school with many different perceptions—and misconceptions—about death, violence, and the use of weapons. Schools can reduce the risk of violence by teaching children about the dangers of firearms, as well as appropriate strategies for dealing with feelings, expressing anger in appropriate ways, and resolving conflicts. Schools also should teach children that they are responsible for their actions and that the choices they make have consequences for which they will be held accountable.

♦ **Treat students with equal respect.** A major source of conflict in many schools is the perceived or real problem of bias and unfair treatment of students because of ethnicity, gender, race, social class, religion, disability, nationality, sexual orientation, physical appearance, or some other factor—both by staff and by peers. Students who have been treated unfairly may become scapegoats and/or targets of violence. In some cases, victims may react in aggressive ways. Effective schools communicate to students and the greater community that all children are valued and respected. There is a deliberate and systematic effort—for example, displaying children's artwork, posting academic work prominently throughout the building, respecting students' diversity—to establish a climate that demonstrates care and a sense of community.

♦ **Create ways for students to share their concerns.** Peers often are the most likely group to know in advance about potential school violence. Schools must create ways for students to safely report troubling behaviors that may lead to dangerous situations. Students who report potential violence must be protected. It is important for schools to support and foster positive relationships between students and adults so students will feel safe providing information about a potentially dangerous situation.

♦ **Help children feel safe expressing their feelings.** It is very important that children feel safe when expressing their needs, fears, and anxieties to school staff. When they do not have access to caring adults, feelings of isolation, rejection, and disappointment are more likely to occur, increasing the probability of acting-out behaviors.

♦ **Have in place a system for referring children who are suspected of being abused or neglected.** The referral system must be appropriate and reflect federal and state guidelines.

♦ **Offer extended day programs for children.** School-based before- and after-school programs can be effective in reducing violence. Effective programs are well supervised and provide children with support and a range of options, such as counseling, tutoring, mentoring, cultural arts, community service, clubs, access to computers, and help with homework.

♦ **Promote good citizenship and character.** In addition to their academic mission, schools must help students become good citizens. First, schools stand for the civic values set forth in our Constitution and Bill of Rights (patriotism; freedom of religion, speech, and the press; equal protection/nondiscrimination; and due process/fairness). Schools also reinforce and promote the shared values of their local communities, such as honesty, kindness, responsibility, and respect for others. Schools should acknowledge that parents are the primary moral educators of their children, and work in partnership with them.

♦ **Identify problems and assess progress toward solutions.** Schools must openly and objectively examine circumstances that are potentially dangerous for students and staff and situations where members of the school community feel threatened or intimidated. Safe schools continually assess progress by identifying problems and collecting information regarding progress toward solutions. Moreover, effective schools share this information with students, families, and the community at large.

♦ **Support students in making the transition to adult life and the workplace.** Youth need assistance in planning their future and in developing skills that will result in success. For example, schools can provide students with community service opportunities, work-study programs, and apprenticeships that help connect them to caring adults in the community. These relationships, when established early, foster in youth a sense of hope and security for the future.

As we have indicated throughout this book, much can be done to prevent the development of behavior problems, especially those seen as precursors to the kinds of antisocial, aggressive responses associated with school violence and other serious concerns for students, teachers, administrators, parents, and communities. Having effective, research-based practices in place enables school communities to prevent problem behavior. As Dwyer et al. (1998) suggest, an important step is to learn the early warning signs of a child who is troubled, so that effective interventions can be provided.

Early Warning Signs

In most cases, children exhibit aggressive behavior early in life and, if not provided support, will continue a progressive developmental pattern toward severe aggression or violence. However, research also shows that when children have a positive, meaningful connection to an adult—whether it be at home, in school, or in the community—the potential for violence is reduced significantly. As Dwyer et al. (1998, pp. 8-11) suggest, none of the "early warning signs" alone is sufficient for predicting who will be violent or aggressive in school, and it is inappropriate—and potentially harmful—to use the early warning signs as a checklist against which to match individual children. Rather, the following early warning signs (not equally significant and not presented in order of seriousness) were offered only as an aid in making decisions about who may need help:

◆ **Social withdrawal.** In some situations, gradual and eventually complete withdrawal from social contacts can be an important indicator of a troubled child. The withdrawal often stems from feelings of depression, rejection, persecution, unworthiness, and lack of confidence.

◆ **Excessive feelings of isolation and being alone.** Research has shown that the majority of children who are isolated and appear to be friendless are not violent. In fact, these feelings are sometimes characteristic of children and youth who may be troubled, withdrawn, or have internal issues that hinder development of social affiliations. However, research also has shown that in some cases feelings of isolation and not having friends are associated with children who behave aggressively and violently.

◆ **Excessive feelings of rejection.** In the process of growing up, and in the course of adolescent development, many young people experience emotionally painful rejection. Children who are troubled often are isolated from their mentally healthy peers. Their responses to rejection will depend on many background factors. Without support, they may be at risk of expressing their emotional distress in negative ways—including violence. Some aggressive children who are rejected by nonaggressive peers seek out aggressive friends who, in turn, reinforce their violent tendencies.

◆ **Being a victim of violence.** Children who are victims of violence—including physical or sexual abuse—in the community, at school, or at home are sometimes at risk themselves of becoming violent toward themselves or others.

◆ **Feelings of being picked on and persecuted.** The youth who feels constantly picked on, teased, bullied, singled out for ridicule, and humiliated at home or at school may initially withdraw socially. If not given adequate support in addressing these feelings, some children may vent them in inappropriate ways—including possible aggression or violence.

◆ **Low school interest and poor academic performance.** Poor school achievement can be the result of many factors. It is important to consider whether there is a drastic change in performance or poor performance that becomes a chronic condition that limits the child's capacity to learn. In some situations—such as when the low achiever feels frustrated, unworthy, chastised, and denigrated—acting out and aggressive behaviors may occur. It is important to assess the emotional and cognitive reasons for the academic performance change to determine the true nature of the problem.

◆ **Expression of violence in writings and drawings.** Children and youth often express their thoughts, feelings, desires, and intentions in their drawings and in stories, poetry, and other written expressive forms. Many children produce work about violent themes that for the most part is harmless when taken in context. However, an overrepresentation of violence in writings and drawings that is directed at specific individuals (family members, peers, other adults) consistently over time, may signal emotional problems and the potential for violence. Because there is a real danger in misdiagnosing such a sign, it is important to seek the guidance of a qualified professional—such as a school psychologist, counselor, or other mental health specialist—to determine its meaning.

◆ **Uncontrolled anger.** Everyone gets angry; anger is a natural emotion. However, anger that is expressed frequently and intensely in response to minor irritants may signal potential violent behavior toward self or others.

◆ **Patterns of impulsive and chronic hitting, intimidating, and bullying behaviors.** Children often engage in acts of shoving and mild aggression. However, some mildly aggressive behaviors such as constant hitting and bullying of others that occur early in children's lives, if left unattended, might later escalate into more serious behaviors.

◆ **History of discipline problems.** Chronic behavior and disciplinary problems both in school and at home may suggest that underlying emotional needs are not being met. These unmet needs may be manifested in acting-out and aggressive behaviors. These problems may set the stage for the child to violate norms and rules, defy authority, disengage from school, and engage in aggressive behaviors with other children and adults.

◆ **Past history of violent and aggressive behavior.** Unless provided with support and counseling, a youth who has a history of aggressive or violent behavior is likely to repeat those behaviors. Aggressive and violent acts may be directed toward other individuals, be expressed in cruelty to animals, or include fire setting. Youth who show an early pattern of antisocial behavior frequently and across multiple settings are particularly at risk for future aggressive and antisocial behavior. Similarly, youth who engage in overt behaviors such as bullying, generalized aggression, and defiance, and covert behaviors such as stealing, vandalism, lying, cheating, and fire setting also are at risk for more serious aggressive behavior. Research suggests that age of onset may be a key factor in interpreting early warning signs. For example, children who engage in aggression and drug abuse at an early age (before age 12) are more likely to show violence later on than are children who begin such behavior at an older age. In the presence of such signs it is important to review the child's history with behavioral experts and seek parents' observations and insights.

♦ **Intolerance for differences and prejudicial attitudes.** All children have likes and dislikes. However, an intense prejudice toward others based on race, ethnicity, religion, language, gender, sexual orientation, ability, and physical appearance—when coupled with other factors—may lead to violent assaults against those who are perceived to be different. Membership in hate groups or the willingness to victimize individuals with disabilities or health problems also should be treated as early warning signs.

♦ **Drug use and alcohol use.** Apart from being unhealthy behaviors, drug use and alcohol use reduce self-control and expose children and youth to violence, either as perpetrators, as victims, or both.

♦ **Affiliation with gangs.** Gangs that support antisocial values and behaviors—including extortion, intimidation, and acts of violence toward other students—cause fear and stress among other students. Youth who are influenced by these groups—those who emulate and copy their behavior, as well as those who become affiliated with them—may adopt these values and act in violent or aggressive ways in certain situations. Gang-related violence and turf battles are common occurrences tied to the use of drugs that often result in injury and/or death.

♦ **Inappropriate access to, possession of, and use of firearms.** Children and youth who inappropriately possess or have access to firearms can have an increased risk for violence. Research shows that such youngsters also have a higher probability of becoming victims. Families can reduce inappropriate access and use by restricting, monitoring, and supervising children's access to firearms and other weapons. Children who have a history of aggression, impulsiveness, or other emotional problems should not have access to firearms and other weapons.

♦ **Serious threats of violence.** Idle threats are a common response to frustration. Alternatively, one of the most reliable indicators that a youth is likely to commit a dangerous act toward self or others is a detailed and specific threat to use violence. Recent incidents across the country clearly indicate that threats to commit violence against oneself or others should be taken very seriously. Steps must be taken to understand the nature of these threats and to prevent them from being carried out.

Practices That Support Responsible Behavior

Well-informed staff development coupled with action plans grounded in schoolwide efforts, like those described in this book to "stay on the same page" with regard to teaching appropriate academic and social behavior, go a long way in making schools safer, more positive places to learn. *Safeguarding Our Children: An Action Guide* (Dwyer & Osher, 2000) provides additional information about "how to" develop safe schools. Schoolwide prevention, early intervention, and intensive services for students with significant behavioral needs are among the evidence-based approaches that are discussed, and, again, they are at the core of the research-based practices described in this book.

Effective *schoolwide interventions* are designed to improve the academic performance and behavior of all children (Dwyer & Osher, 2000, pp. 2-4). The schoolwide foundation includes the following:

- Compassionate, caring, respectful staff who model appropriate behaviors, create a climate of emotional support, and are committed to working with all students.

- Developmentally appropriate programs for all children that teach and reinforce social and problem-solving skills.

- Teachers and staff who are trained to support positive school and classroom behaviors.

- Engaging curricula and effective teaching practices.

- Child- and family-focused, culturally competent approaches.

- Collaborative relationships with families, agencies, and community organizations.

These approaches alone are sufficient for preventing serious behavior problems for many students, but they will not address fully the needs of all students. However, an effective foundation makes it easier to identify students who require additional interventions and increases the effectiveness of additional interventions—both early and intensive. Dwyer and Osher (2000) describe the schoolwide foundation in more detail in Chapter 2 of *Safeguarding Our Children*.

When students fall through the cracks of schoolwide efforts, *early intervention* is necessary to prevent academic failure or behavior problems. Dwyer and Osher (2000) suggest that early intervention, along with an appropriate foundation, is sufficient for almost all students, and they describe how early intervention can be used to respond to early warning signs in Chapter 3 of *Safeguarding Our Children*.

Students whose needs cannot be fully addressed by schoolwide efforts or early intervention require *intensive interventions*. Intensive interventions are individualized to a student's needs and strengths. These interventions often involve multiple coordinated services, such as individualized special education services as well as other school and community supports. In Chapter 4 of *Safeguarding Our Children* the focus turns to intervention approaches and practices that are currently being used successfully to provide intensive interventions to children and youth in need and their families.

Preventing Problem Behavior at School

Efforts to improve general learning conditions at school revolve around preventing inappropriate behavior and teaching appropriate behavior. Effective behavior instruction is as important as effective academic instruction. For example, Nelson and colleagues (1998) argued that "students will behave according to social norms if [teachers] take the trouble to teach those students those norms and supervise them in a consistent way" (p. 4). They proposed a model that emphasized direct interventions within and across all school settings, ensuring that disruptive behavior did not occur or become entrenched (i.e., *preventative* focus) or was corrected (i.e., *remedial* focus). They argued that different types of students (i.e., typical, at-risk, target), varying according to the nature of their problems, need different types of interventions (see Table 11.1). Schoolwide interventions (e.g., effective teaching, schoolwide discipline) are appropriate for students who are not at risk for problems. Targeted or focused interventions (e.g., conflict resolutions, anger management) are appropriate for students at risk of developing disruptive behavior problems. Intensive, comprehensive interventions (e.g., community-based service linkages, school and community partnerships) are appropriate for students exhibiting persistent disruptive behavior patterns.

Kamps and Tankersley (1996) present a similar perspective, describing primary, secondary, and tertiary levels of prevention. Primary prevention improves the life situations of the entire population. Secondary prevention improves the lives of vulnerable individuals by providing assistance to remove them (protection) or improve their functioning (remediation). Tertiary prevention improves the lives of individuals with disabilities by impeding further deterioration in functioning. Kamps and Tankersley consider the prevention of behavioral and conduct disorders most effective and efficient when:

TABLE 11.1 Prevention and Remediation Levels to Meet the Needs of All Children

Student Type	Intervention Approach
Typical (Not at risk for problems)	Schoolwide Interventions (Preventative and Remedial)
	Effective teaching practices
	Schoolwide discipline plan
	Schoolwide classroom management strategy
	Catch disruptive behavior early
	Move to a designated classroom
	Think about behavior
	Debrief and rejoin class
At-Risk (Developing or exhibiting disruptive behavior patterns)	Targeted Interventions (Preventative and Remedial)
	Intensive instruction/counseling
	Anger management
	Conflict resolution
	Self-control interventions
	Consultant-based 1-to-1 intervention
	Intensive academic intervention
Community Interventions (Exhibiting disruptive behavior patterns)	Intensive Comprehensive Interventions (Remedial)
	Community-based connection
	Social service agency coordination

SOURCE: Adapted from Nelson, Crabtree, Marchand-Martella, & Martella, 1998, p. 5, Table 1.

- ◆ It begins with young children.

- ◆ It involves parents as collaborators.

- ◆ It involves cross-setting, multiple, and proactive interventions.

- ◆ Administrators, teachers, peers, and other key people are included in treatment plans.

- ◆ It involves self-management as well as maintenance and generalization within natural environments.

- ◆ It involves collaboration among families, schools, and service providers.

Prevention practices that have been found to be effective are described in this book. However, none of them will be as effective if used in isolation, by one or two teachers or a few classrooms in a school. Building effective prevention practices requires the efforts of the entire school community.

_____ **Putting It All Together**

Reducing violence and preventing discipline problems is not the responsibility of any one group or individual. Administrators need assistance identifying, implementing, and supporting effective interventions. Teachers need help teaching behavior as well as teaching academics. Students need to be taught appropriate social, behavioral, and academic norms and supervised in their learning and demonstration of them. Parents need assistance participating as partners in making schools safer, more positive places to send their children. Reducing violence and preventing discipline problems requires a plan.

Sugai (2000) offered the following guidelines for improving behavior in our schools:

♦ Use a team-based approach to identify, implement, and evaluate best practices. Include administrators, teachers, school psychologists, other support personnel, and parents. Support improvement efforts with budget, personnel, and resource allocations.

♦ Use research-validated practices.

♦ Make behavioral instruction proactive. Teach appropriate social behavior, model appropriate social behavior, give students opportunities to practice and become fluent in expected behavior, and provide plenty of positive feedback.

♦ Provide a continuum of behavioral support. Increase the intensity of the intervention as the intensity of the problem increases.

♦ Use data-based systems to guide decisions. Keep staff informed as to what is currently in place as well as to what is working and not working. Use data on behavior as part of the school's goals.

The opportunities for misbehavior that lead to violence and serious behavioral episodes are greater in a disorderly, undisciplined school (Dwyer & Osher, 2000; Dwyer et al., 1998; U.S. Department of Education, 1998). Effective schools are implementing schoolwide campaigns that establish high expectations and provide support for socially appropriate behavior. They reinforce positive behavior and highlight sanctions against aggressive behavior. All staff, parents, students, and community members are informed about problem behavior, what they can do to counteract it, and how they can reinforce and reward positive behavior. In turn, the entire school community makes a commitment to behave responsibly. Effective and safe schools develop and consistently enforce schoolwide rules that are clear, broad-based, and fair. Rules and disciplinary procedures are developed collaboratively by representatives of the total educational community. They are communicated clearly to all parties—but most important, they are followed consistently by everyone. Effective schools implement strategies like those described in this book.

REFERENCES

Algozzine, B., Audette, B., Ellis, E., Marr, M. B., & White, R. (2000). Supporting teachers, principals—and students—through unified discipline. *Teaching Exceptional Children, 33*(2), 42-47.

Brooks, K., Schiraldi, V., & Ziedenberg, J. (2000). *School house hype: Two years later.* Washington, DC: Justice Policy Institute [Online]. Retrieved March 23, 2001, from the World Wide Web: www.cjcj.org/schoolhousehype/shh2.html

Dwyer, K. P., & Osher, D. (2000). *Safeguarding our children: An action guide.* Washington, DC: U.S. Departments of Education and Justice, American Institutes of Research.

Dwyer, K. P., Osher, D., & Hoffman, C. C. (2000). Creating responsive schools: Contextualizing *Early Warning, Timely Response. Exceptional Children, 66,* 347-365.

Dwyer, K., Osher, D., & Warger, C. (1998). *Early warning, timely response: A guide to safe schools.* Washington, DC: U.S. Department of Education.

Gable, R. A. (1996). A critical analysis of functional assessment: Issues for researchers and practitioners. *Behavioral Disorders, 21*(1), 36-40.

Gunter, P. L., & Denny, R. K. (1996). Research issues and need regarding teacher use of classroom management strategies. *Behavioral Disorders, 21*(1), 15-20.

Kamps, D. M., & Tankersley, M. (1996). Prevention of behavioral and conduct disorders: Trends and research issues. *Behavioral Disorders, 21*(1), 41-48.

Kauffman, J. M. (1996). Research to practice issues. *Behavioral Disorders, 21*(1), 55-60.

Kauffman, J.M. (1999). How we prevent the prevention of emotional and behavioral disorders. *Exceptional Children, 65* 448-468

Langdon, C. A., & Vesper, N. (2000). The sixth Phi Delta Kappa poll of teachers' attitudes toward the public schools. *Kappan, 81,* 607-611.

Lloyd, J. W., & Heubusch, J. D. (1996). Issues of social validation in research serving individuals with emotional and behavioral disorders. *Behavioral Disorders, 21*(1), 8-14.

Mathur, S. R., & Rutherford, R. B. (1996). Is social skills training effective with students for emotional or behavioral disorders? Research issues and needs. *Behavioral Disorders, 21*(1), 21-28.

Nelson, J. R., Crabtree, M., Marchand-Martella, N., & Martella, R. (1998). Teaching behavior in the whole school. *Teaching Exceptional Children, 30*(4), 4-9.

Rose, L. C., & Gallup, A. M. (1999). The 31st annual Phi Delta Kappa/ Gallup poll of the public's attitudes toward the public schools. *Kappan, 81,* 41-58.

Sugai, G. (2000). Instituting school-wide behavioral supports. *CEC Today, 6*(7), 5.

Sugai, G., Sprague, J. A., Horner, R. H., & Walker, H. M. (2000). Preventing school violence: The use of office discipline referrals to assess and monitor school-wide discipline interventions. *Journal of Emotional and Behavioral Disorders, 8,* 94-101.

Taylor-Greene, S., Brown, D., Nelson, L., Longton, J., Gassman, T., Cohen, J., Swartz, J., Horner, R. H., Sugai, G., & Hall, S. (1997). School-wide behavioral support: Starting the year off right. *Journal of Behavioral Support, 7,* 99-112.

U.S. Department of Education. (1998). *Early warning, timely response: A guide for safe schools.* Washington, DC: Author. Available online: www.ed.gov/offices/OSERS/OSEP/earlywrn.html

Wehby, J. H., & Symons, F. J. (1996). Revisiting conceptual issues in the measurement of aggressive behavior. *Behavioral Disorders, 21*(1), 29-35.

Whelan, R. J., & Simpson, R. L. (1996). Preparation of personnel for students with emotional and behavioral disorders: Perspectives on a research foundation for future practice. *Behavioral Disorders, 21*(1), 49-54.

RESOURCES

Algozzine, B., Audette, B., Ellis, E., Marr, M. B., & White, R. (2000). *Demography of disruptive behavior and the need for discipline.* Manuscript submitted for publication.

Brophy, J., & Good, T. L. (1986). Teacher behavior and student achievement. In M. C. Wittrock (Ed.), *Handbook of research on teaching* (pp. 328-375). New York: Macmillan.

Colvin, G., Kameenui, E. J., & Sugai, G. (1993). Reconceptualizng behavior management and school-wide discipline in general education. *Education and Treatment of Children, 16,* 361-381.

Gall, M. D., Borg, W. R., & Gall, J. P. (1996). *Educational research* (6th ed.). White Plains, NY: Longman.

Kauffman, J. M. (1997). *Characteristics of emotional and behavioral disorders of children and youth.* Columbus, OH: Merrill.

Kerr, M. M., & Nelson, C. M. (1989). *Strategies for managing behavior problems in the classroom.* Columbus, OH: Merrill.

Marr, M. B., Audette, R., White, R., Ellis, E., & Algozzine, B. (in press). School-wide discipline and classroom ecology. *Special Services in the Schools.*

Stallings, J. (1975). Implementation and child effects of teaching practices in Follow Through classrooms. *Monographs of the Society for Research in Child Development, 40*(7-8, Serial No. 163).

Stallings, J. (1980). Allocated academic learning time revisited, or beyond time on task. *Educational Researcher, 8*(11), 11-16.

Sugai, G., & Horner, R. H. (1999). Discipline and behavior support: Preferred processes and practices. *Effective School Practice, 17*(4), 10-22.

White, R. (1996). Unified discipline. In B. Algozzine (Ed.), *Problem behavior management: An educator's resource service.* Gaithersburg, MD: Aspen Publishers.

White, R., Algozzine, B., Audette, B., Marr, M. B., & Ellis, E. (in press). Unified discipline: a school-wide approach for managing problem behavior. *Intervention in School and Clinic.*

White, R., Marr, M. B., Ellis, E., Audette, B., & Algozzine, B. (In press). Effects of school-wide discipline on office referrals. *Journal of At-Risk Issues.*

Index